LEADER

Ralph Caplan, Author

D0070947

Cracking the Whip

Cracking the Whip

ESSAYS ON

Design

AND

Its Side Effects

Ralph Caplan

FAIRCHILD PUBLICATIONS, INC.
NEW YORK

Executive Editor: Olga T. Kontzias
Acquisitions Editor: Joseph Miranda
Assistant Acquisitions Editor: Jaclyn Bergeron
Development Editor: Sylvia L. Weber
Assistant Development Editor: Suzette Lam
Art Director: Adam B. Bohannon
Production Manager: Ginger Monaco
Production Editor: Elizabeth Marotta
Copy Editor: Amy Jolin
Interior Design: Adam B. Bohannon
Cover Design: Adam B. Bohannon

Copyright © 2006
Fairchild Publications, Inc.

Library of Congress Catalog Card Number: 2005927978
ISBN: 1-56367-390-8
GST R 133004424

Printed in the United States of America
10 9   8   7   6   5   4   3   2   1   TP 13

for Rachel and Noah

CONTENTS

FOREWORD
by Milton Glaser

I was hoping to write this foreword to *Cracking the Whip* without defining what design is for the millionth time. Like love, art, or truth, an exact description of design is difficult because the subject is simply too large and elusive to wrap up. Like the proverbial iceberg, the top part is visible, but what goes on below the surface is considerably more significant.

Some years ago, I was invited by Queen Beatrice of the Netherlands to speak about design to a small group of invitees whom the queen felt would be interested in the subject. The queen, who acts more like an ombudsman than royalty, sculpts and has a deep involvement in the visual arts. An aide informed me that this mini-conference had been nine years in the making and that the next subject would be Antarctica. The eminent Italian designers, Gae Aulenti and Mario Bellini, had also been invited, as well as Ettore Sottass and Philippe Starke. (The last two were unavailable, if memory serves.) At the conference, where the queen's subjects had gathered after a state dinner in the Amsterdam town hall, Mario Bellini told the following story:

> I was at the Trienniale in Milano when a man approached me and said, "I know you, aren't you Mario Bellini?"
> "I am," I acknowledged.
> "You're the guy responsible for all those design chairs," he went on. It struck me at that moment that the man

was using the word design as an adjective to describe a certain kind of style, as though Chippendale or colonial furniture had not been "designed," but simply manufactured.

A more enlightened view of the word would give design a more significant role in human culture. After all, design cannot be separated from intention, which is what differentiates us from all other species. Like it or not, I seem to have inadvertently stumbled onto a definition. An old friend of mine, Jivan Tabibian, explained it this way: "Design is the introduction of intention into human affairs." Not bad, but not quite complete. Below the surface of the definition, the economic function of design and its ability both to stimulate behavior and to create pleasure needs clarification. Not to mention the insistent role of "beauty," which emerges without being necessarily intended.

No one has written more lucidly on the intersection of purpose and consequences in the design world than Ralph Caplan. His writing is conversational, enormously funny, and deeply penetrating. He's great fun to talk to, and come to think of it, his conversation is more like writing than talking, since he habitually speaks in complete sentences and paragraphs. He has thousands of amusing personal anecdotes, some of which end up in his essays. While he talks to you, his alert eyes are scrutinizing your face for any sign of response or approval. He pays attention to what's obvious, which is not as easy as it seems and is a key to the pleasure we derive from reading his work. The great lesson of 20th-century education seems to be that in order to inform your audience, you first have to entertain them. Caplan understands the principle, but his most satisfying writing is driven by indignation. For instance:

> Why, for example, do people talk at movies? Clearly it is because they are accustomed to talking at home

while watching television. But why do they talk while they are watching television, if not from the certainty that they would not be missing anything if they shut up? The acceptance of words as background has carried over to print. If TV talk is the verbal equivalent of Muzak, graphic designers are the visual counterpart of talking heads, charged with communicating the unnecessary to the unneeding.

At heart Caplan is a moralist, who understands that the subject of "design" permits him to write about anything from an ethical point of view. He writes as though he believes that there is no such thing as popular culture, only culture itself. He is our own Jonathan Swift and has defined our practice as well as any one else in our times. We're lucky to have him around, and I envy the pleasure you'll have reading these essays for the first time.

PREFACE: PERIPHERAL VISION

The essays in this book, many of which appeared first as columns in design magazines, are written from a peripheral point of view. That is, they reflect design as seen out of the corner of my eye, rather than studied. I think everyone but designers sees it that way most of the time.

Well, almost everyone. A friend of mine in Chicago was a nun back in the days before nuns took to wearing mufti, as if they were clerical workers. The wimple that Sister Mary Irma wore functioned as blinders do on a horse, shutting out the periphery and forcing her to focus, literally, on the straight and narrow. Whatever she missed seeing, she missed by choice: avoiding distraction is intrinsic to the nun's discipline. An uncommonly perceptive scholar and poet, Sister Mary Irma looked hard at life; but, like the Girl from Impanema, she looked straight ahead.

Looking straight ahead limits perspective as well as distraction. Peripheral vision—which in a sense is what you see when you aren't looking—is a distraction, the ocular equivalent of noise and unintentional eavesdropping. For designers, it can also be a precious gift, offering a preview of side effects that might appear in the wake of their work. Because the field is so broad, side effects of design can crop up when least, or never, expected. Deliciously applicable to almost everything almost everywhere, the design process is inclusive to the point of nondefinition. If it were a religious denomination, Design would be Unitarianism. That breadth allows—in fact, compels—considerable latitude; and these essays rove freely from hardware stores to fashion to pasta and corporate culture, exploring mysteries like the stuff we keep and wish we'd gotten rid of, and the stuff we throw away and wish we'd kept. They report on the verticality of New York City, on tourism as a lifestyle, on art, craft, and the imperfections of bathrooms.

As Willie Nelson says, "It's all the same song."

A critical friend of mine remarked that my essays were discursive. It didn't sound like a compliment, but I wasn't sure.

"Is that good or bad?" I asked.

"Oh," he said, "I just mean that reading them is like watching someone crack a whip—you see it go left and right, this way and that and every which way, and you know it's going to crack somewhere, sometime, but you haven't a clue as to where or when."

I don't always have a clue either—that's how peripheral vision works. I knew what discursive meant, but was insecure enough to look it up anyway. Webster's Collegiate Dictionary gives two seemingly contradictory meanings: "a: moving from topic to topic without order" and "b: proceeding coherently from topic to topic."

Of those two extremes, I tend to favor the first, finding more satisfaction in randomness than in system. Although the book is a collection of ideas about the design process, many of the essays in it are topical. Well, they were written when they were written. I have revised a number of them, updating specific allusions in some cases and, in others, applying what my editor calls "the Jack Benny rule." If a fair sampling of prospective readers know that Jack Benny was a comedian, it is not necessary that they also know any of his routines. Still, some names and events will not ring a bell with every reader. Although I have tried to minimize those, I take comfort in believing that, with the daily proliferation and improvement of search engines, looking up an occasional reference is not a daunting challenge. When in doubt, Google.

Where gender is concerned, updating has been more problematic, particularly in respect to indefinite pronouns. Often, *his* has been changed to *his or her*, but not in every case. I have tried switching randomly from his to her, but the practice drives copy editors to marginal road rage. Denise McLuggage, in her prefatory note to *The Centered Skier* confronts the dilemma with a charming belligerence.

I not only find *his or her* ungainly in use, but I bristle at the implication that everywhere it is not used, and *his* appears alone, then that *his* is intended to be exclusively masculine. . . . I do not feel excluded by mere pronouns and sincerely trust that no one else will either. But if someone does, I refer him to God. She will explain.

Writing personal essays about design seems like a paradoxical undertaking. Design projects are in major respects impersonal, dependent on mass production, and undertaken on behalf of clients and customers, rather than the designer alone. But one of the most valuable contributions designers can make is the infusion of personality into projects that would otherwise have none. This is not "self expression" but self application—the act of bringing individual talent and intuition to bear on general needs.

Cracking the Whip is addressed to anyone who cares about design. That could be anyone. Like Moliere's character who had been speaking prose all his life without knowing it, I had been interested in design for years without knowing it, until I began writing about it. Some of you may find that you have been interested in design without knowing it, until you began reading about it.

—RALPH CAPLAN
NEW YORK, 2005

ACKNOWLEDGMENTS

Gathering a group of already published essays into book form looks like a one-man job. Actually it takes, if not a village, at least a neighborhood. Peter Bradford proposed and initiated this project, and Joshua Passe produced a prototype of the book for presentation. Many of the essays appeared first in design magazines, where they profited from the attention of editors Annetta Hannah and Chee Pearlman at ID, and Martin Fox, Julie Lasky, and Joyce Rutter Kaye at PRINT. Steven Heller, editor of the *AIGA Journal* and of *VOICE*, has been a valued advisor.

The staff at Fairchild Books has been consistently helpful and encouraging. I want especially to thank Olga Kontzias and Sylvia Weber for editorial direction, and Adam Bohannon for design.

As always, my wife, Judith Ramquist, collaborated in each stage of the book's preparation with patience, energy, and critical judgement.

Cracking the Whip

1

Identity Crises

Who we are, who we wish we were, and who we wish to say we are easily get confused in a mobile, transient society. We change roles, hats, color, gender, and steal each other's identities. Personal growth manuals exhort us to "reinvent ourselves," as if we were entering a witness protection program. Time is money? Names are money! Identities are fungible, and can be traded and traded on. Identity theft is a crime so common and so easy to execute that credit card companies hardly try to catch the thieves, preferring to recoup their losses by raising prices.

There is as much concern with identity in design as in psychology, but in design the focus is on someone or something *else's* identity. If, as has been claimed, every*one* is responsible for his or her own face after 40, it is not true of every*thing*. Because our artifacts and environments are not responsible for what they look like, the designers who shape them have to be. And because corporations find it so hard to control what they look like, such once simple matters as thinking up a product name and designing a logo have been distended into corporate identity programs, "global ikonics," and "branding."

One of the themes in this section is the use of names as verbal beards to shield the persons and operations behind them. Words and images, already routinely pressed into service to obscure meaning rather than express it, are used to obscure identity as well. Spin is the name of the game, and perhaps in a sense it always has been. Some of the following pieces explore new rules and new plays.

Names and Faces

In the years between *Cleopatra* and *Who's Afraid of Virginia Wolf?* a friend of mine suffered a peculiar form of misery. His name is Richard Burton, and women kept calling him up to flirt with him, propose to him, and ask whether he was "the real Richard Burton." He always replied that he thought he was as real as anyone else, but was beginning to question it. "One thing I am sure of," he told me, if not his callers, "It's no fun having the invasion of privacy that comes with fame if you can't have Elizabeth Taylor along with it."

His parents were to blame, of course, but how could they have known? Naming a child is always a risky business. So is naming a business; and the effort to minimize the risk has given rise to an executive mystique. There are numerous firms in the country that specialize in naming companies, products, and processes. One of them goes in for psychological probes of a name's emotive consequences. Another analyzes names for "audio appeal, visual appeal, image, and equity." Still another checks out the foreign language implications of names that are acceptable in English but might not be in, say, Korean. (Did you know that the Korean word for athlete's foot is *Wal-Mart*? It isn't, really, but that's the kind of intelligence this firm digs up.)

Still, products, like people, survive the worst of names. What could be sillier than Hotpoint for a refrigerator, less inviting than "Wasteking" for a kitchen range, or more obnoxious than "Noxzema" for a complexion salve?

The interiors of New York City buses carry a poster advertising the services of a local beauty salon. The copy reads:

DISCOVER HOW TO ACHIEVE
A FACE OF YOUR OWN

This astonishing invitation is graphically illustrated by a photograph of a handsome woman putting on a mask. The woman wears no makeup. The mask looks exactly like the

Originally published January 24, 1965 in *QUOTE*, as the column "Crossfire."

woman, except that the eyes drip mascara like a bleeding black ball and the mouth is the color of rotting salmon. In short, it looks like the faces in other ads and on other women. This, presumably is the face of her own that she has discovered. She achieves it by putting it on.

That thousands of passengers see this poster daily without either smashing it in rage or rolling on the floor in laughter is indicative of the protective insensitivity we have developed for survival in the modern world. A mind conditioned by nightly TV to watch sufferers work their way through esophageal canyons of acid reflux can cope with this sort of thing by day.

Actually, almost every woman I know already has a face of her own. The problem is not achieving it, but liking it enough to reveal it. The test for authentic people used to be whether they had the courage to be themselves. Soon it may be whether they have the courage to look like themselves.

Person, Place, or Thing

Although I have always aspired to be one of those people who knows where the bodies are buried, not until recently had I ever visited Grant's Tomb, located at the point where Riverside Park and I both peter out. The security guard greeted me with the effusive cordiality that comes with having no one else to greet. This is, after all, not Yosemite. I had the place to myself until a couple came in and began reading the captions. "Look," the woman exclaimed. "The last recorded act of his life was proofreading!"

That seemed like a wimpy way to end a career of military and political victory, but her reading was correct. Grant ended his life proofreading his memoirs. In them he confessed, "I think I am a verb," explaining that a verb expressed "to be, to do, to suffer and I have done all three." An admirable statement, even if Grant stole it from Buckminster Fuller, who famously said almost 100 years later, "I seem to be a verb."

It is unsurprising that a genius in military strategy and a genius in anticipatory design strategy should arrive at the same insight into their grammatical selfhood. If you're going to go through life as one of the parts of speech, a verb is the right thing to wear.

At our best we experience each other as verbs, but we identify each other as nouns, always the easiest garment to slip on in an emergency. Name tags are mandatory in a world where the number of people one meets expands in inverse proportion to one's capacity for remembering what they are called. I have made my peace with name tags, but it is an uneasy truce.

How uneasy was dramatized for me at an event called Neo-Con. In the political media, *neocon* is a mildly pejorative term describing people who, having been zealous liberals in their youth, have become even more zealous conservatives in their AARP years. But in the furniture industry, NeoCon is a mas-

Originally published May/June 2001 in *PRINT*, as the column "Peripheral Vision."

sive trade show held annually in Chicago's Merchandise Mart. Name badges at such an event function as a security measure to keep competitors from spying and eavesdropping on each other. Since my corporate mission is to spy and eavesdrop on everyone, I wore no badge, explaining when challenged that my name badge was unlisted. My friend Joe Stone was coveting an array of badges laid out on a registration table, hoping to hide his identity behind one of them.

"Are these last year's name badges?" he asked the young woman guarding them. "May I have one?"

They were not and he could not. Why would he even want one? she wondered. What good would it be?

"Joe here collects them," I told her. "He has the largest collection of trade show badges in the free world."

"An interesting hobby," she said cheerfully. I would never have thought so, but she may have a point. Certainly the field offers anecdotal variety. People who would never cheat at poker do it with name badges, which are often the best available means of convincingly pretending to remember someone you don't. "Of course I remember you. You're . . . why, you're . . ." you say, vainly looking at a woman's lapel for a tag that turns out to be attached to her belt.

NeoCon was not the only furniture show where I have had an identity crisis. At the first International Furniture Fair in New York's Javits Center, I appeared on a panel with two ergonomists (one of whom was named Archie Kaplan, an egregious misspelling that added to the confusion to come) and a craftsman from England who made chairs of glass. I liked him but was terrified by his chaise lounge with jagged edges. On stage a table was set with our name placards in place, and I said lightly, "What if we each sat behind someone else's name card?" I did not expect to be taken up on this proposition—I did not even think it was a proposition—but a man who designs glass lounge furniture for a living is ready to escape the ordinary when invited. "Excellent," he said, promptly sitting in my place and leaving me nowhere to sit but in his. The moderator saw what had happened, but was too shocked to correct it, introducing him as me, me as him, and calling on me (him) first. In a glorious exchange, he (as me) attacked his own designs as irresponsible and I (as him), defended them. The dialogue went like this:

"I am deeply offended by your disregard for the safety and comfort of the user, all for the sake of style," he said.

"I resent that, Caplan," I said. "No one has ever been killed or even cut in one of my chairs."

"Maybe not yet," he conceded.

It was the only panel discussion I have ever unreservedly enjoyed, and I think of it whenever I get a splinter.

Name badges are simple enough but can be complicated by design. I have seen some that display the name of the event at a scale readable across a football field, and the name of the person in the type used for the bottom line of an eye chart, thus putting the emphasis on the one piece of information everyone already knows.

At a college reunion only my bifocals enabled me to read the name badge of a woman I encountered and thus retrofit her into the memory of the girl she had once been. When name and person came into focus, I cried out, "Christine!"

She took off her glasses, switched to trifocals, and inspected my lapel.

"Ralph!" she said. We embraced, something I do not recall our ever having done when we were students. Now I wonder what or whom, in that shared senior moment, we were embracing. Our memories? Our old selves? Our names?

James Baldwin wrote a book called *Nobody Knows My Name* at a time when not everyone did. Today, you should be so lucky. Your name is a magnet for homeland insecurities. The government knows your name. Stores know it. Creditors know it.

Junk mail perpetrators incorporate it into their lists. Spam mongers guess it from your e-mail address. The stuff of public directories, individual names nevertheless remain laden with private meaning. Nothing sounds to the ear or strikes the eye quite like your own name.

The Japanese are noted for the high seriousness with which they regard business cards, but no culture I know of takes name badges seriously. Yet we stand naked until named. Nudity was the signature of Abner Dean, a popular cartoonist of the '40s whose characters were always naked. In one of his drawings, though, the people do wear name tags. The caption reads, "Everybody has to have a label."

Well, everybody does. Name tags, like all inventions of the devil, are both pernicious and necessary. The first human impulse was to be a verb, to act: pluck the fruit, eat it, find fig leaves to cover the mystery of our most private parts. It must have been the serpent who adorned the fig leaf with copy, simultaneously introducing into newly minted humankind the proper noun, the pronoun, and with them the concept of ownership. "Hi. I'm Adam."

I think I am a gerund.

Crossing Over

At seven A.M. the only vertical bodies in the park are dog walkers, power walkers, and joggers. Those categories are impure. Some joggers have dogs. Some power walkers are unempowered. Some joggers *are* dogs—a Dalmatian named Buck laps me twice each morning. They are, like Faith Hill, Linda Ronstadt, and Audra Macdonald, crossovers, performers who do not know their place or want to.

But everybody has more than one place. Even in Los Angeles, you are a pedestrian the moment you step out of the car. For most of my adult life I have been described as a nondesigner, an epithet lodged in the lexicon of negative status somewhere between noncombatant and nonperson. As often as not, however, I am a designer, just as many designers I work with are, at any given time, not designers but someone else entirely, never mind who. They are downright protean, but so are we all.

When asked how he was able to turn the poet in him off in order to make documentary propaganda films, Dylan Thomas answered "I didn't have to. I'm only a poet when I am writing poetry." As was the Greenwich Village street character Joe Gould when he wrote his celebrated couplet: "In winter I'm a Buddhist/In summer I'm a nudist." Doggerel in this case is worth plumbing for connections. Heavily influenced by Buddhist thought, the Japanese psychiatrist Morita, a contemporary of Freud, formulated a therapy that holds, in the words of its leading western exegete, David K. Reynolds, that "What I do now is me."

What you do now is you. Although design is not usually an altruistic undertaking, the world in general is badly enough designed that there is no dearth of opportunities for designers willing to cross boundaries wherever and whenever they are

Originally published March/April 1996 in *I.D.*, as the column "Counterpoint."

needed. But there is also abundant opportunity and—more importantly—necessity for "nondesigners" to do what designers would do for them if only they could. Specialists from a multiplicity of fields commonly cross over into design when they require new tools that nobody, yet, has provided them with.

Once, while giving a talk to a large audience whose members ran the gamut of design disciplines, I tried to frame the presentation in a way that might include the interests of all. I was astonished afterwards at the number and variety of people—architects, graphic and industrial designers, even a land planner—who claimed I had outlined a way of working that was peculiar to them. When a member of the audience told me warmly that he had designed his entire practice along the lines I had been describing, I asked him what kind of designer he was. "I'm an eye surgeon," he said.

That surgeon, Malcolm McCannel, insisted that I go to Minneapolis to see what he meant. He had invented a number of techniques and products used by eye surgeons around the world, but that impressed me less than the design attention he had given to his offices and examination rooms. Every aspect of the practice was thought through from the standpoint of a patient anxious about vision, treatment, and insurance coverage. The result was a humane system calculated to minimize the patient's confusion while heightening the clarity of the doctor's judgment. We became friends and Malcolm became my ophthalmologist serving until I needed help nearer at hand.

As I do now. Last summer I had to have an eye operation. Since the removal of tonsils at the age of four, I have never had another operation of any kind and resisted this one for years. Something else I have done for years is suffer through the details of other people's operations. So indulge me: I have earned the right to bore you about mine. Actually, it's not all that boring. For one thing, my affliction has an exotic name:

spastic entropion. My lower lid would involuntarily fold in, causing the lashes to scratch the cornea. The condition is correctable by a minor procedure, although in my case (when telling people about your operation, it is mandatory to make sure they know yours is a special case) one procedure was not enough. "Mr. Caplan has a very interesting eyelid," the surgeon told a colleague. No one has ever said that about me before.

Like my friend McCannel, this surgeon, Dr. Peter Michalos, is a very large man whose hands look better suited to logging than to corneal sutures. (The late Charles Addams, who was a patient, made a drawing of Dr. Michalos as Lurch.) "How come eye surgeons are always big guys with big hands?" I asked him.

"Actually, it's not important that our hands be dainty," he said, "but that they be steady. All we do with them is hold instruments. It's the instruments that are delicate."*

Michalos began to explain my problem to me by drawing a picture of my eye from the patient's perspective, a technique once commonly used by industrial designers, which accomplished the dual purposes of communicating and showing off. Designers as different as Henry Dreyfuss and Jay Doblin taught themselves how to draw upside down for the benefit of clients sitting across a desk. (Once, after having lunch with Doblin, I was reproached by a waiter for defacing the table-cloth. Though Doblin had done it, the damage was on my side of the table, and drawn from my point of view.) I was not surprised to learn that Michalos, too, was a designer.

Everyone knows the joke about the guy who has lost his glasses and can't look for them until he finds them. Everyone

*My misconception was evidently a common one. The protagonist of Ian McEwan's 2005 novel *Saturday* is a brain surgeon. In his experience, "Most people in their first consultation take a furtive look at the surgeon's hands in the hope of reassurance. Prospective patients look for a delicacy, sensitivity, steadiness, perhaps unblemished pallor."

who needs glasses knows, too, that it is no joke. Similarly, the people most likely to need eye drops have poor vision, arthritis, and diminished manual dexterity: the very conditions that make eye drops necessary make it difficult to self-administer them. Michalos has addressed the problem by designing the On Target Eye Drop Delivery System, a plastic eye mask with two female sockets. You simply screw the eye-drop bottle into the socket (which fits the three standard bottle sizes) and release the medication while looking through a light hole that mechanically aligns your eye to receive it. Since the mask is dark, the patient never sees the drop coming.

Michalos has also designed the Flipframe, a set of eye glasses for women who can't put on eye makeup while wearing glasses, but can't see where to apply it when they're not. A single lens flips from side to side and up, enabling the user to keep one eye on the other.

Crossover professionals slide into design from across borders without asking anyone. I have for years been beguiled to the point of obsession by the label on Dr. Bonner's Pure Castile Peppermint Soap, where the density of the type is rivaled only by the intensity of the messages. The product proclaims itself ideal for bathing, shampooing, washing cars and whitewall tires, removing ticks, brushing teeth, shaving, disinfecting pets, rinsing pesticides from fruit trees, and cleaning other soaps when they get dirty. But the copy is not confined to pitching this wondrous product. It is studded with dazzling personal pronouncements on good and evil, contraception, freedom of speech, and Essene morality. For all that, the majesty of the label is not in the content but in the superb achievement of fitting all that type around a quart bottle. Here is the graphic counterpart of clowns in a tiny circus car: the mind knows all those words can't possibly fit on a label that size, but the eye proves that they do. And all are perfectly readable, if not always comprehensible. Could anyone but a graphic designer have managed such a feat? Hard to imagine. Would any graphic designer have managed it? Harder to imagine.

I can hardly wait to read them all again as soon as the sutures come out.

Giving Up the Ghost

A singing group called Milli Vanilli had won a Grammy Award in 1990 as "best new artists." When all the vocals on their album were discovered to be the work of other voices in other rooms, the award was rescinded, creating a controversy on ethical standards in the music industry.

The quintessential TV interview question—"How did you feel when . . . ?"—was put to one of the singers whose voices were heard when a group called Milli Vanilli mouthed their lyrics. The singer shrugged. "It's true," he said, "it wasn't their singing. But then, in all fairness, it wasn't our faces."

Few who are ripped off can accept it with such grace. The assignment of credit has always been tricky, and the more complex and collaborative design gets, the trickier it is. Anyone who has ever worked in a design office knows how often the line "designed by John Jones" is, at the very least, an oversimplification. Yet accuracy, not always easy to establish in any case, would make for cumbersome and boring credits and would perhaps misleadingly suggest a diffusion of responsibility.

In the film *Lady in the Dark*, Danny Kaye based a production number on the frustration of the moviegoer who, each time he thinks the film is about to begin, finds that it isn't. Not yet. Not until the director, assistant director, color technician, cinematographer, costume designer, and makeup artist have been given their due. Those were the good old days. Because today's films would *never* begin if that were the practice, most contemporary credits are listed at the end. The audience stumbles out in the dark, turning its back on the passing parade of best boys, best girls, gaffers, schnorrers, grips, grunts, stunt consultants, optical radiation specialists, animal casting directors, hair stylists, and the couple down the street who catered the on-

Originally published May/June 1991 in *I.D.*, as the column "Circumstantial Evidence."

location snacks. With an exquisite sense of self-parody, the producers of *Silence of the Lambs* even credited the assistant moth wrangler.

Well, how else would you know? On the other hand, who needs to know? Not the audience. I have never met a film cultist devoted enough to follow the work of his favorite gaffer. The importance of credits lies within the industry, and their proliferation says something about the right to fairness, the need for recognition, the sense of participation, and the power of unions and agents. It also says something about how movies are made. As it happens, I *like* reading names, and however tedious people find those running lists, they do drive home the idea that movies are not made by individual men, women, or children.

Neither are most designs.

Although multitudes of designs have been done by X but identified as the work of Y, I don't know of a design counterpart to ghostwriting—the practice in which X deliberately creates work for Y to present as his or her own. Except in fiction. Howard Roark, the hero of *The Fountainhead*, ghosted a building under the name of an inferior architect purely for the satisfaction of getting it built; but few architects are so pure of heart. On the other hand, not many architects blow up their own buildings, as Roark did, either. Pity.

A writer I had never heard of (with good reason, for his name was suppressed in the interests of professional ethics) died recently, and I was struck by the candor of the obituary. "He was," the obit said, "the ghost writer for autobiographies of Liberace, Ed McMahon, Mike Douglas and Henny Youngman. He was also the ghost writer of Bob Hope's *I Never Left Home*." Coincidentally the same day's paper described Caroline Kennedy's appearance at the law firm "where Theodore Sorensen, who wrote some of her father's most famous words, is a partner." In these times we are all willing, even eager, to stand up and be counted. No one thinks it strange when Peggy Noonan, who had some of Ronald Reagan's insights, writes a book about her life as his mind. And no one cares that automobile tycoon Lee Iacocca's autobiography was not exactly autogenerated. After all, he didn't build cars either.

Ghostwriting seems wrong to me, but even if it didn't, I can't imagine doing it with any satisfaction. Nevertheless, I confess to having ghostwritten three speeches, each with its own rationalization.

Once I wrote a speech for my then boss, an executive who, because of his job title, was expected to know something about design, but didn't. Under the circumstances I decided I would be more embarrassed by what he would say on his own than I would feel compromised by writing something for him to say.

The second occasion was a campaign speech for a political candidate. My rationalization was that no one would elect *me* to a high office, and they might elect him. They did, by a margin so slim that I mused afterwards that it could have been my phrasing—"I invite you to join me in a political adventure"— that put him over. My confession in this case is compounded by a subsidiary confession: I enjoyed it.

Those two were *pro bono*. My third transgression was for hire. It began with a phone call from someone at CBS: "I want to know if you can come up with five minutes of funny remarks for Mr. Paley to say at his 80th birthday party."

"I could never come up with anything as funny as what you just said," I replied. But I accepted the assignment, on the grounds that nothing so bizarre should be cavalierly dismissed. After two meetings with Mr. Paley I wrote five minute's worth of birthday humor. I liked what I had done. I learned later that he hadn't liked it, and had hired someone else. I also learned that I had been the third writer hired.

Nothing in my ghostly career had prepared me for the

spookiest experience of all: being ghosted. As one of a dozen or so subjects in a promotional publication for a paper company, I was informed that participation would be made as painless as possible by a ghostwriter, who would interview each of us and write brief statements for us to have said. The ghost in this case turned out to be an engaging writer with credentials so impressive I wanted to ask him the classic question addressed to hookers in movies and in life: With all your advantages, how did you get into this?

What I asked him instead was, "Is this really going to be ghostwritten? Won't that make you a ghostwriter?"

He had none of my hangups about it. "I guess so," he said pleasantly. "I don't know what else you'd call it. My name won't appear anywhere, and I think the statements will be more effective in the first person."

We talked. His questions were probing and sensitive, and I struggled to answer them. When I saw the draft I was not disappointed exactly, but I was uncomfortable. He had written almost nothing that I had not actually said during the interview. On the other hand, he had written almost nothing that I would have written for myself either. It was a workmanlike job, thoroughly professional. I had no right to complain, and I didn't. What I did was sit right down and write myself a statement.

My own.

What's Yours?

Victor Papanek declined to patent his designs, explaining "I feel that ideas are plentiful and cheap, and it is wrong to make money off the needs of others."

I don't know how money is ever made *except* off the needs (real or imagined) of others, but the issue here is not money but the rights to what it can not entirely buy.

The late Dr. Gerald Fagan, when he was a resident psychiatrist at a boys' school, relieved the guilt of students who masturbated by reminding them, "It's yours, isn't it?" But it isn't always so easy to know what belongs to us. The protection, and even the identification, of what's yours has been vastly complicated by technology. As media for distributing ideas are multiplied, amplified, and reduced in price, ownership of so-called intellectual property becomes increasingly ambiguous. Even the ownership of hard goods has been softly defined for generations. In Arthur Miller's *Death of a Salesman*, Willie Loman's refrigerator and car are falling apart at the same time as he is. "Once in my life I would like to own something outright before it's broken!" Willie cries. "They time those things. They time them so when you finally paid for them, they're used up." In the audience we smile and nod in recognition, for we are an audience and a society of renters.

The rights to what we do own are subject to interpretation. When film mavens objected to Ted Turner's colorizing black-and-white movie classics, he replied, "The last time I looked, I owned them"—his way of saying he was entitled to make them all mauve if he wished, or to keep any one else from seeing them.

Are there public rights to private property? The nadir of my adolescence was not acne, or being turned down by May Allen for the senior prom, or even being suspended from high school. It was a strike by ASCAP—the American Society of

Originally published May/June 1998 in *PRINT*, as the column "Peripheral Vision."

Composers, Authors and Publishers—and until it was settled, radio stations were prohibited from broadcasting music or lyrics produced by its members. I don't remember exactly how long it lasted, but for what seemed like forever the only songs we heard were in the public domain, usually by Stephen Foster. We understood dimly that the rights of creators to the material they had created were at stake, but we wanted the music back. If the concept of intellectual property was in legal vogue then, none of us would have thought it applied to "Darn That Dream" or "Flat Foot Floogie with the Floy Floy."

The inheritance of intellectual property is more problematic. The son of a vaudeville comedian, having been given his father's name at birth and taken over his father's act when the old man died, proudly advertised in the trade papers: "This act is not a copy. It is a legacy." Today, Dickensian court battles rage over whether families own in perpetuity the *images* of their celebrity ancestors.

I love a Gershwin tune, but if I can't play one without paying, whom do I pay? Not George and Ira, who have no further use for royalties. The Gershwin Family Trust? Well, why not? If families can inherit money, why shouldn't they inherit songs that can be turned into money? One reason is that cultural resources not only enrich us but enrich each other through us. Our copyright laws have always acknowledged this by providing only temporary coverage, after which the private holdings become public domain. But temporary anything has a way of becoming at least semipermanent. Copyright law has been extended over the years, and the Supreme Court has approved extending it an additional two decades. (Had that been in effect during the ASCAP revolt of my youth, nothing but Baroque would have been public domain.) A Gershwin trustee warned that without such protection, "someone could turn Porgy and Bess, into rap music." A dreadful prospect, I guess, but folklorist Steve Zeitlin, noting that Gershwin's opera itself drew on African American musical traditions, asks, "What could be more appropriate?" Zeitlin finds it similarly ironic that Disney, having freely used "Snow White" and other public domain materials for major productions, anxiously seeks to protect forever the sanctity of Mickey Mouse, which strikes some people as a Mickey Mouse idea.

Designers know the danger of letting work go unprotected—the danger not only of theft by competitors but of erosion through the negligence of managers who can't see, don't care, or have designs (and designers) of their own. The graphics standards manuals, devised as security systems, have often been ineffective because the people who understood them were not in control of their implementation.

Intellectual property implies the commodification of what cannot be commodified. If we protect it, why not protect emotional property as well? When William Styron wrote about the Nat Turner uprising, blacks challenged his right to write about the slave experience, on the grounds that it belonged to them collectively and exclusively. A comparable possessiveness attaches to the Holocaust as a phenomenon uniquely applicable to Jews but not to the Gypsies and gays who were also sent to Nazi death camps, or to the Armenians and Rwandans slaughtered at other times under other auspices. When David Leavitt based a novel on the homoerotic autobiographical writing of Stephen Spender, the elderly poet sued, telling Leavitt to get his own sex life instead of appropriating someone else's old one.

But Leavitt was writing fiction, in which personal experience may be transferable. In Charles Williams's *Descent into Hell*, Pauline tells Peter about a recurring event that terrifies her. He can't do anything about the recurring event, but he offers to carry the fear for her, just as he would carry a parcel or her books. It's still *her* fear, he explains, but with him as designated schlepper, she won't have to do the fearing.

No one has yet copyrighted an idiosyncrasy or patented a neurosis, but James Thurber has shown us the way: A character in a Thurber story steals another man's dream. Another character in a Thurber cartoon has a friend accompany him to the doctor's office, where he registers the unprecedented medical complaint, "I've got Bright's disease and he's got mine."

"What's mine is yours" is the posture of a saint. "What's yours is mine" is the ideology of a mugger. Frankly, I do not know how to reconcile them. I think I understand rights and privileges in respect to owning things—whether one-off or mass produced. If I find a rock, it's mine. If I fashion it into a tool, it is more decisively mine, because my hands shaped it and my imagination told them how. If it is mine, then, since I am no saint, it is not yours. You have therefore been served with a moral injunction not to covet my rock and a criminal code forbidding you to take it if you do covet it. However, if I give it to you or leave it to you, the rock is yours, with all the rights and privileges pertaining thereto.

Thereto is the rub. What rights and privileges pertain to the rocks in your head? And where do they go when your head is gone? Some things that are yours are part of you. No one *can* take them from you, but it hurts when they try. To be plagiarized is, as Steve Heller indicated recently in *PRINT*, to be "violated." This can be accomplished with dazzling chutzpah, as when a journalist in London took a couple of pages from an article of mine, then *quoted* me in an additional paragraph from the same article, putting me in the curious position of agreeing with myself.

Sometimes what looks like plagiarism is simply coincidence. But not all coincidence is entirely coincidental. After driving to Wesleyan University to hear the brilliant Suzanne Langer lecture on signs and symbols, I was disappointed to find that she really had nothing more to say on the subject than I had already said in a lecture of my own. Driving home, I figured out why. My ideas *were* as good as hers, but only because they were hers to start with! I had absorbed them from reading her books.

Talking Wrong

When I was asked to recommend "a typically American play," for a visiting group of Chinese industrialists, I suggested the tap musical, *Bring in 'da Noise, Bring in 'da Funk*. It's not exactly *Our Town*, but, driven by movement and beat rather than language, the show seemed a good choice for people who spoke little or no English.

Our interpreter, Ms. Wu, looked spectacularly like the ingenue in any of Bruce Lee's early Hong Kong films. Her English, learned in, and never before exercised outside of, Peking, was impeccable. When we reached the theater, however, the marquee gave her pause. What, she wanted to know, did "funk" mean?

What indeed? "There is no exact equivalent in Mandarin," I told her. I was stalling for time, yet I knew from past experience that there would never be enough time. I have a history of trouble with *funk*, having used the word confidently for years without ever finding out what it means. When I proposed naming a rock group "The Motherfunkers," the idea was rejected scornfully because "It doesn't make any sense"—a curious criterion in a guild whose members include Jefferson Airplane, Phish, and Mott the Hoople.

In the theater lobby I spotted a vendor of tie-in merchandise who was selling hats like the one Savion Glover wore in the show. The vendor was wearing one of the hats himself.

"Man," I said, "you're my man. Please tell this young lady what *funk* means." The vendor turned suspiciously toward Ms. Wu. "Funk? Like, funk means whatever you want it to mean," he said.

"She has never heard of it before," I said. "She doesn't want it to mean anything. She wants to know what it does mean."

He rose to the occasion with a dazzlingly inventive exegesis

Originally published February 1997 in *PRINT*, as the column "Peripheral Vision."

of Talmudic complexity. It was authoritative, hip, and thoroughly incomprehensible. And, I suspect, funky.

"That pretty much covers it," I assured Ms. Wu.

"I see," she said inscrutably. "And what does "da' mean?"

That I thought I could handle myself. "'Da" is simply the word *the* mispronounced, I explained. But, she persisted, if, as I claimed, "'da" was incorrect English, what was it doing in the title of what I claimed was a major American cultural event? As a professional in-factory translator, Ms. Wu knew that communication is hard enough even when you're trying to get it right. Why, she wanted to know, would anyone deliberately talk wrong?

Why would anyone deliberately talk wrong? I tried to tell her.

For verisimilitude. That's how some of the characters portrayed in the show would talk, and how others would try to talk in order to be accepted by them

For humor. I described the scene in "*Airplane!*" in which two black hipsters talk to a nun in English while English subtitles run across the bottom of the screen. The film was made long before Ebonics was introduced into the teacher training agenda of the Oakland, California, school board—another case of life ripping off art.

Because some things sound more right when they are wrong. When I was in training as a Marine Corps radio operator, a good deal of attention was paid to protocol: "Bluebird, this is Thunder. How do you read me? Over." *Over* meant that the ball was in Thunder's court and Bluebird was now waiting, not talking. When either of you wanted the other to talk, you said *over*. When the conversation was complete, the speaker signed off by saying *out*. That was final. *Over* required a response. *Out* precluded a response.

"Over and out," therefore, is a contradiction in terms.

"No transmission can be both over *and* out," the sergeant would hiss when we screwed up. "Out means that it's over. Get it?"

None of that satisfied me. Did it satisfy Ms. Wu? Luckily, the curtain went up before I had a chance to find out, but her question evoked other mysteries that occupied me through the first act. Why, I wondered, not for the first time, do I receive announcements of events featuring speakers whose names and credentials cannot be read because they are printed over a photograph in noncontrasting type? Like other civilians, I have no patience with that.

Designers do, and are impatient with our impatience. At Cooper Union a few years ago, the cognitive psychologist Donald Norman observed that, although the occasion was a design symposium, the design of the program made it impossible to read. A literalist in the audience shouted back that the program was possible to read, if you knew how. This was true, but it was hard not to sympathize with Norman, who thought he should be able to find out where and when an event was taking place, without help of parent or teacher.

The Society of Environmental Graphic Design was scolded by the disability activist George Covington for the willful illegibility of their publications. Of course, since Covington is legally blind, almost all the printed communication he encounters is illegible; but that was all the more reason for making it readable by *someone.*

Designers customarily bury urgent messages in graphics that are far less decipherable than anything they would use to communicate with a cleaning woman or the IRS. Why, Ms. Wu might ask, would anyone deliberately design unclear messages?

Well, *For effect.* Deviation gets attention.

For exclusivity. If you have to "know how" to read a poster, you are one up on anyone who doesn't know how. Professions, like fraternal organizations and street gangs, require codes of their own.

For the illusion of depth. In the absence of complex ideas, we can always make simple ones obscure. Well, Andre Gide pleaded, "Do not understand me too quickly." Graphic designers, for better and worse, are helping to see that no one does.

Prepare to Come About

In the film version of *The Cider House Rules*, Candy Kendall takes Homer Wells to the site of a drive-in movie and explains seductively, "Privacy is what drive-in movies are all about."

The line is faithful to the function of drive-ins as described in John Irving's novel, but it surely is not what Candy, or anyone else, would have said in the early '40s. It is, however, exactly what she would say in 2000, having rehearsed it incessantly through most of the '90s. As the century closed, a spokesperson for the Jenny Craig weight-loss company divulged the corporate strategy in hiring Monica Lewinsky to pitch their product: "She is someone who truly wants to change her life in a positive way, and that's what Jenny Craig is all about." It's also, I guess, what Promise Keepers are all about. And Head Start and psychotherapy and the Great Books program and New Year's resolutions and marriage vows. Is it possible that all of them, including Monica, are about the same thing? To say that X is what Y is all about is at best an oversimplification, at worst an outright lie. (This applies equally to the insistence that X is *not* what Y is about, as in Hillary Clinton's modest disclaimer: "The campaign is not about Rudy Giuliani or me, it is about the issues.")

We entered the new millennium twitching with language tics picked up in the last one. The end of the day. The bottom line. The cutting edge. Pushing the envelope. (Does anyone ever open the envelope to see whether there is anything in it but junk mail? No, because that could lead to a slippery slope). And we still tell each other what things that are not about anything are about.

As shorthand for thoughts too long to finish, or too complex to face up to, the device was useful. "What's it all about, Alfie?," theme song from the eponymous movie, was a

Originally published March/April 2000 in *PRINT*, as the column "Peripheral Vision."

rhetorical question expressing the ineffable character of life itself. In the Willie Nelson road film *Honeysuckle Rose*, Dyan Cannon tries to deflect the pity of fans grieved by her husband's infidelity when she asks, "Isn't betrayal what country music is all about?" Well, betrayal really was what a lot of country music was about before it and the artists who create it crossed over.

But when a man at a lawn party I attended pointed an empty champagne flute into the scenery and said, "I think I'll take a little walk down there and see what that lake is about," I was irritated into retaliative rudeness.

"I'm not a limnologist," I said, matching his pretentiousness with my own by calling attention to my knowing what a limnologist is, "but I'm pretty sure that lake is about water."

Shortly after that I began noticing, with annoyance, that basketball is all about integrity, winning, control, or teamwork, depending on which sports colorist I was listening to. Leadership, compassion, responsibility, freedom, and inclusion are what the Republicans or Democrats are all about, depending on which political colorist is spinning. An hour of TV surfing will inform you that fiber is what any given breakfast cereal is all about, unless it is the one that is about both fiber and flavor; adventure is what a car is all about (except for the car that is all about safety and the two that are all about innovation), and access is what the Internet is all about. It is all about excess, too, but the commercials don't tell you that.

The tendency to see, or pretend to see, everything in terms of what it is "about" imposes a simplistic formulation that obscures the legitimate instruments of aboutness. Articles are about something. So are pictures and jokes and even an occasional speech. Books are usually about something, but it is not always easy to say what it is.

The last big publishing sensation of the last century was the Harry Potter series of children's books, which dominated the bestseller lists one after another, then all together. I began reading them out of curiosity, which was immediately accompanied by admiration and delight. If I still don't quite understand contemporary kids, it is clear that J.K. Rowling, the author of the Harry Potter books, understands us both. The phenomenal success of her work has generated acres of analysis, much of it in the form of such assurances as: "these books are not about witchcraft, they are about heroism." On the other hand, the conclusion that these books *are* about witchcraft has led to their removal from schools and libraries by the same forces for good that keep saving us from *The Catcher in the Rye* and the Teletubbies.

In truth, the Rowling books are about both witchcraft and heroism. Also about faculty politics, bullying, favoritism, good and evil, and—as I suppose any explication of wizardry must be—about role-playing.

They are also about what all fiction is about: story. Until he goes off on a scholarship to Hogwarts, a preparatory school for wizards, Harry Potter lives with his aunt and uncle and their pampered and odious son, all of whom mistreat him cruelly. Unlike Harry, they are Muggles—people who have no potential for magic.

Muggle families generally breed more Muggles, but every so often a Muggle child is discovered to have nascent magical powers that can be nurtured into wizardry. Hermione Granger, the young heroine of the series, is one such person, and through diligence and sound mentoring is already developing into a witch of distinction.

Wizard families generally breed more wizards, but occasionally a Squib appears—a person born into a wizard family who has no magical powers. So the Harry Potter books are about the emotional difficulties of being an outsider.

Most compellingly, these books are about a parallel universe and the imaginative energy it takes to sustain it. All children suspect there is another life running alongside this one somehow, and that they belong in it. Designers think they can create one.

Creating a parallel universe of any kind suggests a shadow cabinet of designers. When preparations for the 1964 New York World's Fair seemed to be hampered at every turn by bureaucratic stupidity, a class at Parsons was assigned the task of designing an alternative Fair. But since the student project had no real constraints, and the official one had nothing going for it except constraints, the latter was the one that got built.

Constraints, we learn at Hogwarts, are as intrinsic to wizardry as they are to design. Wizards are forbidden to distort time capriciously. Budgetary discipline is essential to responsible wizardry: Top-of-the-line broomsticks and wands are costly and competition is intense. Moreover, life and work in a parallel universe are perpetually constrained by the universe parallel to it, where Muggles are a majority. Since an estimated 80 percent of clients are Muggles, designers have much to learn from the Hogwarts curriculum.

Having no potential for magic is tantamount to a deficiency of imagination. Muggles distrust imagination because they do not understand it, having so little direct experience of its pleasures. Muggles are the people who ask writers, "Where do you get your ideas?" They get jobs on network television where they ask people whose families have been wiped out how it feels to have their families wiped out. Muggles, by definition, just don't get it.

Running on Empty

Folks who put their confidence in the promise of computers to eliminate paper from life and work are now complaining that the machine has double-crossed them. True, the technology that augured a paperless revolution has not diminished the amount of paper we deal with. This, however, is not because the machine has betrayed us but because we betray it. The simplest way to eliminate unwanted paper from the corporation and the home is to reduce the number of things that are written but needn't be. Then, reduce the number of things written that are needlessly duplicated, distributed, and saved. Most memos fall into one of those categories. Whether faxed or e-mailed, they are created chiefly because the resources for sending them exist, enabling us to communicate what doesn't need to be communicated to people who wouldn't need to know it if it did. The same processing speed that could make the reduction of memos easy makes their proliferation easier still.

All our media are largely given over to things that are better left unsaid. Some of them never had to be said in the first place. Others once did—the saying of them was crucial and was attended to—but they don't have to be said over and over again. Technology is not the problem, of course. It never is. Unfortunately, it is not the solution, either. The problem, as we say of sex and violence and bad manners, is the culture.

I sit in a plane that sits on a runway at O'Hare. We have been here for most of the afternoon, with occasional trips back to the gate to replace the fuel consumed by the idling engines and air-conditioning system. We are not waiting to take off. We are waiting to learn if we *will* take off, if the afternoon flight to La Guardia has been canceled, rerouted, or just forgotten. It is customary at such times to vent one's anger at whatever airline holds you hostage, and my seatmate mutters on

Originally published July/August in 1999 in *PRINT*, as the column "Peripheral Vision."

cue, "This is what you have to expect if you fly United." I nod, but he and I both know that this is what you have to expect no matter what airline you are stuck with, and the United crew members on this occasion are unfailingly polite, responsive, and eager to provide as much help as possible, which is just about none at all. The flight to La Guardia is not long enough for a movie, but the runway time allows for a double feature and selected shorts, to which we are treated with frequent interruptions by the captain.

"This is your captain again," he would say. "We have been unable to confirm any departure information. I'll give you an update as soon as I can get one." True to his word, he broke into one of Robert De Niro's best lines to say that there was still nothing to say but he would be back soon if there were any further developments or, as it turned out, even if there were not.

I didn't mind the interruptions—I had already seen the De Niro film and the captain's dreary messages were no less sparkling than the dialogue in it—but I was irritated by the feeling that I had been through this before and could not remember where. It took me an hour or two to place the experience, probably because it was too common to isolate. The wave of familiarity had nothing to do with air travel; it was the experience of being at home. What we were hearing from the captain sounded like a parody of, or homage to, television news.

"We'll be back with more on Baghdad" (or Monica or Jon-Benét Ramsey) they say, but when they come back it is only to reveal that there is nothing more to say, which does not stop them from saying it in detail. Experts are interviewed to confirm that they don't know anything either, although they know how to put things into perspective by laying out background and possibilities, which they call "options," as if there were some way we could act on them. The experts often truly *are* experts. It is not their fault that there is no news, although they collude by appearing as guests in the first place. But the regulars—the anchors, the Cokies and Sams and Peters and Pauls—are contractually committed to talk without cessation, even if it is nonsense. They do not always talk nonsense and may even prefer not to; they simply are not assigned enough meaning to fill the time and space allotted for it between commercials. CNN carries the heaviest burden, since the other networks have mandatory breaks for entertainment.

That's not much of a break. It has been amply recognized that entertainment and news are not exactly different universes. Seinfeld was lauded for breaking new ground with the concept of a show about nothing, but network news departments had broken that ground long before. It is not true that no news is good news, because when there is no news there are still news programs, and their intensity is heightened by running on empty. Unlike people using cell phones, whose body language eloquently expresses that there is nothing urgent or even interesting about the calls, newscasters have to make believe. The journalistic tradition of the scoop guarantees that when there is nothing to say or to show, there is a fierce competition to say and show it first. Thus, the tragedy of John F. Kennedy, Jr.'s, downed plane became the occasion for an orgy of newsless reporting. In the absence of information, opinion was substituted. But in the absence of information, none of the opinion qualified as informed opinion. The opinions prepared for the anchors to read were supplanted by the opinions of experts and of so-called real people. At such times, the distinction between experts and so-called real people is lost, for the realest of people are as platitudinous as the least real news analysts. We don't know any more than the pros do.

After one of the bodies was identified, an NBC interrogator

asked an expert where and when they would find the other bodies. He replied that it was hard to say. Being a real person myself, I could have told her that; but I would not have bothered explaining why it was hard to say. The expert did: "If they are not in the fuselage," he explained, "that could indicate that they are somewhere else."

The malady is not specific to our time, but the scale is. People have always talked about nothing. It was called small talk, and was useful for getting over the awkwardness of a ride with a stranger, a meal with a relative, or a high school date. But small talk has become downright infinitesimal. Paradoxically, at the same time it has become bigger, expanding to fill our days and nights, its function not to help us through insignificant encounters but through daily life.

Why, for example, do people talk at movies? Clearly it is because they are accustomed to talking at home while watching television. But why do they talk while they are watching television, if not from the certainty that they would not be missing anything if they shut up? The acceptance of words as background has carried over to print. If TV talk is the verbal equivalent of Muzak, graphic designers are the visual counterpart of talking heads, charged with communicating the unnecessary to the unneeding.

Nonprofessionals—designers who have other day jobs—are in a better position to resist, for their work is generated on a need-to-say because-there-is-a-need-to-know basis. Not many logos are commissioned on that basis but labels often are (That's why there is an impassioned demand for truth in labeling and no call at all for truth in logoing). Il Forteto is an agricultural cooperative community in Vicchio, Italy, where, on 600 magnificent acres studded with the remains of a 16th-century estate, the members produce a range of superb cheeses. Admiring the splendid and lucid labels on wheel after wheel of cheese, I asked sales and marketing director Stefano Sarti, one of the commune's founders, who had designed them. "Flavio," he said. Was that a designer or a firm? I wondered. Milan? Bologna? "No, no. You met Flavio," Stefano reminded me. "Flavio makes the ricotta."

Expectations

There are thousands of books on how to write. Some of them are good, but I'm not sure that anyone learns how to write from them. The books most useful to writers (like those most useful to designers) are as likely to be off the subject as on it. One that manages to have it both ways is a classic I found in a secondhand book store when I was a student. It is called *Becoming A Writer*, and it has absolutely nothing to say about structure, pace, point of view, organization, diction, or any other element of craft. The author, Dorothea Brandes, had another agenda.

It is hardly a hidden agenda, for at the outset Ms. Brandes bluntly stakes out the book's territory: "If it is successful it will teach the beginner not how to write, but how to be a writer; and that is quite another thing." Her book lives up to that bizarre promise. There is a chapter called "What Writers Are Like." There is a chapter called "The Writer's Recreation." There is even a section at the end of the book called "Coffee vs. Maté," which advises: "If you tend to drink a great deal of coffee when in the throes of composition, try replacing one half of it with maté, a South American drink much like tea, but stimulating and innocuous. It can be bought at any large grocer's." It couldn't be bought at any large grocer's in my town, so it was years before I tried maté. It certainly tastes innocuous. It stimulated me to go out for coffee.

Her beverage of choice is suspect, but Dorothea Brandes is onto something germane to most occupations. If there is a significant distinction between writing and being a writer, isn't there an equally significant distinction between designing and being a designer? Isn't that also "quite another thing?" But I wonder about the sequence. Should a beginner learn first how to be a carpenter and only then learn how to drive a nail in straight? What if you practice *being* a painter until you get

Originally published January/February 1990 in *I.D.*, as the column "Circumstantial Evidence."

good at it, and then discover you have no talent for painting? Don't you need a life before you start practicing how to behave in it?

It was Socrates who said, "The unexamined life is not worth living." When we studied that in Philosophy 101, my classmate Robert Q. Bedford came up with Bedford's Corollary to Socrates' Law: "The unlived life is not worth examining." In the film *sex, lies and videotape*, the character played by Andie MacDowell says, "My life is shit. It's nothing like I thought it would be." The juxtaposition of those two statements suggests that the unexpected life is not worth living, but the most interesting people I know lead lives they didn't expect and are glad of it. I propose Caplan's Codicil to Bedford's Corollary to Socrates' Law: The unexamined life is not worth expecting.

Figures of Speech

Q: What is a metaphor?
A: For cows to graze in.

Okay, so it isn't funny. It wasn't funny in the fifth grade either, but it drove us kids to the dictionary to find out what a metaphor really was. Children use metaphors all the time, but rarely have occasion to talk about them. Designers, on the other hand, talk about metaphors incessantly, without necessarily showing any interest in their true function.

In her 1978 book *Illness as Metaphor*, Susan Sontag analyzed the metaphorical approaches to tuberculosis and to cancer, which she had. Ten years later, in *AIDS and its Metaphor*, she recalled her earlier writings: "By metaphor I meant nothing more or less than the earliest and most succinct definition I know, which is Aristotle's, in his *Poetics*. 'Metaphor,' Aristotle wrote, 'consists of giving something a name that belongs to something else. Saying a thing is or is like something-it-is-not is . . . the spawning ground of most kinds of understanding, including scientific understanding, and expressiveness.'"

It can also be a spawning ground for misunderstanding. Sontag, who died of cancer in 2005, showed how the wrong metaphors—war, invasion, the body as a battlefield and so forth—represent illness and the ill in ways that obscure our understanding of both. *AIDS and its Metaphors* was written, before the metaphorical pattern she describes was reversed in Operation Desert Storm, where medical imagery—"surgical strike"—was applied to a military operation with equal distortion. In that case, the operation was successful, but the patient lived. For our next invasion of Iraq the metaphor had become "war on terror," although terror (unlike terrorism) is intrinsic to the human condition and cannot be taken by force

We are enjoined by all the teachers and usage manuals in our lives never to mix metaphors, but mixing is not the worst

Originally published November/December 1993 in *I.D.*, as the column "Counterpoint."

thing that can be done to them. When Senator Byrd declaimed on the Senate floor that "Gridlock reared its ugly head," it was funny that he mixed the metaphors but sad that he missed the point. The failure to understand that gridlock has, in fact, no head to rear would be trivial if it did not betoken a senator with no head for understanding gridlock. Whether in Congress or at a traffic intersection, gridlock is not a monster attacking us, but an expression of our own unwillingness to yield and our inability to think of consequences.

When the Aspen Music Festival's $7 million concert hall opened, the architect Harry Teague called it "a metaphor for a gigantic musical instrument being excavated . . . a buried treasure to be re-examined every time you go there." But he did not put most of this splendid building underground as a metaphor, but as a means of keeping it visually below the height of the Music Tent that is an Aspen landmark. I think he meant that, since a concert hall is in a sense a musical instrument, a buried concert hall might stand as a metaphor for the precious experience of discovering music.

The image is fine, as long as the acoustics are good. Designers, after all, use language as everyone else does: to say what they mean, or to keep from saying what they mean, or to say what they don't mean, or to conceal that they don't mean anything. Metaphors can serve any of those purposes. But, as with other powerful resources, we need to use them sparingly, resisting the urge to draw on them just because they are there. Forced to choose (as no one ever is) between Raymond Loewy's "Never leave well enough alone" and Charles Eames' injunction, "Innovate as a last resort," I choose Charles. Using last-resort techniques as the first line of defense is bad design strategy, as evidenced whenever an unarmed person is shot by a nervous police officer.

Symbols generally deserve as much respect as fire and other dangerous elements. "Always keep your lapels clean," my father warned. He never wore, and did not approve of anyone else wearing, political buttons. A small-town grocer, he knew that many of his customers, and all of his fellow Rotarians, were Republicans, and he saw no reason to offend them (particularly the customers) by displaying his preference for the other side. Were he alive today, he would feel compassion for AIDS victims and would contribute to the cause, but he would not wear a red ribbon any more than he would tie a yellow one around a tree.

L.R. Shannon, a personal computer columnist for the *New York Times*, remarks that "computer professionals love metaphors, or at least believe computer nonprofessionals learn best with them. The metaphor for Lotus Organizer is a notebook. The metaphor for Windows is a desktop. The Dynode metaphor is an address book."

As someone who has trouble with the difficult passages in *DOS for Dummies*, I admit to limited computer literacy. But when it comes to metaphors, there are experts on my side. Theodore Holm Nelson, distinguished fellow of Autodesk, Inc., writes: "In the old days, you tried to understand the various input commands. . . . Today, you try to understand what the icon means. Instead of 'you don't understand computers,' it's now 'you don't understand the metaphor.'"

Dismayed by the "tedious array of icons . . . supported by the new Metaphoric Ideology," Nelson says of the desktop metaphor: "We have to tell the beginner how it looks like a desktop, because it doesn't (it might as easily . . . be called the Tablecloth or the Graffiti Wall).

"*The metaphor*," says Nelson, who must be the most spirited italicizer since J.D. Salinger, "*becomes a dead weight*. Once the metaphor is instituted, *every related function has to become a part of it*. . . . It becomes like a lie or a large government project," growing in complexity and guaranteeing inconsistency. The Mac's garbage can is "a hideous failure of consistency . . .

which means either 'destroy this' or 'eject it for safekeeping.'" Nelson's comments appear in *The Art of Computer Interface Design*, a book published by Apple in a remarkable display of corporate valor and apparent objectivity.

"The alternative to metaphorics is the *construction of well-thought-out unifying ideas*," Nelson says; and getting rid of "metaphorics" in software design might make me free at last. But in design generally we can never afford to lose the power of metaphor. All the more reason to approach it with care.

A young designer shows me some sketches he has done for a project. "They look interesting," I say. "What exactly are they?"

"Oh," he says, "nothing yet. They are just conceptual."

The term was once used to describe drawings that expressed an idea without specifying the details of implementation. Now it refers to drawings that have no ideas behind, or in, them.

Discomfited by the suggestion that conceptual drawing implies a concept, the designer shifts ground. Or at least nomenclature. "They are," he says, "just metaphors."

"They are not!" I say.

"Well, what do *you* mean by a metaphor?" he asks.

"Look," I say, "If I call you a horse's ass, that's a metaphor."

"Why is that a metaphor?"

"Because you are not actually a horse's ass. When I say you are, I'm trying to say something more graphically than I could in nonfigurative language."

"So you're really saying I'm *like* a horse's ass."

"No. That's what I'm really meaning," I say, "but that's not what I'm saying. To say you are *like* a horse's ass is not a metaphor. It is a simile. Designers never talk about similes. Maybe that's next."

"Will this be on the quiz?" he asks, but I am in no mood to return the sarcasm. It occurs to me that it would have been more gracious to have applied the epithet to myself, rather than to him. I still feel the sting when I remember the poetic cruelty of a drill instructor on Parris Island, South Carolina, who held our wretched platoon of misfits at attention while he assessed our prospects. Shaking his head in contemptuous wonder, he bellowed his conclusion: "None of you would make a pimple on a Marine's ass!"

Now *that* was a metaphor, and no one had to hit the help key to find out what the icon really stood for.

Words and Pictures

Under the auspices of the United States Information Agency, I once did a gig in Belgrade with a designer who introduced his slide presentation by saying that one picture is worth a thousand words. He then regaled the audience with what must have been, by that standard of measurement, the equivalent of a two-volume book, although curiously he did not do it in silence. If, I thought maliciously, one picture is worth a thousand words, why did he need so many of them, when the pictures were right there?

It was an idle thought, reawakened a day or two later when we played Zagreb. "One picture is worth a thousand words," the designer asserted again. The audience smiled and nodded approvingly, although they may have been hearing something else in the simultaneous translation. I was not smiling, or nodding either for that matter. I was counting. The statement itself consists of only seven words, and I imagine it is about the same length in Serbo-Croatian. If it were true, you could say it with one picture and still have 993 words worth of meaning left on the picture chip. The designer, however, wasn't saying it with one picture. No one ever does. In Zagreb, as in Belgrade, he was saying it with words. You couldn't blame him, and I didn't. There are occasions when words are the instruments of choice, more efficient for the purpose, even in translation.

That ancient adage about the relative economy of words and pictures was hardly new material either to us or the audience. The original Chinese proverb was less modest: "One picture is worth more than *ten thousand* words." Why would designers, who are ordinarily not averse to hyperbole, reduce the verbal inflation rate by more than ninety percent? I suspect it's just that American designers are more literal than Chinese sages. The latter work their craft in a tradition that calls for a poetic

Originally published November/December 1987 in *I.D.*, as the column "Circumstantial Evidence."

sense of hyperbole, and they recognize a figure of speech when they see (or say) one. The wall of a thousand Buddhas in Beijing, for example, hasn't really got a thousand Buddhas on it; the name means that it is "as though" there were a thousand. No one's counting. No Chinese sage (or peasant either) ever seriously posited a word-to-picture exchange rate of ten thousand to one. The proverb simply tells us that there are circumstances in which a picture can be clearer, quicker, more moving than any number of words carrying the same message.

The annals of graphic design are loaded with examples of this unsurprising phenomenon. An issue of the old *LIFE* magazine; George Lois's *Esquire* cover of Sonny Liston as Santa Claus; Dugald Stermer's *Ramparts* cover of South Vietnam's Madame Ngu in a Michigan State cheerleader's costume; the hundreds of ads for products ranging from scotch to college education that feature an Eames lounge chair as an indicator of affluence and taste; the myriad television commercials for casual clothing and designer cologne that suggest in pictures what to say in words would offend Jerry Falwell.

There are, however, even more frequent circumstances when *no* picture can adequately convey what words can. Plainly it is a matter of cognitive complexity and of the kind of message to be communicated. Even more plainly, it is a matter of whose words and whose pictures. One picture by Stieglitz is probably worth a billion words by Jackie Collins. Six words by almost anyone are worth a thousand pictures by me. The mistake is to assume that words and pictures are somehow natural competitors, fighting for the same message turf. Actually there is plenty of meaning to go around. In communication design, words and pictures are mutually supportive, and can't easily be substituted for one another, any more than people can. It depends on what you need them for. (One good violinist is worth a thousand accountants, but not at tax time). One of the few cases I know of a direct word-for-picture swap is Milton Glaser's I♥NY, and that is a simple one-for-one exchange, as with hostages or second basemen. Glaser's version has a strength, charm and ingenuity not found in the verbal declaration. Or at least it had when he designed it. Now that the device has been ripped off all over the world, the heart simply reads as the word, having become what George Orwell called a "dead metaphor," one that over time loses its metaphorical charge and takes on the weight of just another word.

Just another word was more than I had time for, when I agreed to limit my remarks at a conference in San Francisco to two minutes. No problem. The audience would consist almost entirely of graphic designers, most of whom came into the world believing that one picture is worth you know what.

I prepared to attack them with a talk consisting, by actual count, of exactly one thousand words, a triumph of exactitude over style and substance. I could not do it in two minutes, however. I am a man of few words, but it takes me a long time to get them out. According to my neighborhood psycholinguist, people speak at an average speed of 150 to 200 words per minute. This means that even someone at the high end of average would take at least five minutes to say one thousand words. Since my speed is below average (I have been clocked at 112 when excited), I had to discard most of my prepared notes. The entire talk, however, was published in the *American Institute of Graphic Arts Journal*, on the grounds, I guess, that my thousand words can be read as fast as anyone else's, even though they take a lot longer to hear.

In design for print, words are routinely removed by a surgical specialty called art direction, because reading takes time and "people don't read." It does take time, and a lot of people don't read. But a lot of people don't see either. The one-picture/thousand words fallacy is the kind of conventional design wisdom that rarely gets questioned. There were other examples at the San Francisco conference. Upon receiving an award for corporate design leadership, the CEO of the sportswear company Esprit proclaimed, as have scores of others before him, that "Good design is good business."

That bromide unnerves me each time I hear it. Not that it is entirely untrue, but it is recited as if it were an equation, in which case good business would be good design. That ain't necessarily so, as evidenced by a flyer advertising the twelfth annual Design Management Conference and reminding us, "Designers know that most of the biggest selling products are mediocre. Note the packages in supermarkets, the appliances in discounters, or the ads on TV." Does that mean that mediocre design is even better business?

The late Arthur Drexler divided the world into two classes of designers. The first was "inundating the whole western world and parts of Asia with unnecessary objects . . . and they and their designs must be resisted." The second category existed "only in the narrow cracks left between really large-scale industries. In the United States they can make furniture and glassware and lamps, but not automobiles."

Good design, Drexler was saying, from the vantage point of the Museum of Modern Art, may be good business if you are Herman Miller or Rosenthal, but not if you're General Motors.

I don't believe that either. Good design is *everybody's* business, as are good management, good engineering, good customer service, good sex, movies, food. Nobody spends much time arguing the point, because everyone takes it for granted—who wants bad anything? I remember, back in the days when Jane Fonda was a popular name to drop, seeing her described on a cereal box as "one of America's favorite health advocates." Not an impressive distinction, since there are no serious sickness advocates. Health needs no advocates, because no one is against it. Its desirability is taken for granted.

Because its desirability is *not* taken for granted, design does need advocates, but not cheerleaders waving a simplistic slogan. Any maxim can be misleading if not qualified. Less is more—more or less. You get what you pay for, some of the time. And, under certain extreme circumstances, one picture may be worth a thousand words.

Image and Reality

In a political season the mind naturally gravitates to images. A designer's mind is never far from them in any case. But the most familiar public vehicle for designed images is political.

Not that the public isn't deluged with designed images of other kinds. It's just that nonpolitical images are encountered after the fact: the logo off the drawing board and on the screen, the picture already in print. Political images, on the other hand, are designed in the nation's most conspicuous electronic show windows. The smoke-filled back room has given way to the Crystal Palace.

Astute politicians have always manipulated images, of course, but never before have they done it so unapologetically. "I have nothing to hide," our politicians say in effect. "I formulate my image before your very eyes and, because this is a democracy, make you privy to how I do it." The contemporary American politician is a magician who not only shows how the trick is done; he keeps trying it out in front of the audience to see whether it works and whether it is the right trick for the purpose.

Consequently, our public awareness of politics is less a sensitivity to issues and laws than a sensitivity to image engineering. There is an incredible, but hardly refreshing, candor in all of this. In 1984 Presidential candidate Walter Mondale wanted Vice-Presidential candidate Geraldine Ferraro to help him convey an image of boldness—an image all the polls (and all the pols) agreed that he desperately needed and could find only in outside resources. At the same time, his supporters explained that Ms. Ferraro's selection in itself "demonstrated" boldness. In other words, her role is to make him look bold; but his very willingness to assign her that role *is* bold. The image does not project reality but creates its own. By a curi-

Originally published September/October 1984 in *I.D.*, as the column "Circumstantial Evidence."

ous technique of definition, you genuinely are what you seek to seem.

In campaign politics, it is worse to look indecisive than to be indecisive, particularly if these are really the same thing. At some point in the opposition between image and reality, however, one of the two emerges as more important than the other—at least, more important to us. If a political candidate has the image of being "trigger-happy," he may not get elected. If he really is trigger-happy, we may not live to care whether he is elected or not. If a manufacturing corporation has a poor image, its sales figures may plummet. But if the firm's products are of poor quality, we may not get the laundry clean or the heart transplanted.

This is called an image problem. As the techniques of image manipulation get better, the image of the people who create and use them gets worse. The trades most sophisticated in improving the client's image are curiously impotent when it comes to their own. Public relations people complain that they have a bad press, although their expertise presumably consists in influencing the press. Advertising agencies find it easier to convince people that drinking Pepsi-Cola makes you young at heart than to convince people that advertising is a noble undertaking. Political consultants may succeed in making George W. Bush look compassionate or Joseph Lieberman look innovative, but they seem unable to create for themselves the sort of public trust they manufacture for others.

Before beginning his dictionary, Samuel Johnson called on Lord Chesterfield for financial support. He was turned away. The door to Chesterfield's London townhouse became an image of rejection. For all his subsequent success and fame and greatness Johnson never overcame the slight, remembering all his life the image of "the inhospitable door." When I was a child our family custom was to regularly visit a relative who was no gladder to see us than we were to come. My father, struck by Johnson's phrase, applied it to the door of the relative's house. "The inhospitable door" is how it was always described in our family. (Inhospitable or not, we went dutifully, tradition having a higher priority than perception.)

That was not a gratuitous image. In both Johnson's case and our family's, the image projected by the door corresponded with the reality behind it. This is more likely with some artifacts than with others, and doors are particularly suitable for the purpose. When people are behind their closed doors, the doors themselves take on personalities.

If that is anthropomorphism, at least it is self anthropomorphism. That is, "the door doesn't want to open" not because you ascribe human desires to it but because it projects human impulses. The computer not only doesn't want to open, it may not even want to speak to you until you have done your homework. (Computers are like Parisians who reply to your French by indicting you for not speaking it right.) Whether computers can "think," or even "feel," is hotly debated. Not here. Not now. It is enough that computers and other products evoke emotions in us. They can make you welcome or unwelcome (doors) summon guilt (the light that says my computer is on when I am not) seduce you (convertibles, wine bottles) and fight you for the control of your life. When somebody enters a room and unthinkingly turns on the television set without consulting the schedule, he or she is responding not to a particular show, but to the object itself.

We condescend to people who believe objects have spirits inside them. But that belief is sounder than the belief that spirit can be added to the product from the *outside*. Yet clients who expect designers to endow them with a credible image are asking for precisely that.

They can't have it. Oh, images can be conferred—makeup artists and plastic surgeons do it all the time. But credibility— which has to do with *deserving* the projected image—can't be supplied that way. Designers do enhance the credibility of their clients and the force and clarity of their images; that is an important part of what design is for. But it is done by creating something new or discovering something already present. Either way, responsible image building entails working with what is truly there. If image is a problem, reality is where to look for a solution.

2

Object Lessons

T hings are in the saddle, and ride mankind," Emerson complained at the height of the first industrial age. He feared that the objects we own were beginning to own us. Henry Adam's juxtaposition of The Dynamo and the Virgin advanced the same concern and the Luddites, seeing a threat to livelihood as well as quality of life, acted on it.

Our paradoxical discomfort with things—the very things we love and that we use to define ourselves—is more complex now. Object lessons are more comprehensive today because the objects are, and so are the dilemmas they bring. The threats the Luddites thought they faced have not entirely vanished, nor have Luddites. But the ever increasing room for debate about whether machines can think gives rise to other provocative questions: If they can, so what? Could they be programmed to feel?

Technology has caught up with hyperbole. The phrase "totally new concept," so tritely used to introduce products that are anything but, has outlived its uselessness, for we have become accustomed now to confronting concepts that really *are* totally new. And totally unexpected. In our living rooms, home offices, shirt pockets and purses are machines that can do what we thought only we could do, and more.

To ask what things mean to us now is to wonder whether there will come a time to ask what we mean to them.

MoMA and TruValue

I can't fix anything and almost never try to. Since this disciplined abstention limits my need for tools, you might expect it to limit my interest in hardware stores as well. It doesn't. Hardware stores rank with bookstores and bed as environments of choice, and I spend time in them every chance I get. As design experiences they are almost invariably superior to the kind of shops that used to be called "good design stores" and are now simply called "design stores." I admire shops like Moss, and the showroom and catalog merchandiser Design Within Reach, but for pleasurable encounters with product design they don't match TruValue.

This is not because hardware stores have more elegant merchandise, although you can find plenty of that in them, especially if they sell marine hardware. It is simply that there is in the diversity and breadth of useful gadgetry an unaffected vitality that few specialty shops can match. The inventory of a hardware store is assembled to make money, and toast, and coffee, and tight seals, and three-quarter inch holes; the inventory of a design store is intended to make money and "statements." Have you ever seen a design statement as interesting as a chain saw?

Hardware stores are not the only retail sources of design exuberance. Camera shops and magic supply houses are equally inviting. So are stores that sell camping and hunting equipment. My high school friend Max Green owns such a store in our western Pennsylvania hometown. I not only don't fix things, I don't shoot things either, although I qualified as marksman in boot camp. But Max Green's window—full of rifles I have no wish to fire and pup tents I hope never to sleep in or even pitch—is more engaging and informative than most museum design shows.

Not that most museum design shows are stiff competition.

Originally published May/June 1987 in *I.D.*, as the column "Circumstantial Evidence."

"A woman preaching," Samuel Johnson said, "is like a dog's walking on his hind legs. It is not done well; but you are surprised to find it done at all." He was wrong about women, and even about some dogs, but the principle applies to design in a museum, which often relies for impact on the Johnson Effect. That is, the excitement, if any, is derived less from the quality of the exhibition than from the shock of finding designed objects in an art museum at all. "Isn't it interesting to see a socket wrench in a museum," we think, although it shouldn't be all that interesting almost fifty years after an assortment of nuts and bolts and computer innards was displayed at the Museum of Modern Art.

Art museums have historically been ambivalent about design, and designers have tended to return the compliment. "I don't design for museums," Henry Dreyfuss liked to say; and I liked to reply that I hoped nobody did. Designers shouldn't design for museums any more than mummies should die for them. Nevertheless they are our most promising vehicles for critically interpreting the things we live with. What we need are design museums that are as enlightening as hardware stores, and as much fun.

The C-Word

Alfred University is not an easy institution to understand, and I don't. Its famous college of ceramics is part of the State University of New York, while its liberal arts, business, and engineering colleges are private. But you don't have to understand Alfred to be attracted to it, as I am after taking part in a symposium there on "Craft and Design."

Before the symposium began, speakers were invited to freshen up in the Dean's office, an offer I couldn't refuse but did not look to for revelation. My spirits lifted, however, when I found Boraxo in the soap dispenser. There is something heartening about a design school where even deans get their hands dirty.

Once I called Michael Lax, an Alfred alumnus, and was told that he was unavailable and would have to call me back. The reasons people give for being unable to come to the phone almost invariably involve the putative presence of other people, as in "I have someone with me" or "She's in a meeting." The most refreshing explanation I have ever heard was, "I'm sorry. Miss Applewhite can't take your call right now. She's working."

As it turned out, Michael was working too. "Sorry," he said when he returned my call. "I was up to my elbows in plaster." There was then, and is now, a paucity of industrial designers who spend much time up to their elbows in plaster. In design the emphasis shifts as soon as possible from shaping the thing to solving the problem, from making it to making it happen. The designer moves as soon as possible to the process of addressing someone else's needs—the client's, the consumer's, the distributor's. That difference is one of many points of abrasion that make craft and design ill at ease with each other (and that would bind craft more closely to art, where its proximity is equally suspect).

Originally published January/February 1995 in *I.D.*, as the column "Counterpoint."

Yet well meaning people keep trying to bring craft and design together with results that, as with matchmaking generally, can be simultaneously instructive and confusing. A few years ago I served as a juror for a competition intended to encourage the development of a sense of design among practitioners of the crafts. This seemingly reasonable purpose was announced in the call for entries, which explicitly invited craftspersons to submit work they regarded as especially strong in "design values," which the sponsoring organization shrewdly neglected to define. Submissions ranged from the exquisite to the banal, with most of them falling between those extremes; in that respect the competition was no different from most design competitions. But the jury deliberations were very different. I remember, for example, asking what a particular vessel was for, and being told complacently that "the entry form doesn't say," as if the function of an object were incidental to judging its quality. There was a coffee cup that was enchanting in its way, except that its way included a perverse resistance to sitting evenly in the saucer. When I asked whether cups and saucers designed for each other, shouldn't be expected to fit like hand and glove (or at least like cup and saucer), I was told: "These are not meant to be your everyday dishware." Well, they were not my ordinary dishware, which was much less handsome and much more useful.

The assumption was that their status as craft made the cup and saucer irrelevant to the act of drinking. But why should the standards of nobler forms be any less exacting, less humane, less intelligently executed than run-of-the-mill objects? In factory-made dishware, even minimal quality control precludes mismatched cups and saucers. If, as Ezra Pound said, "poetry has to be at least as good as prose," why doesn't craft have to be at least as good as mass production?

It could be argued that craft is so close to art that it seeks to soar beyond the product. But designing a product well also entails going beyond the product, to where the user is. Design posits a user.

In the absence of design criteria, crafted objects are defined in terms of innovation, real or imagined—just as they are in marketing and public relations—as if innovation were somehow good in itself. With me abstaining, our jury awarded a special "innovative design prize" to a table knife that, instead of lying at the side of the plate, stood upright on its cutting edge, although not for long.

Design is directed to a need, and therefore to the person who has it. Craft is not oblivious to need, but the priorities are different. Not even the worst craftsperson is likely to make a cup that would not hold water, but not even the best craftsperson finds that concern at the top of her agenda, presumably because it is a purpose so easily achieved by everything from coconut shells to used soup cans.

Craft and design are both too rich for assignment to a single meaning. Design means developing a plan for carrying out an objective, but in our culture it also means the decoration on a sheet of wallpaper. Craft means the skillful performance of a complex operation, but it also refers to a complex of leisure pursuits that end in the production of artifacts derisively called artsy crafty.

As craft and design became separated from each other, the vision, never very satisfactory, of the designer as "artist in industry" was supplanted by the vision of the designer as "the conscience of industry." Unfortunately, conscience is not a function that can be performed by X on behalf of Y. It cannot be farmed out. Yet, metaphorically at least, conscience must be lodged somewhere. Could craft be the venue of choice?

The sociologist C. Wright Mills thought so and used that idea as the basis for a stirring charge to designers, ending with the astonishing assertion that "the highest human ideal is: to be a good craftsman." Wright was not speaking of craft as a process, but of craftsmanship as a value, a value he saw as "the common denominator of art, science and learning and also the very root of human development." Yet for all the towering height that ideal gains from Mills's eloquence, it is, like all ideals, attainable only by work, which in fact was intrinsic to his thesis. Mills conceived of craftsmen as "cultural workers," a concept shared by the silk screen artist Sister Corita, who, when asked to state her philosophy of art, shifted the conversation to South Sea islanders she had read about who had no word for art. "They don't need one," Corita claimed, "because they just do everything as well as they can, which is what we mean by art."

There is a kind of protective elitism in the disassociation of design from craft. In college I took a seminar with a prominent poet who was at the time in psychotherapy and had been encouraged to stop suppressing the drama of her life. By way of practice, she told the class about an affair she was having with her plumber. "I just wish," she said with a lyrical sigh, "that I had discovered the crafts earlier," a confession all the more intriguing for its implication that plumbing is a craft and poetry is not. Elitism, as it always has, works both ways. On the one hand there is the ceramist who feels superior to the designer because her teapot does not actually have to produce tea. On the other hand there are the designers who spend their days in boardrooms and feel superior to anyone who gets their hands dirty with work.

Designers can't plunge their arms in plaster because they spend too much of their time in meetings, although nothing in design and art school curricula prepares them very well for that. As in professional life generally, the distance from physical work leads to a romanticization of it, so that as our economy, and designers with it, becomes focused more on service and distribution than on actually making things, the people stationed at the outposts furthest from reality seize on ways of describing themselves that are wholly unrealistic but that hearken back to a lost reality. So advertising and public relations agencies love to refer to their operations as "shops."

At bottom, as Sibyl Moholy-Nagy wrote, designers are "lovers of paint and metal," and design can hardly shed its craft component without suffering a loss—first of identity, then of character. The old standard industrial design school course "materials and methods" is profoundly boring as a curricular designation, but, in the hands of a master craftsman-teacher, the subject begins to look like the soul of design process. Arthur Pulos, who was such a teacher, reminds us in *American Design Ethic* of rich design legacies like "the fingerprint in the clay, the scar of the adze on the wooden beam, the facets of the hammer on metal" that mark the forming of material to human use.

Assuming that they are rooted in the same impulse to create something, where do craft and design diverge? I think it is at the point where the emphasis shifts from creating a form to meeting a need. The practice of design addresses the user in terms of a job to do, an irritant to remove, a strategy to formulate, an itch to scratch. The practice of craft is closer to elemental form giving. The statement it makes may seem to be "I made this for you," but it really is, "I made it for myself, and *therefore* for you."

Personally I envy anyone who can say "I made this." Designers usually cannot, for the scale and complexity of contemporary design projects requires collaborators. Craft, more direct and immediate, requires individual responsibility for, and ownership of, the process. George Nakashima made a Nakashima table in a sense that Frank Gehry can never make a Gehry building.

Crafts were for a long time associated with a particular order of materials; craftspeople worked in wood and wool, but not in polypropelene. Not now. Today, craftspeople, like designers, work in synthetic materials, and they do it without guilt. That is, without aesthetic guilt. The guilt now comes from the damage we do in synthesizing the materials and the damage they do by refusing to go away. The guilt comes from our raiding the planet for materials it will one day no longer provide. Rosewood, like the rainforest it comes from, is an endangered species. That may be the ultimate paradigm shaft.

Shifting from form to need marks the separation of design from craft in still another way. Design, once a matter of shaping objects, has moved increasingly beyond objects to strategies, systems, software and situations. Our sages have been telling us for years that process was becoming more important than product, that our national economy has metamorphosed from a factory for manufacturing goods to a bureau for providing services; from owning things like cars and TV sets, to renting functions like transportation and communication. The design critic Edgar Kauffmann, Jr., saluted what he named "the new immaterialism," seeing it as an exciting opportunity for designers. It was and is. But an immaterial craft is harder to envision. What is the use of craft in a world of virtual reality?

Well, surely one use must be to feed our hunger for the other kind of reality—the real thing, the genuine article that, like us, can be bumped into and held and resented and loved. Bran Ferren, one of the most high tech of technocrats, insists that the technology of special effects developed because "reality isn't good enough." Maybe. But virtual reality isn't good enough either.

Paradoxically, the need for craft, like the need for design, also moves beyond the object. Does anyone *need* another bowl, another coffee mug, a keepsake box, basket, nut dish? Did anyone really need a nut dish in the first place? It's not that we need those particular things, but that we need things, things made of stuff. Satisfying that need is a design problem that looks to craft for help. When the information network promises to eliminate any reason to travel or to touch something palpable other than a keyboard or a mouse, we search all the more intensely for the personal and the tactile.

The tactile *is* personal. Why else would sexual harassment be an issue? Strictly speaking, ceramics is the process of fashioning something out of clay and firing it. But clay is not only the stuff pots are made of; it is, according to both Old and New Testaments, and I suspect the Koran as well, the stuff *we* are made of. Maybe we need to be fired, or fired up.

The polemic *Bad*, by Paul Fussell, is subtitled *The Dumbing of America*. Just as catastrophic for designers is the *numbing* of America, the state in which we become so far removed from the processes by which our artifacts are made that we don't understand either them or ourselves. Craft in design can help close the gap between us and the things we live with. It is an antidote to numbness.

Exquisite Distinctions

The lecturing I've done has entailed spending a lot of time in hotels, which turned out to be instructive. It also meant spending time in that curious gray area known as the question period. That was instructive too. There is a pattern to the questions people ask about design. They ask what design is, and what designers do. They ask how to tell good design from bad. They almost never ask what design is *for*.

I always ask. And am surprised by the enormous range of answers. There are more functions in heaven and earth than are dreamt of in all our philosophies, and design is a process applicable to so many of them that it is easy to forget one of the most important: As I was reminded recently, design is an instrument for making distinctions.

I was having breakfast alone at an inn in a midwestern university town. The two men at the next table were talking about the growth and direction of one of the university's professional schools. What the school needed at this point, they agreed, was "an improved marketing plan." The rest of the conversation was marketing talk; I redirected my attention to the eggs with home fries.

I guess schools of higher learning need marketing plans, although I wish they didn't need to call them that, and the dialogue at the next table showed how deeply the language and values of business have penetrated the groves of academe. I have an affection for both educational institutions and businesses, but there is an important difference between them. The men at the adjacent table (eggs over easy with cinnamon toast; short stack with Canadian bacon) seemed not to be aware of it. Yet that very difference is part of what makes education valuable for human pursuits in general, including business.

George Bernard Shaw complained that "the public does not

Originally published January/February 1987 in *I.D.*, as the column "Circumstantial Evidence."

make exquisite distinctions." He was writing of the public he knew. Today he might have dropped the adjective, for we live in a world where it is increasingly difficult to make distinctions at all. Distinctions between institutions are blurred; distinctions between people we live with and people we watch on screen are blurred; distinctions between *things* are blurred.

Design can help with the last of those maladies, but it doesn't always. Once I ordered a home exercise gadget from a catalogue. It did not reduce my waistline but it increased the volume of my mail. Lands End, Sharper Image, Crate & Barrel, Neiman-Marcus, Williams Sonoma. . . . The list is endless, and you can't escape by leaving home because every airline provides a similar catalogue in the pocket of the seatback in front of you.

Not that I want to escape. I like looking through catalogues. What disturbs me is that I often have no idea what I am looking at. James Thurber claimed that Harold Ross, who founded *The New Yorker*, had a disconcerting habit of poking his head into a writer's office and asking, "Is Moby Dick the man or the whale?" I have never asked that. But I have looked at catalogs and asked, "Is that the trouser press or the talking scale? Is that the telephone tap detector or the portable copy machine?" There are, of course, ways of finding out. Some catalogues have descriptive captions letter-keyed to the photographs. *H* is the radar detector and not the microwave oven. *A* is the air filter, and *B* is not its clone but an answering machine. *D* appears to be the electronic white sound generator but really is the electric boot dryer.

Eradicating differences through design is not exactly new. In 1964 the British magazine *Design* ran a piece complaining that, although the engineering of an American projector was truly revolutionary, its styling had "the restrained curves, the chromed bezel of everything else" introduced that year, whether projector or stereo receiver. I remember it well, since

I wrote the piece. "Everything else" was a calculated exaggeration; all I meant was that appliances and other products tended to look shockingly alike. The prevailing "clean design look" was not only carried from brand to brand but from object to object, so that the precision look of laboratory instruments showed up on stereo equipment and dictating machines.

Making distinctions through design was becoming confused, I felt, with "conferring distinction," or pretending to. One of the principal equalizing media in the sixties was brushed aluminum, which, in the hands of a mechanical stylist, could bestow "distinctiveness" while sacrificing distinction. Styling may confer, or rather proclaim, a momentary distinction on a product that has none in fact; but design always has another agenda.

Achieving an all-purpose look took some doing in the sixties. Now it may be the line of least resistance. In 1964, IBM brought out its System 360, which used microminiaturization to increase speed and reduce size. By the seventies, as Victor Papanek points out in *Design for Human Scale*, people were examining the implications of "extreme microminiaturization," which, combined with new materials, could wipe out the limitations that technology and function imposed on design. This, it was feared, could lead to preposterous excesses in appearance design. To some extent it did, but a curious counter tendency has persisted. Now that everything really *can* look like everything else, a lot of things really do.

Designers are often hired to create artificial distinctions, but the design process is more useful for creating real ones and for clarifying those that already exist. We have always needed to distinguish between brands; between product lines; between a particular product and others in the same field. More than that, we have always needed to see what things are and what they mean. Design can show us. But only when elegant solutions are based on exquisite distinctions.

Consequences

For a very long time now I have owned and admired a book called *Ideas Have Consequences*. This does not mean that I have read it or that I ever will. The title, inextricably combining the obvious and the profound, is intriguing enough.

Design has consequences is a proposition of the same order. Whatever the consequences, designers are responsible for them, and therefore for trying to anticipate them. We like to talk about such consequences as boosted sales and reduced production costs. We *have* to talk about such consequences as the destruction of resources and the proliferation of material waste, and about performance failures that bring designers back to the drawing board.

A singularly charming design by designer Louis Nelson is his own lake house, which I enjoy seeing most weekends from the other side of the lake. He has a neighbor with a leaf blower. So do I. Louis complains about the noise. So do I. But because we are both cowards, we complain to each other, rather than to the perpetrators. That makes for peace, but not quiet.

One Sunday morning he phoned to call my attention to what sounded like a chain saw massacre on my side of the lake.

"I hear it," I said indignantly. "Better than I can hear you."

Still, I tend to exonerate my neighbor from primary responsibility, finding fault with the gadget as much as with the gadgeteer. The National Rifle Association people would blame my neighbor: "Leaf blowers don't make noise," they would say. "People make noise." They would be as wrong about that as they are about handguns (which people also make.)

I shouted into the phone. "Someone like you designed that leaf blower," I reminded Louis. "Design has consequences."

Originally published November/December 1991 in *I.D.*, as the column "Circumstantial Evidence."

I knew where that came from. The Chicago marketing consultant Richard Latham was a reformed, or, as they say in AA, *recovering* industrial designer, who headed one of the nation's leading design offices. They had redesigned a snow blower to improve appearance, safety and market share; but Latham had doubts about it. "What happens to the peace and quiet of a winter morning when you have six of these in one block?" he asked. "I think mashing your senses on a bright snowy morning is worse than mashing your leg."

Imagining consequences is as important as anything else designers learn to do. At best, it means never having to say, "It seemed like a good idea at the time."

It is hard to believe that "Have an airport nice day" could have seemed like a good idea to anyone at any time, but the Port Authority of New York and New Jersey once instituted a "niceness training program" in which airport workers were instructed to greet passengers that way. What's wrong with it, of course, is not the stupefyingly tin-ear banality of the greeting, but its willful disregard for what's wrong with airports and the people who work in them. Apart from the cruelty of requiring workers to utter it, much less utter it repeatedly, much less with a straight face, consider the consequences of so blatantly insincere a slogan sung out to passengers already driven to tears of rage by blocked access lanes, overbooked flights with unreliable schedules, misleading signage and personnel who are uninformed, indifferent, and powerless to help in any case.

My late friend Jack Roberts once required the receptionist at his advertising agency to answer the telephone, "Carson Roberts. Have a happy day!"—a greeting I found especially irritating since, because of the coastal time difference, by the time I called him my day had already been cast in concrete or gloom, whichever comes first. Jack himself once called his own office after a dismally unsuccessful client meeting, and got a taste of his own medicine, or at least his own sugary placebo. "It's too late to have a happy day," he growled, and ordered that the salutation was never to be used after noon Pacific Coast Time. Sometimes we can adjust for consequences.

But not always. Jack's splendidness as a human being made it possible to forgive him for inventing the happy face that smiled at us ubiquitously from a multitude of surfaces that would have been happier without it. The face was at its worst a promotional graphic on the beach towels and memo pads Carson Roberts handed out to clients and friends. Only with multiplication were the oppressive design consequences felt.

Charles and Ray Eames were healthily frightened by this prospect. As a chair approached prototype stage, and as they approached a grudging satisfaction with how it looked, they would ask essentially the same question Latham did: "What would it be like if there were fifty of them?" Renowned for their daring departures from tradition, they understood how hard it is to foresee the consequences of tampering with established form.

Like chairs, knives, forks and spoons work pretty well in our culture. It may have taken a while to get them right, but by the time you and I arrived on the scene they had already proven themselves as implements for eating western food. This does not make them impervious to design assault, a truth I rediscovered most recently upon buying flatware for the cottage near the roaring leaf blower.

I was perfectly happy with the tableware we already had at the lake, which was made for American Airlines. Don't jump to conclusions. The set was a gift from Niels Diffrient, who had designed it with the meticulous care he brings to all his work. It served us well, although the scale was disconcerting, and dinner guests sometimes asked whether a movie would be shown on this flight.

The set we replaced it with is elegant, lovely, Scandinavian. So is the designer, whose portrait was displayed in the showroom. My wife was more attracted to the presentation qualities of the knife: it stood on edge. I agreed that a knife standing on edge made for an unusual and handsome place setting, but worried that cutting into a juicy piece of meat would transform it into a messy object to put back on the table cloth. She pointed out that we hardly ever have a cloth on the table, or a piece of meat either for that matter. Also, once you began to eat, you would simply lay the knife on the edge of the plate as you would any other.

I wish. For I had not foreseen that the knife not only *needn't* lie flat—it *won't*. It won't stand up on plate edges either. It works beautifully on Astroturf, but on other surfaces the knife rejects virtually every position assigned to it. I was about to hurl it to the floor in frustration (my tableware manners are no better than my table manners) but that wasn't necessary. Like its companion pieces, the knife crashes to the floor of its own volition when anyone tries to clear the table.

Big deal. Any product-friendly user can learn to operate the knife in time. What difference does it really make in an era when no one cuts meat or even spreads butter anyway? The knife is only there to round out the collection, as couturiers say.

But this is not so much a collection as a dysfunctional family. The meat and salad forks are so nearly identical in size and shape that no one can set the table without first matching them tine for tine. One of the spoons is too large for a tablespoon but too small for a serving spoon. The other is too small for a tablespoon but too large for a teaspoon. Placement problems aside, don't expect to measure sugar or cough syrup with these spoons.

Don't expect to eat gracefully with them either. The handles are rounded and weighted to spin helplessly in the hand when applied to any food more resistant than gruel. The only way to attack a firm cantaloupe with the spoon, for example, is to clutch it in the fist like a shillelagh. The rounded handles, however, do not cause the implements to roll off the plate. They only make the fall easier. What makes this falling inevitable is that they are weighted at the end. Not the business end. The far end. The end of the handle!

In this respect, the design is impressively faithful to human development if not to ergonomic logic. The human body's heaviest single component, the head, is balanced on the frailest supporting structure, the spine. It is a design not conducive to walking upright, but if we don't like it we can always crawl. Mimicking the arrogance of nature, our flatware handle is designed to overcome the spoon's Aristotelian urge to rest in a bowl. These implements must be kept in your hands at all times, like a purse in a New York restaurant.

Designs described as having stood the test of time have not only been tested by time but shaped by experience over time. Their forms are not arbitrary. Ironically, the very fact that they have evolved to be functional leads designers to redesign them as if their functioning can be taken for granted, as if they will continue to work regardless of what is done to them in the name of visual innovation.

It can't and they won't: evolutionary forms are as fragile in design as they are in biology. They may be made to work better, or be supplanted by something that does. But not unless the designer inquires every step of the way into the consequences that ultimately make design consequential.

Theoretically Challenged

Where design theory is concerned, I have a theoretical deficiency. I know people who think design needs theories to give it credibility. In other fields, the order is reversed. Credibility—that is, the meriting of confidence—comes from the payoff. Einstein won our respect for the alleged brilliance of two theories—a general one and a special one—that somehow led to the equation E=MC², although few of us understand either the theories or the equation. He won our affection through the power of his personality and personal history. But what gave him credibility was that the Bomb went off. And what gave physics its subsequent credibility was not theories but the fact that physicists could make things that work.

Designers also make things that work. But in design, the working and the theorizing are not related as they are in science. If a scientific theory works, it is considered sound—at least sound enough. For scientists, theories are tools. Like other tools, they do not have to be perfect for all occasions: there are no scientific Renaissance tools; there is no mathematical counterpart of the Swiss Army knife. It is enough if a theoretical tool is effective for a particular job. And although Newtonian physics has been supplanted by more sophisticated theories, the earlier physics can still be used to explain some phenomena accurately and is therefore valid for that purpose. If theories do not work, they are regarded as unsound or at least inadequately tested. In this respect, they differ vastly from theories that carry no operational burdens and therefore cannot be checked out.

If we have to talk about theories, then we have to make distinctions. There are comprehensive theories and conjectural theories. A comprehensive theory consists of a system of propositions that coherently account for a complex phenome-

Originally published November/December 1984 in *I.D.*, as the column "Circumstantial Evidence."

non such as those observed in economics or medicine or even law.

Such theories explain and simplify phenomena. But *simplify* does not simply mean to make simple; it means to make as simple as possible. Electromagnetics isn't simple, it's complex. The second law of thermodynamics is not simple. Marxism is relatively simple, but so what? The goal of a comprehensive theory is to make something as simple as is consistent with fully accounting for it.

Unfortunately, in design, as in many other fields today, there is a strong drive to do just the opposite: to complicate description in the belief that complication in itself represents substance and depth. So we borrow arcane language from disciplines historically associated with substance and depth. In design the mathematical term *parameter* is used to mean nothing more than constraint; the engineering term *feedback* is used to mean nothing more than response; the logics term *paradigm* is used to mean nothing more than model; *viable* (a biological term) is used to mean feasible. Or, often as not, to mean nothing at all.

Comprehensive theories are required to handle complexity. But I am not sure design entails the appropriate complexity very often. It seems not to be in the blood and bones of the profession and may therefore be absent from the heart as well. In *Theory and Design in the First Machine Age* Reyner Banham writes:

> The devices that characterized the Machine Age were the products of intuition, experiment or pragmatic knowledge—no one could now design a self-starter without knowledge of the mathematics of electricity, but it was Charles F. Kettering, not mathematics, that invented the first electrostarter on the basis of a sound grasp of mechanical methods.

As for conjectural theory, that is simply a reasoned hypothesis. The detective says, we don't have a motive but we have a theory. That's more my style, and I suspect it is more in line with the sort of theory useful in design practice. I believe that the designer's theory ought to be directed toward the use and the user, rather than toward design itself. I don't care whether interior designers have a theory of design, but I do hope—if they're doing offices—that they have a theory of work, illuminating how it gets done and by whom. I don't care about industrial designers' theory of form nearly as much as I do—if they are designing stereo components—about their theory of sound, or their theory of indoor recreation. That's what I hope they know about. That's the kind of theory I hope will inform their vision.

If we needed an example of what happens when designers let their attention shift from field to force, we need look no further than the observations of the most famous semioticist of our time, Umberto Eco. Writing about the communicative aspect of objects, Eco discusses the "statements" that objects make. Remember when product designers used to talk about chairs that made statements? They learned that in design schools and from design critics. Chairs do make statements, and should, but surely the most important statements they make ought to have something to do with sitting down. This, however, is usually not what our most conspicuously designed chairs are talking about. And that is Eco's point.

During the fifties, Eco argues, "paradoxically, in aiming to make functional objects, designers tried to accentuate the communicative functions of those objects; and instead of producing objects that communicated the way they could be used, they produced objects that communicated the design philosophy. That is, the object did not say "This is how you use me,' but rather said 'I am a perfect design object.'" Eco takes an example from Italian cutlery. Inspired by the Scandinavians,

Italian designers began producing more beautiful forks with short prongs that made the statement "I am a modern fork." They were modern indeed, and we all admired them and showed them in our magazines and museums and gave them awards. But they were of no use for eating pasta, which has a certain vogue in Italy. For pasta you needed the anonymously designed long pronged fork, which made the statement, "If you plunge me into a mass of fettucine, I will accept the cargo."

It is important to notice that these badly functioning designs were praised for "elegance." But elegance as theoretical scientists apply it is quite different. The *elegance* of a mathematical formula is that it explains a phenomenon beautifully, with no parts left over. In design, elegance is more readily perceived as a property of product than of process. If we had more elegant theories, we might look to design for more than elegance.

In the serious comic movie *Gone Are the Days*, Ossie Davis plays a black preacher in the rural south, crusading for civil rights. Ruby Dee plays a scullery maid. The preacher is exasperated by his inability to arouse the scullery maid to an interest in civil rights legislation.

"You are a disgrace to the Negro profession," he complains. "Don't you have any race pride?"

"I got plenty of race pride," she replies. "But there ain't much call for it in my line of work."

That's where design theory is today: there ain't much call for it in our line of work.

Are the Things We Save

I have never seen a mortician who did not enjoy his work or a mover who did. Moving is a truly egalitarian transaction, equally disagreeable for both professional and client. My office is being moved and it is as hard on me as on the people who do the loading and unloading. The pain is emotional. To move is to pack, or at least to prepare to pack. This entails confronting all the action piles that have not been acted on, the accumulated books and magazines unread and passed on from move to move, the found objects that there is no longer any point in finding: invitations to dinners already eaten, announcements of conferences that have been over for years, letters that were left unanswered with regret but apparently without catastrophe, projects that never happened, projects that never should have happened.

Packing is commonly a precipitous activity that does not leave time for understanding what is being packed, why it has been kept, and what use it will be in a new location. I understand why I have held on to certain things, and why I keep moving them from place to place. (*Procrastination: Why You Do It, What To Do About It*, for example, is a highly recommended book well worth packing and unpacking because I fully intend to read it someday.) But in the process of sorting and thinning files, I discover items that I cannot remember acquiring, or that I dimly remember saving but have no idea why, or that I intended to write about but never did. For example:

A bundle of pamphlets held together with a rubberband. One, about the effects of family stress on job performance, is called *Work is a Family Affair*. Some of the other titles are *When You Are Facing Divorce; Drug Abuse Facts; Signs of Pill Dependency; Dealing with Adolescence; Cocaine Involvement Test; To the Young Person Leaving Treatment; People, Problems, and Supervisors*.

Originally published January/February 1988 in *I.D.*, as the column "Circumstantial Evidence."

The problems these pamphlets deal with are serious. But they are not at present *my* problems. I am not facing divorce or abusing drugs, and I have no adolescents left to deal with. Why had I collected this small library of comfort and intervention? I had no idea until I examined the pamphlets and noticed that each one carried the name and telephone extension of the employee assistance program manager at an international corporation.

Then I remembered. A couple of years ago I attended some meetings at the corporation's local headquarters. While we were having lunch in the company dining room, I noticed a rack of reading materials, all of them about similar subjects: crisis intervention, alcoholism, debt, gambling, legal difficulties. One of my hosts explained that the corporation maintains an active counseling service for employees, with confidentiality assured.

The literature rack is a powerful graphic statement of the changing role a corporation plays in the private lives of its employees, and the depth and severity of our routine personal problems. The counseling might be confidential, but the distribution of information was uncomfortably public. This rack was not for browsing: there were no magazines on display to lighten the load or help disguise the focus of your attention. I took all the pamphlets I could carry.

A flyer from the University of Michigan promoting a publication called *Simulating Future Worlds*, and promising to reveal "techniques and applications that enable designers, architects and urban planners to plan and design without risk." I suppose I was encouraged to keep the blurb by the prospect of risk-free design, but discouraged from ordering the book by the conviction that there is no risk-free design in any of the future worlds I care to simulate.

"Art Prostitute" reads the business card of Dennis Carmichael, who appears to be at home in the world's two oldest professions. I am not sure where I got this, and there is no area code on the card.

A classified ad for a nude house cleaner. No area code here either, but the ad appeared in a New York City neighborhood service journal.

An announcement of a conference on "Designing Facilities to Survive Terrorist Attack," sponsored by the Institute of Security Design in Washington. Both the institute and the design specialty were new to me. With such presentations as "Vulnerability Analysis by Threat Scenario," this was a design conference that meant business long before September 11, 2001, made it everybody's business.

A note reminding myself to find some excuse for writing about the Screwpull, invented and designed by a wine-loving retired executive named Herbert Allen. The simplest, most reliable corkscrew I have found, it consists of a plastic sheath and an incredibly strong and sharp friction-free steel helical wire. The wire is lined up by the sheath to pierce the cork exactly at the center. You simply turn the handle as you would with any corkscrew; and when the wire reaches the optimal gripping length, the sheath stops it from going any further. As you keep turning, screw and cork rise easily out of the bottle. It is always useful to remind ourselves that many of the world's most useful products are designed by people who are not product designers.

A full-page photographic ad in the July 19, 1981, issue of *The New York Times*. The photo shows a tree-lined college campus, with a handsome young man seated on a bench, a book in his hand and another on the bench beside him. The ad is not pushing campuses or books, but clothing. The clothing, like the books and trees, is generic. The student is wearing a sweater over an open-necked shirt, slacks, and a tweed jacket. He is wearing, in other words, exactly what college men wear.

In ads. In college stereotypes. In college movies. In college novels. Even in some colleges. The copy plays on this familiarity, shrewdly releasing a barrage of clichés to match the clichés in the picture: "Think good taste. Think true classics. Tradition. . . . The jacket shown: imagine it on the quad . . . in an ivy covered hall . . . in Harvard Yard."

But why does the headline read: "Introducing Polo University—A New Concept in Menswear From Ralph Lauren"? How can something be both a copy of a classic and a new concept?

There is the hint of an answer in Witold Rybczynski's *Home*. "The 1980's fashion for Ivy League clothes" was, according to Rybczynski, "Lauren inspired." I had assumed that it was Ivy League inspired, and long before the eighties. But that was a less innovative imitation. The first Ivy League copies were directed to the non-Ivy League: the image might be Harvard Yard, but the address was the school of agriculture at North Oomasaw State. Polo University, however, *is* a new concept of sorts, for it is our first university of style. No classes or professors, no campus, no admission requirements, not even a losing football team. Just the look and the cost.

Worth Having?

One of the most interesting items in a show called "High Styles," at the Whitney Museum of Art, was a blown-up photograph of the 1958 General Electric wall-hung refrigerator. The museum was unable to locate the real thing, and for good reason: neither manufacturers nor buyers expected it to become a museum piece.

I could have led them to one, for my parents were the first, and last, people in our home town to buy the unit. Neighbors used to come into the kitchen to contemplate it—much as they would have had it been a museum piece even then; but they were less interested in its "high style" than in the prospect of its falling through the floor when someone slammed the door.

They needn't have worried. The refrigerator door wasn't used all that often, for the unit developed mechanical problems almost immediately and nobody local could fix it. It was soon augmented by a white free-standing refrigerator of the very kind the GE model was designed to make obsolete.

It hangs there still, no longer an object of wonder except to people who wonder why in all these years my father hasn't gotten rid of it. I know why. My father believes it is too good to throw away. It is not good enough to *give* away, but it cost too much to discard. So he uses it as a storage cabinet.

Industrial designers continually shape products that outlive their usefulness; normally when that happens, however, they enter the distribution system of second-hand stores, trade-ins and scrap dealers. Product designers rarely have to face the consequences of a consumer like my father.

For other designers, that situation is more common. Graphic designers spend a large part of their working lives designing materials that fall in the category of not-good-enough-to-keep-but-too-good-to-throw-away (NGETKBTGTTA). The category does not include coffee cans, used tooth brushes, automobile

Originally published September/October 1985 in *I.D.*, as the column "Circumstantial Evidence."

tires, and similar artifacts that are too good to throw away because there is always something more you can do with them. Nor does it apply to containers that are not good enough to keep but that you aren't *allowed* to throw away, such as the giant packing boxes with acres of tailored styrofoam in which television sets, VCRs, and personal computers are delivered. These have fulfilled their function as soon as the product has arrived safely, but the consumer is enjoined from ever getting rid of them by the company's announced refusal to repair anything that isn't returned in the box it came in. I know a couple who gave up skiing because the closet occupied by their ski gear was needed for the packing cases Sony told them they must keep for the life of their stereo. (The same couple has never removed the informative labels stitched to their pillows.) NGETKBTGTTA is a psychological prohibition, not a legalistic one.

A midwestern corporation conducted an in-house training program a few years ago in which each participant was required to state his primary job objective. One group member was the pilot of the corporate jet. "My primary job objective," he said, "is not to crash." Graphic designers often have a comparable objective in designing promotional literature. A brochure is needed for a major trade show. Strategies and tactics are discussed. An approach is developed. A copy platform is drafted. Rough sketches are made. Dummies are prepared. Photography is commissioned—perhaps requiring a crew to go to the Himalayas or to Youngstown, Ohio, for local shooting. Illustrators may be called in. Paper stock is chosen and ordered. Copy is redrafted, and refined, and polished, and corrected. And every one of those steps involves approval or disapproval, struggle, and deadlines. The piece may be magnificent. It may be pedestrian. It may be utter schlock. It may win the highest awards of the design community, where awards of some kind are given to something or someone almost hourly.

However the product's life experience turns out, its first objective is very much like the pilot's: not to crash. Not to be left on the literature table or dumped into a hotel wastebasket. In a sense, the product's primary function is not to be thrown away. The result is a category of design consisting of elegant publications that you receive, open, admire, flip through, and possibly even read, but never pick up again, or want to. None of the normal avenues of disposal are open to you, however. You can't leave the used volume on an airplane seat or donate it to a thrift shop. You are stuck with it. Built into the design is your inability to discard it without guilt.

Guilt in this case is the consumer's problem, not the designer's. But, ironically, in many cases the designers *are* the consumers. Paper companies, printers, engravers, photographers—everyone with products and services to sell to designers —produce a cascade of rich materials, usually superior in production quality to the most expensive books and magazines. Moreover, they are free. But once you have read an ingeniously designed volume, magnificently bound, containing a beautifully printed and illustrated, carefully documented essay on the evolution of form in coat hangers, once you have leafed through the efforts of five top photographers interpreting the street signs in their favorite cities, will you want to do it again? Once you have looked through a portfolio of serigraphs lovely enough to frame, will you frame them? No. Will you look at them again? No. Will you even remember having seen them? Probably not. But they must be kept. Keeping is what they are for. Of course these graphic products are not really about coat hangers or street signs or boats or fish; they are about paper and printing and good will. The message is not the medium, but it is an excuse for it. And often a good one.

Such gratuitous literature is the antithesis of junk mail, which is infuriating not because of what it is but because of what it isn't. Since junk mail can be thrown out without being opened, it wastes little time. Junk mail, like junk food, goes down easily. But in the process it reminds you of the real mail you didn't get today. It is not that one minds hearing from Common Cause or Time-Life or even the Franklin Mint. I cannot imagine buying anything from the Franklin Mint; I can almost not imagine anyone who does. But mail from them ought to be easy enough to ignore. And would be, except that every communication from the Franklin Mint carries a message: this is not an invitation to a party or a personal letter from an old friend, this is a reminder that you *have* no friend, that for you there *is* no party, that the check is *not* in the mail. What is in the mail instead is a solicitation for the first edition of memorial subway tokens from the great underground systems of the world. That hurts. NGETKBTGTTA mail doesn't hurt. It just takes up space in bookshelves and psyche.

I have long admired the "Great Ideas of Western Man" series of advertisements that made Container Corporation better known for its institutional advertising than it ever needed to be for its products. My admiration was rewarded when I received a handsomely bound volume containing all the ads in the series, plus a history of the campaign. With it came an equally handsome reproduction of each ad, printed with a quality that museums would be happy to emulate if they had corporate budgets. I was thrilled. As the years wore on, however, the thrill wore off. Like most graphic materials that are too good to throw away but not good enough to keep, the ads and the folio that contains them are oversized. They demand a special shelf. They are, as ads used to say, "suitable for framing." But nothing as elegant as this can be framed out of KMart. The kind of framing they are suitable for is studio framing—at a cost of a few hundred dollars a frame. In any case, I don't want to frame them. I really don't want to see most of them again. Neither do I want to keep moving them every time I move me. Some of them are magnificent. I wish they were schlock.

The Trouble With Design

A college friend of mine worked two off-campus trades while studying for the ministry. He served as pastor of a tiny church of great passion but indeterminate denomination, and he was a magician. Both callings required him to perform on weekends to unsophisticated, small town audiences, but the congregation appeared to be more accepting of his unorthodox theology than the magic show audiences were of his imperfect prestidigitation. Bob was not a particularly skillful magician, and a lot of his material, which he bought by mail order from a magic supply house in Chicago, flopped. But even when he tried a difficult trick that worked, he would come back to the dormitory bemused, complaining that practicing magic in the sticks was a no win business. "If you mess up, they scoff and hoot," he said once. "You're derided as a clumsy oaf, and I can understand that. But even when you carry off the most complicated illusion without a hitch, there are people in the audience who want to make clear that no one's putting anything over on them. 'There's a trick to it,' they say accusingly. 'That's just a trick.'"

"Of course it's a trick," I said. "What do they mean?"

"They mean," he said, "that it isn't real magic."

"Maybe you ought to stick to preaching," I said.

Moses turned a stick into a snake, and vice versa. That was a miracle. Penn and Teller can do the same thing. That isn't. One was real magic, the other is a brilliant performance. "The magic of design" and the logic of design are inextricably related, for the seemingly magical freedom in the design process is exercised only in the presence of logical constraints.

The freedom is only seemingly magical, because its use is a matter of craft. But when tricks are raised to art, when they

Originally published September/October 1989 in *I.D.*, as the column "Circumstantial Evidence."

transcend what we can expect from talent, experience, or concept development, the *effect* is magical, an effect produced by the collision of talent and constraint.

When I first got involved with design and the people who do it, I wondered why bestowing awards on each other had become so dominant a professional activity. It looked incestuous. It isn't. A major frustration of the design process is that it has to be practiced with and for people who don't understand it. Then it has to be shown to your mother, who doesn't understand it either. Juried shows take their meaning from the fact that they are judged by people who know what the work entails because they do it too. And that's a very important kind of judgement, much more satisfying than the judgement that says wow or jumps to the bottom line to determine whether the design is good. There is a bottom line, and it matters. But it isn't the only line that matters, and it depends on all the lines that go before, many of which mark various points at which design decisions are made.

The bottom line is crucial information, but as instruments for assessing design excellence bottom lines are like baseball statistics, which, as mathematicians keep telling us about all statistics, have no memory. Baseball is the sport closest in character to real, or nonsporting, life. For all its occasions for heroism, and the multi-million dollar salaries paid to the heroes who exploit them, baseball is a game loaded with the false starts, misunderstood signals, errors, rain delays, and boredom of everyday living. The intricacies of the rulebook disguise the fact that baseball is governed by Murphy's Law. A baseball game, like an individual lifetime, isn't over until it's over, unlike, say, a football game, which is over the moment there is too little time remaining for the score to be tied. Simultaneously exalted and pedestrian, baseball lends itself to fantasy more convincingly than other sports do. Some cases in point are *The*

Natural (novel and film), *Field of Dreams* (novel and film), Nancy Willard's *Things Invisible to See* (novel) and *Bull Durham* (film). However much these vary in literary and filmic quality, they all deal in extremely modest fantasies, as if the authors never forgot that, however miraculous the most spectacular plays in baseball look, they are wholly allegiant to the laws of physics.

So, for better or worse, is design. At a university convocation, one of the speakers, a pleasant fellow with the air of having arrived directly from the sixties, resonated with everything the human potential movement had revealed about the environment, the war, being in touch with yourself, and doing your own thing. His challenge to design students was simple and clear—at least it sounded clear while he was saying it.

"Design a miracle!" he told them. He liked it so much he said it again. "Design a miracle! That's what we need now."

The students were enthralled. Here was an assignment more interesting than laying out a magazine or a poster or an ad, and requiring no research. Their eyes gleamed. They were on fire. They would do what he told them to.

Or would they? I believe he meant well, but it was to my mind exactly the wrong thing to tell design students. Not because it is idealistic, but because it is a contradiction in terms. For the charge to design a miracle ignores the fact—and designers ignore it at their peril—that the design process is grounded in constraints.

That's the trouble with miracles: they are antithetical to design. You may love miracles, and I do. You may long for them, and I do. You may even perform them—I don't, although some of my best friends are miracle workers. But you can't *design* a miracle, which by definition is a phenomenon that occurs in defiance of constraints. We speak of the miracle of flight, but we can fly because such designers as the Wright Brothers, Sikorsky, and Paul McCready learned something about aerodynamics and the behavior of materials in a material world. Lindbergh could cross the ocean as a matter of design, but he couldn't float across a room the way Peter Pan did. He couldn't levitate either.

Sometimes, when I work with design students, I ask them if they've ever written poetry and if the class is large enough, there's a good chance that some of them have. Then I ask if any of them has ever written a sonnet, and there's almost no chance that any of them has. (If they're design students, there is a good chance they've never read one either.) Then I propose that we write a sonnet in class.

We begin with the ground rules. A sonnet has 14 lines. Its meter is iambic pentameter. Regardless of the kind of sonnet we choose, the rigid rhyme scheme means that half the lines are in a sense dictated by the other half. To students it looks like prison.

To be sure, that classroom experiment is no way to produce poetry. But unfailingly it produces a sonnet that meets all the technical requirements of the form, and usually contains a line or two that can be read without cringing. The best lines are often those that were created only to complete a rhyme.

Why introduce design students to sonnet form? Because even the most miraculous Shakespearean sonnet is no miracle. Because in design, constraints not only come with the territory, they are a means to making the territory productive. "I never could write free verse," Robert Frost said, "because I didn't know where the stops are."

The standard constraints in professional design include deadline, budget, distribution, materials, production processes, and corporate politics. At any given time, we may resent any one of them. If only they didn't need it by Thursday. . . . If only the budget allowed more color. . . . If only it could be produced at lower temperatures. . . . If only they didn't have to fit into containers. . . . If only there wasn't so much explanatory copy. . . . If only it didn't have to be approved by a committee, or by people who think like a committee.

Those constraints are what the designer pushes against to shape the project. Designers need to know where the stops are, then figure out how to work within and through them elegantly. That's the trouble with design. There's a trick to it.

Disabled by Design

The term *universal design* is used to describe design that is accessible to people with disabilities, but that includes most of us sooner or later. "The elderly and the handicapped" is a redundancy that reminds us that the handicapped are not an alien species: they are everyone's future. Despite plastic surgery, Botox, and Canyon Ranch, there is at present only one known alternative to getting old.

Consequently, even a professional concern with universal design is likely to be personal. The English industrial designer Kenneth Grange has for years been involved in designing a bathroom that would be safe and convenient for the elderly. I asked him how he had become so focused on that particular problem.

"It was an accident," he said. "My Mum came to stay with us, and she couldn't use our bathtub. Then we discovered that she couldn't use her own bathtub either. It turned out that my Mum hadn't taken a bath for years!"

It's always somebody's Mum. Or Dad. My own interest in this subject began when I realized that what was really handicapping my father was not his Parkinson's disease, but the fact that his ability to negotiate the environment despite the limitations of Parkinson's was at every point blocked by the design of his house and the sidewalk in front of it.

He could work, and insisted on going to his store every day. But he couldn't climb down stairs, so he couldn't get to the car unassisted. He couldn't climb up stairs safely either, and that's where the bathroom was. He could bathe himself. But he couldn't lower himself into the tub or lift himself out of it. What handicapped him, and handicapped me when I helped him bathe, was not a disease. It was design. He died of Parkinson's, but he was disabled by design.

My in-laws, on the other hand, lived for several years in a

Speech given, May 1992, to the First Universal Design Conference, published August 1992 in *Interior Design*.

new house that was thoughtfully equipped for the possibility that the inhabitants might grow old. Yet as soon as my father-in-law went into a nursing home, my mother-in-law ordered the grab bars removed from the bathrooms. "Mamma," my wife protested, "You may need these yourself someday." "When I do," my mother-in-law said, "I'll have them put back. They're too ugly to have up in the meantime."

She was right, for they were the products of an industry that was slow to acknowledge that the disabled have a right to both access and style. Of course styles change. I had to wear glasses before I even got to the first grade. Hardly a major disability, but kids who wore glasses were mocked and called "four eyes." We were all taught that "sticks and stones may break your bones but names will never hurt you," and we all knew that it wasn't true. Anyway, it was not my impaired vision they were mocking by calling me four eyes, but the prosthetic I had to wear. A prevailing cliché in movies of the time was the scene in which she takes off her glasses and he notices for the first time that she is beautiful. Dorothy Parker wrote her famous couplet, "Men seldom make passes/at girls who wear glasses" during that period. Who could have guessed that, some 50 years after the development of contact lenses, glasses would be worn by models and stars and marketed as fashion accessories?

For that matter, who could have guessed that the word *girls* would no longer be acceptably juxtaposed with the word *men*? I wish we were as sensitive to hurtful design as we now are to hurtful language. Both imply failures of recognition. Successful designs evoke in the user a feeling of identification with, and gratitude for, someone who understood what was needed. I appreciate a design that recognizes me because I can recognize myself in it. It is the absence of such recognition that has alienated blacks, women, the elderly, and the disabled. When, in the '60s Johnson and Johnson introduced the "flesh-colored

Band-Aid," the black comedian Godfrey Cambridge asked just whose flesh they had in mind. Yet another comedian of sorts, George Covington—Vice-President Quayle's special assistant for disability policy—warned legislators, "I don't want to hear any of you say 'wheelchair bound,' unless you're talking about kinky sex."

Covington understood that euphemism obscures recognition. "Senior citizen" conjures up no image of either seniority or citizenship, but registers someone's discomfort with the fact that if you get older long enough, you become old. No one is sure exactly when it happens anyway. The psychologist Ira Progroff complained that he could never have a mid-life crisis because in order to have one he would need to know how long he was going to live.

Home, John Ciardi said, is where the cork comes out of the bottle. If it is my home, the cork comes out most easily if I use a Screwpull (see page 84). The Screwpull was not designed with me in mind. It was designed because the designer's wife had arthritis, and because he was frustrated by frail old corks that would crumble when punctured. I don't have arthritis. Yet. And I don't have wine old enough to present a corkage problem. What I do have is congenital klutziness. But the attention to user need that informs this product makes it right for *my* need. In making a corkscrew his wife can use, the designer has made one that *I* can use too. If a toilet seat in an airport is accessible to Itzhak Perlman, I can get into the same booth. And I want to (not while he's in it), because it has room for my luggage.

If something is truly designed to meet someone's particular needs, it is almost certain to address more general needs as well. That's why the Velcro closures designed for shoes worn by the disabled are so appealing to *anyone* whose shoelaces get knotted or come untied. That's why the safari jacket is the ideal garment to wear in hot American cities. That's why the classic fishing tackle box became the standard makeup container for actors. That's why the wheelchair technology developed for, and in some cases by, athletes can be incorporated into better wheelchairs for people who are not candidates for the Para Olympics, but who simply want a better way to get around.

At the same table where the cork comes out of the bottle, the knives, forks, and spoons fall off the plate, because the flatware is designed for presentation rather than for eating. Then how come I can eat with it anyway? For the same reason I can sit in almost any chair. I have a bad back and so do most chairs. But I can maneuver my back into a tolerable position, and I have to because the chair can't. As long as our environment is rigid, we have to be flexible. Badly designed products work because we can adjust to them. But surely one of the purposes of design is to make the built environment fit *us*.

Instead, *we* squirm to fit it. We accommodate. We compensate. Here is one way to define disability: We are disabled whenever we are incapable of adjusting to inadequate design. Universal design means shifting the burden of adaptability from us to the products that serve us. It is design for people who cannot always meet the environment halfway.

That's the Size of It

Question: How many men does it take to replace a roll of toilet paper? Answer: Nobody knows. It's never been done.

With the development of indoor plumbing came the discovery that the population may be divided into two kinds of people—those who replace the paper to be pulled over the roll, and those who position it to be pulled from underneath. One way of doing it manifests an innate sense of rightness; the other is perverse, awkward, and out of harmony with nature, like chalk across a blackboard or a tooth. I am not about to tell you which is which. The advice columnist Ann Landers got so many heated letters on the subject one season that she declared a moratorium on printing them.

You don't have to be a Feng Shui master to know how serious this is. The humblest, and often the smallest, objects, designed for the most trivial of pursuits, ultimately function as tuning forks to the universe. They show us how the world works.

I don't mean exactly that God is in the details. (She is, but she's everywhere else too.) I mean that life's largest lessons are most lucidly illustrated in the pettiest examples. That's why we use a carrot and stick to explain foreign policy options like force versus incentive, but no one uses the geopolitics of Henry Kissinger to explain the difference between a carrot and a stick. Objects speak more clearly than politicians do, and more profoundly too, regardless of scale. "Do not understand me too quickly," André Gide once said. Our buildings and our products might say the same thing if we let them get a word in edgewise. When the Seagram Building rose in New York, the industrial designer Peter Muller-Munk called it "preachy." Well, it was; but so are Good Grips.

As environmental graphic designers remind us, some of the

Originally published November/December 1995 in *I.D.*, as the column "Counterpoint."

most revealing signs of our times consist of the signage itself. Barney Greengrass the Sturgeon King is a Manhattan landmark that went bicoastal in 1995 with a Los Angeles branch, which for authenticity serves a molecularly reconstituted version of New York's fabled tap water. One thing that only the East Coast Barney Greengrass the Sturgeon King had, however, was a convenience store across the street called the G —— Deli. The mysterious blank represented a strategic saving of face and money, the store having opened as The G-Spot Deli, to capitalize on the erogenous geography that was trendy at the time. An angry outcry caused the owners to paint over the offensive language, while protesting their innocence (they insisted the phrase stood for Gourmet Spot) and keeping enough of the name to put off buying a new sign for awhile.

The term "G-spot" was retired as sexual nomenclature before ever being pressed into general metaphorical service. We were not as lucky with the term "hot buttons," which, almost as soon as it was dropped from junior high locker room use, was picked up by marketing people, who spoke, and speak still, of "finding the customer's hot buttons." Worse, the news media took it on. The day I learned that real men don't change the toilet paper roll, I heard an NPR news analyst speculating on whether a political candidate could win by focusing on "hot button issues."

National Public Radio right now deserves our compassion and needs our support. All the more reason to strip the hot buttons off its uniform, for the phrase demeans women while it grossly distorts the process of reaching customers, voters or any other human beings. Sex, marketing, and politics are all too complex to yield their rewards at the press of a button. To believe they will is as simplistic as believing an exhibit is "participatory" because visitors have to push a button in order to hear a taped message.

To be sure, many of our most important actions are initiated by pushing buttons, but the act is misleading. The computer boots when I push a button, but only because someone else has rigged it to do so. Market and political effectiveness depend on understanding, rather than manipulating, people. Design is a way to build that understanding into products and policies.

Buttons are fun. Our fascination with them surely has something to do with the combination of tininess and power, the finger on the button. Little things can be dangerous because their smallness is so seductive. The enormous appeal to designers in Nicholson Baker's novel *The Mezzanine* was his concentration on such diminutive moral issues as the character of shoelaces. After reading the book I tripped on mine, but I still like small things better than big ones and find parts more interesting than wholes. As a rule I prefer indexes to expository books, footnotes to articles.

My predilection for miniatures led me to study the display of pills in the window of a homeopathic pharmacy near my office. They were all tiny, for one size apparently fits all ailments in homeopathy, and in fact no ailment is required. I was especially taken with a bottle labeled Placebos full of minipills made of "the highest quality turbinado sugar." Seduced by the perverse charm of a medication guaranteed by the manufacturer to be inactive, I bought a bottle, wondering whether a placebo plainly labeled placebo would militate against the placebo effect. Not, apparently, in homeopathy. The theory, as I misunderstand it, is that you cure an ailment by taking microscopic doses of substances that induce symptoms of the very malady you are treating. Seems logical, then, when nothing is wrong, to take a substance that will induce no symptoms at all. Since the job of a placebo is to do nothing, size is not an issue.

That's about the size of it. Small is beautiful, E.F. Schumacher said, and designers loved him for saying it, even if they were unwilling to put the principle into practice. Big is beautiful too; sometimes what matters is scale, not size. To consider scale in design is to consider human scale, since humanity is where most end users are found. For a provocative delineation of what human scale might mean, I know of nothing better than a '50s movie called *The Incredible Shrinking Man*. In the climactic scene the protagonist, by now bug size and still shrinking, is in the basement fighting for his life against an attacking fly or flea or mosquito. The battle is played out against the backdrop of a Martinson's coffee can, which takes on the grandeur of the Coliseum. I like to think that the producer used the Martinson's can because, like me at the time, he had a bunch of them on hand and not, as would be the case today, because some product placement agent arranged a deal. The struggle is as terrifyingly memorable as Fay Wray in the arms of King Kong at the top of the Empire State Building. The shrinking man escapes by sliding through a finely meshed window screen, which the insect is too large to pass through. Once on the other side of the screen he is absorbed into a world larger in scale than the one he has spent the movie shrinking from, as the voiceover, mystical and utilitarian, asks whether there is really any difference between the infinite and—the infinitesimal.

Small Wonders

Everyone who owns a lot of books has had this experience. A repairman arrives, looks with awe at the crammed shelves and asks, "Have you *read* all these books?"

The question used to irritate me. "Not yet," I would grudgingly confess, implying that as soon as he replaced the cable box or the window pane or the gasket I would get back to polishing off the few volumes I had not yet finished reading. But of course the irritant was not the obtuseness of the visitor's question but my own awareness that I had not read all, or even most, of the books I own, and was beginning to face the likelihood that I never would. The weight that made the bookshelves sag lay just as heavily on my sagging conscience.

That's how it was until I encountered, in one of the books I *have* read, the following advice from Arnold Bennett: "In buying a book, be influenced by two considerations only. Are you reasonably sure that it is a good book? Have you a desire to possess it? Do not be influenced by the probability or improbability of your reading it."

So I shed my guilt and began buying books I had not the slightest intention of reading. Not only, as Bennett counsels, is this behavior perfectly proper; it is, in the case of certain books, preferable. From that insight I advanced to the liberated position I now hold: I don't have to read a book in order to write about it.

Two unread (and, for that matter, unbought) books I admire are *The Footnote* by Anthony Grafton and *The God of Small Things* by Arundhati Roy. Mr. Grafton is a British scholar. Ms. Roy, if you believe the dust jacket photograph, is an Indian writer of transcendent beauty. Someday I may buy their books, someday

Originally published January/February 1998 in *PRINT*, as the column "Peripheral Vision."

I may read them.* In the meantime, I find them exemplary on the basis of their titles alone, for they call attention to a neglected but critical design force: the fascination of the diminutive.

Designers love bits and pieces, miniature models, takeouts, boxes, sidebars—information that comes at the eye the way soundbites attack the ear. The footnote is one such device, much maligned because it ordinarily shows up in books that are dense and difficult. Composed of material that cannot be incorporated into the main stream, footnotes are leftover ideas, just as widows are leftover type. This makes them all the more attractive. The harder it becomes to concentrate on resolutely nonvisual text, the more one's eye is drawn to the bottom of the page, or to anywhere else. Although the diminished size might be expected to discourage reading, the typographic difference actually encourages it, suggesting an escape from the text, and the possibility of rescue.

The Footnote may help save the honor of the footnote, a device typically seen as an example of pedantic fussiness. That is a bum rap. I have always enjoyed footnotes, not because I am scholarly but precisely because I am not. In the kind of books that have them, footnotes are invariably more interesting than the text, and often more rewarding in the long run.

The formal role of the footnote is to interrupt. Its functional role is to digress. Nothing is more to the point than a good digression. When what it digresses from is dead or deadening, a footnote can be an intrusive call to life.

But the appeal of footnotes is more substantive than distractive. Where the form invites, the content seduces. In the social sciences, footnotes tend to be reduced case studies—where the stories are! If the subject is agriculture, the footnotes are where farmers are found. If the subject is economics, the footnotes are where the money is, literally the bottom line.

*Since writing this, I have bought both, read one.

Nicholson Baker's *The Mezzanine*—an extraordinarily engaging novel is shot through with footnotes, their scale wholly appropriate to the theme and plot, which explore the cosmic magnitude of the insignificant and trivial. The protagonist leaves his office at lunchtime to go shopping for a shoelace (left) to replace one that has snapped. That is the whole story, and a rousing good yarn it is too, but you'll admit it is small.

But although small is beautiful, it may also be hazardous, the danger being that the part will be taken for the whole. Worse, if the parts satisfy, we may not even think a whole is needed. The current promiscuous use of quotations is a case in point. Recently I heard a speaker say, "I want to share with you a quote written by Mark Twain." But Mark Twain, prolific as he was, never wrote any quotes as such—no one but ghostwriters do. There are no quotes until someone is quoted. Since a quote exists only after it has been removed from the scene of the crime, there is a sense in which most quotes are, by definition, out of context. The notion of quotation as a literary genre is perfectly in keeping with a nation that is being soundbitten into senselessness.

Handwriting

You may never have wondered what it is like to look into the eyes of 450 calligraphers, but if you do wonder I can tell you. It makes you acutely aware of the wretchedness of your own handwriting. I know because I have just come from the 9th International Calligraphy Conference in Santa Clara, California.

Embarrassed by my unstylish hand, I began by confessing that I would much rather talk to calligraphers than write to them. Even as I said it, I realized that this must be the kind of thing everyone says to calligraphers, just as, when you meet a mathematician, you're impelled to confess that you cannot do long division and can't balance your checkbook. Mathematics of course hasn't much to do with checkbook balancing, and I don't think calligraphy has much to do with handwriting. In any case, mine didn't keep me from feeling considerable kinship with calligraphers.

Long before that, I had discovered poetry and noticed that each of the Knopf volumes carried a colophon of a few lines about the typeface and about the book designer W. A. Dwiggins. Dwiggins was not only a wonderful typographer, he was also the founder of the Society of Calligraphers, an organization that appealed to me because it was imaginary and had no members.

Poetry is taught in schools as if the look of it doesn't matter, but of course it does. Alfred Knopf knew that, so did children. Only teachers seemed not to know about the connections between sight and sound, between how things look and what they mean. Poets like Gerard Manley Hopkins and e.e. cummings wrote in a way that was significantly visual, confirming the childhood experience that letters could dance their way into words and go on dancing even when the words themselves meant nothing that you could be sure of.

Originally published November/December 1989 in *I.D.* as the column, "Circumstantial Evidence."

Aware that the shape of type on a page is an important component of their art, poets have also seen punctuation as an important resource. The insistently lowercase e.e. cummings used punctuation marks as the lyrical equal of words, performing the acrobatics of parenthesis. In non-lyrical equal everyday writing, commas are sometimes considered fussy, even prissy, like dotting i's; but in the craft of verse they are as necessary as nails, and the Filipino poet Jose Garcia Villa used them so abundantly he was called "the comma poet." One of the poems in his book *Have Come, Am Here,* has no words at all, consisting entirely of artfully placed commas.

The artist Corita Kent, formerly Sister Corita, wrote extraordinarily sensitive letters in an italic hand so lovely that I wondered how she would handle something prosaic, like driving instructions or reminders to feed the cat. Later I came to see that, in her hand, nothing was prosaic, and that the calligrapher's craft could properly be directed to whatever needed doing, whether an invitation to a royal wedding or an announcement of softball practice. The scribe, according to Edward Johnston, "keeps the idea of usefulness constantly before him," as all designers should.

The renowned type designer Herman Zapf recommended that calligraphers apply their craft to the alphabets on the screens of their PCs. (Do calligraphers *have* PCs? I asked them and was informed that some do.) Zapf pointed out how clumsy, illegible, and crude the existing alphabets are, a problem that kept many graphic designers away from computers, although obviously not very far away or for long. "New alphabets as an expression of our time are needed worldwide," Zapf said, "for workstations, screens and other digital equipment."

Developing such alphabets would mean facing the kind of dilemma industrial designers confronted when Formica was introduced. To disguise it with a fake wood grain surface was regarded as dishonest and sleazy by designers who had been taught that a material ought to look like what it is. But it was hard to say what Formica, used honestly, *should* look like? It had no look of its own, no self to be faithful to: it was a blob of glop.

The computer alphabet isn't even a blob of glop. Until summoned into existence by a fingered keyboard, it is literally immaterial. But the same question applies: what should it look like? As if it came off the quills or brushes of calligraphers? Or like those sad typewriter fonts that pretend to be script? Unlike wood, which gets its character from a living tree, Formica has no roots. And unlike calligraphy—which gets its character from the talent and sensibility of the calligrapher— the computerized alphabet has no hand but the one the designer simulates.

It is in the end a problem of design.

Transformational Products

All our newspapers are cluttered with private advertisements delivering public messages. I am not talking about personals—those classified nuggets coded to describe an advertiser's qualifications and availability for relationships too various to spell out. I am talking about the large display ads placed by persons who, discouraged by the constraints of letters-to-the-editor columns, crave a roomier venue. The messages themselves are often religious, often political, often impossible to categorize or even to understand. They depart from standard advertising protocol in their sincerity and the fact that they have nothing to sell but lots to tell.

A man bought space in my local paper to challenge the notion that the violence in streets and playgrounds is caused by the violence seen on television. Violence, he argues, is caused not by the content of television, but by the set itself. Here is one paragraph's worth of his tightly reasoned case:

"Television has created an inverted situation where the child's principal source of education is *smaller* than the child and is *dominated by it*. In addition, the set is passive. This *represents a total reversal of nature's order*. . . . The set remains unreactive. . . . A hand-held controller turns it *on* and *off*. . . . To the child's developing mind this controller is an instrument for eliminating disliked things and getting what it wants."

Whether or not you find this line of argument as attractive as I do, it reminds us that television as a product development appeared to be merely innovative when it really was transcendent. (All the more ironic that it should be used to sell products that purport to be transcendent when they are at most novel.) When television was nothing more than a manufacturing promise, it was a relatively modest one: radio that you could see. When the first sets appeared, the medium was

Originally published March/April 1994 in *I.D.*, as the column, "Counterpoint."

revealed as an *unkept* promise. You could see it all right, but what you saw was clumsy, tentative, and amateurish.

How quickly it sneaked up on us as a major—some think *the* major—force in our lives. Not, however, without warning from prophets who, in the tradition of their trade, were dismissed as bearers of evil tidings. There is something disturbing about this, the prophets said. And they were told not to worry, it's just another entertainment device.

It's more than an entertainment device, the prophets protested, and usually less than entertaining.

OK, came the response, but it's just another informational medium, like magazines and radio.

This one is different, the prophets sulked.

Lighten up, they were told. Sure there are differences, but not basic ones. Television is not different in kind. It is different only in degree.

They were right. But the prophets were righter. When a difference in degree reaches a certain magnitude, it becomes equal to, and indistinguishable from, a difference in kind. Products that transform degree into kind might be called transformational products.

The A-bomb was one. Once we had absorbed the scale of destruction, we tried to minimize the scale of the change it represented. This is something different, the prophets insisted. Not *really* different, they were told; it's just a more sophisticated weapon, like a high-tech spear. Again, the judgment was technically correct but irrelevant. A weapon so sophisticated in its manufacture, so primitive in its purpose, and so unknowably devastating in its effect was unlike anything that had come before.

Surely the computer is the most pervasive example of a product so radically different in degree that it equals any difference in kind. Its deceptive name evokes the pedestrian expectations of its creators—a device to make counting and organizing data more efficient. In the history of industrial nomenclature there may be more boring entries than "computer" and "data processing," but you'd need a computer to find them.

Like nuclear weapons, the computer was described by advocates as just another tool. And it is, differing only by degree from a power drill or an adding machine. But that degree is so vast that it may as well be a new species of artifact. The computer does nothing we can't already do, people argued; it just does it faster. Maybe. But it does it so much faster that it has changed our concept of doing. And it can do almost anything.

Versatility in objects has always had a slightly comic aspect—the sofa that becomes a bed; the vacuum cleaner that reverses its jet engines to inflate rubber rafts; the walking stick that doubles as a sword; the Swiss Army Knife that is harder to carry than a tool kit, harder to hold and use than any tool, and—with its ear-wax remover, nail file, pipe cleaner and potato grater—is the single most convincing reason the Swiss avoid war at all costs. But the computer's versatility operates at another level entirely. It is a tool for the hardest of jobs, whatever they happen to be.

Television, nuclear weapons, computers are all products—designed phenomena that were dependent on discovery but brought into being by people whose mission was to produce them. The anti-depressant drug Prozac is like them in that respect, and also in respect to its popularity and the issues it is beginning to raise. Peter Kramer's extraordinary book, *Listening to Prozac*, describes the drug's radical departure from other drugs in its apparent capacity for affecting the self, moving beyond the treatment of an affliction to the redesign of the personality. Dr. Kramer has enriched medical discourse with the phrase "cosmetic psychopharmacology," causing a variation on an old television commercial to run in my head. "Madge, what can I do for my dry, dishpan personality?" "Prozac," Madge recommends, adding, with a wink in her voice: "You're soaking in it."

Kramer notes that, unlike lithium and imipramine, "Prozac was not so much discovered as planfully created. . . . Whereas lithium is the simplest of chemicals, an element, unpatentable, its usage discovered by a solitary practicing doctor with no eye toward profit, Prozac is a designed drug, sleek and high-tech." He wonders whether this designed quality has influenced the drug's reception by making specifiers and users both more susceptible to its blandishments and more likely to distrust it.

Is Prozac just another drug? Or is it, in its power to transform rather than heal, the harbinger of a new use of prescribed medications? In describing its status as a designed drug, Kramer may be offering a clue. Prozac's predecessors—Miltown, Valium, Tofranil—were, he says, just model changes. Although penicillin was surely a transformational product, and the Model T presaged one, designers in pharmaceutical laboratories or body-styling studios are not normally responsible for transformational products. Design public relations has identified thousands of "totally new concepts" and "breakthroughs," but design practice has more to do with the continual refinement of what already exists.

What already exist for Prozac are billions in sales. Dr. Kramer stated recently that we are all within three degrees of separation from Prozac. Immediately after reading that, I put it to a somewhat inelegant test. For one day, every time the phone rang I asked whether the caller knew anyone on Prozac. All of them did (one said she didn't know anyone who wasn't on it), with the possible exception of a man who was calling to sell me MCI or Sprint or a prime lot in Florida. He didn't answer the question, but his surliness at being distracted made it clear that he was not taking it himself.

Teddy Bears and Bar Rails

Tactility is the missing ingredient in a lot of design. The slogan "high tech/high touch" that was popular several trends ago, said that the more sophisticated our technology, the greater our demand for a compensatory warmth. If so, it addresses the problem only to the extent that a slogan can address a problem, which is hardly at all. In any case, high tech/high touch always seemed more alliterative than substantive. Technology can be high or low on a developmental scale, but touch doesn't particularly lend itself to vertical evaluation. Except in basketball, high touch is no better than any other kind.

We talk about function and form as if one has to do with performance and the other with appearance. But both, as it happens, have to do with either the reality of touch or the suggestion of it. The artist Richard Artschwager says that "sculpture is for the touch. Painting is for the eye." He speaks of his desire to create "a sculpture for the eye and a painting for the touch." But sculpture generally is for the eye, although you can touch it if you're close enough and the guard isn't looking. And any Van Gogh is a painting for the touch, even if you can't get close enough to touch it. No matter how highly visual, the design process, which so often has to do with tools of one kind or another, cannot steer clear of the sense of touch for long.

And who would want to? Not only is it pleasant (as in shiatzu) and efficient (as in high torque), touching is one of the first necessities of life. A mass of research, according to an new report, indicates that "in the early months the tactile sense is, neurologically, the most mature sensory system." Touch, in other words, is our first reliable connection with the world.

Yet in a period when we are adjured by human potential faddists to touch each other, and when museums have

Originally published March/April 1988 in *I.D.*, as the column "Circumstantial Evidence."

reversed their centuries-old position, and begun mounting "please touch" exhibitions, designers find it difficult to restore tactility to activities that have been stripped of it. There are Esalens to help us get in touch with our feelings. But how do we get in touch with our hardware?

One answer is: software. Forty years ago, by happy accident, I stumbled onto computer graphics. Or rather I stumbled onto two computer graphics pioneers. George Michael and Bob Cralle, computer specialists at the Livermore Radiation Laboratories in California, were experimenting with computer-generated animation when probably they should have been doing whatever the real work of a radiations laboratory happens to be. The images they produced were primitive, but dazzling nonetheless, and full of promise. Their dreams were ahead of the game. Brilliant, indefatigable, zealous, they were True Believers, looking confidently ahead towards a day when books would be replaced by the computer, and all the information in a good university library could be stored on a disk.

Their argument was convincing but unappealing. "I don't want information storage and retrieval," I protested, "I want books."

"What for?" Cralle taunted. "You'd have the same words and the same meaning."

"But it wouldn't feel the same," I argued. "I like books. I like to hold them and smell the binding glue and riffle the pages and stick my thumb in them to keep my place while I make a note."

"Ah hah," Cralle responded, "You want the teddy bear effect. No problem. Once we have advanced to the point of eliminating books, we will know how to program into a computer the way books used to look and smell—for anyone who needs that."

I needed that; but no thanks. Not that way. For it wasn't the teddy bear effect I wanted, it was the teddy bear itself. A book in the hand is worth a hundred discs. I want the weight of the book bag, the thud of dropping it on a table, the shotlike sound of closing a book you're glad to be done with. You can't write your name on the flyleaf of a computer, or press a flower between its pages.

Touch is important to readers. It is also important to writers, whose rewriting is complicated by first drafts that pose as polished manuscripts. Hemingway didn't use a typewriter because the result looked too final, too much like printing. Hard copy, though, *is* printing. Writing on a computer offers its own sensuous teddy bear effect. Word processing is not a faster kind of typing, but a wholly different experience. Because the keyboard offers no resistance, even a bad typist can float through a work session as silent as an Indian canoe on a hidden creek. There is danger here. Words, like fish, want to fight and be fought for.

The high-tech young woman who showed me how to use my program understands computers and knows how to explain their operation to dummies. Certain functions are toggle switches, she pointed out. That is, you do the same thing to turn them on as to turn them off. It was a lucid way to make their use intelligible to me, but emotionally it was off center. The functions are like toggle switches in essence but not in feel. Toggle switches go click! Thus they belong to the large category of things that feel like how they sound and vice versa. A baseball hitting a bat, the scratch of a real pen on good paper, a basketball bouncing confidently on a sidewalk. The sound could be duplicated. It could be synthesized by Casio and sold in the percussion section of Manny's Music Shop. But the feel resides in the design.

To assess the loss of tactility we need to remember low tech. Consider the sensuousness of a bar—not a barroom, but the slab of polished mahogany itself, backed by shining glassware that tells you how it will sound when it knocks on wood. To see such a bar is to know how it will feel to your forearm, how it yields spilled liquors to the barman's quick pass with a rag.

Now make a technological leap. We think of automotive design as if all we did with cars was drive them and look at them, but we do much more. Dick Latham, the Chicago industrial designer turned marketing guru, was asked why he drove a tiny Alfa Romeo.

He didn't have to mull it over. "It sounds so wonderful when I shift gears that I shift gears all the time. And I keep opening and shutting the door, because when you shut the door it sounds like it's full of ice cream."

While my friends Michael and Cralle were plotting the extermination of teddy bears, Gerald Gulotta was designing some drinking glasses that were a delight not just to behold but to hold. At the bottom there was a sort of plinth around which the drinker's finger pleasurably and naturally curled. It functioned gloriously as the digital equivalent of a bar rail, and you didn't have to leave home to enjoy it.

The current generation of designers have been robbed of constraints by the same technology that has given them the means to invent their equivalents. At the same time that technology—microminiaturization in particular—was making it stylistically unnecessary to do anything, it was making it possible to do everything. If an answering machine, a word processor and a burglar alarm were all essentially contained in a chip, they could be housed in the same kind of box. But they could also be housed in almost any shape a designer responsibly (or irresponsibly) chose. Conventional industrial design wisdom holds that an object ought to look like what it is and does. But now we have objects whose function is so remote that it offers up no clues about form. Designers have to work it our for themselves like armchair detectives. Functional modernism emphasized the revelation of a product's working parts. But now there are likely to be no working parts visible to the naked eye or palpable to the bare hand. Initially that was true of highly specialized instruments, used mostly in laboratories. Today it applies to calculators, lighters, alarm clocks, VCR's, and other equipment of daily living. As critic Michael Sorkin writes, "Home is where the state of the art is."

Well, what better place to enjoy it?

How Do It Know?

Instead of the information you ask for, people give you the information they think you want. "Is there still a shoeshine parlor on the second floor of this building?" I asked a pretty young woman at the Merchandise Mart in Chicago.

She looked down at my feet. "You don't need a shine," she said.

I didn't want one. I wanted the shoeshine parlor. But, like much that I long for these days, it was gone, and with it the mysterious sign on the wall. There was nothing typographically interesting about the sign. The mystery was the message:

THIS BUSINESS IS OWNED AND OPERATED
BY A MEMBER OF MENSA.

I knew what Mensa was—an organization of people with abnormally high IQ's; but I have never known what Mensa is for. I see no reason why people with abnormally high IQ's should not organize if they wish, but I don't see any reason why they should either. This is not sour grapes. The probability that I am not qualified for Mensa makes me no more envious than the certainty that I am not qualified for the DAR. You play the hand you are dealt. Or, in Mensa's case, the head.

Still, I wondered how much the proprietor's IQ mattered to the clientele. Polishing shoes is an honorable craft, but not a highly cerebral one. The skills are rudimentary, the decisions few and simple. Brown, black, or neutral. Cream shine or wax.

While shining my own shoes, I heard a radio news brief about a job applicant in New London, Connecticut, who was rejected by the police department because he tested "too smart" to be a cop.

Smart people have always irritated and threatened the rest of us. "Too smart for her own good" usually means too smart for the *speaker's* own good. Or, in the case of designers, for the

Originally published May/June 1997 in *PRINT*, as the column "Peripheral Vision."

client's own good. When William Golden was in charge of design and advertising at CBS, he described a designer's dilemma: "Business regards him simply as a tool of communication, while the designer feels *he* has something to say. He undoubtedly has. But it can be pretty irritating, for example, to pick up a telephone, only to discover that instead of transmitting your message, the damned thing is not only talking back to you, but is talking about something else."

Golden's remark was hyperbolic, a witty figure of speech, only a few years ahead of its time. Today it is hard to find a phone that does *not* have a message of its own, or, for that matter, its own list of other phones to call. And as telephones outtalk us, other inanimate objects outsmart us.

In Golden's day, smartness was attributed to us rather than to our artifacts. Street smarts, for example, were a property of cab drivers and hustlers, not of the streets themselves. No longer. The world is incessantly creating, or at least advertising, "smart" designs. Saab has developed "a smart seat belt/smart air bag combo." Mercedes *names* a car "Smart." Airline magazines advertise smart pillows, smart cameras, smart sunglasses, and toothbrushes that are at least reasonably bright. *Wired* salutes a new product as "brilliant." Paper companies tout paper smart enough to outfox temperamental printers. A furniture company offers an award-winning smart chair.

Well, I would be happy with a chair that won an award for ergonomic design, but intimidated by one that got a MacArthur grant. How smart do we want designed objects to be anyway? If a layout could adjust text and art to the ability of individual readers, would readers be served or patronized? The French illustrator Andre François said, "I would gladly type the letters if my secretary would make the decisions." But she (for it was a she) wouldn't make the decisions and neither will Microsoft Word. Our instruments and their software bear no policy burdens; they bear only tidings—glad, evil, or irrelevant.

When such jokes were current and permissible, there was one about the hillbilly challenged to name the greatest invention of all time. Without hesitation he chose the thermos bottle. "It keeps my coffee hot and it keeps my lemonade cold," he explained. "How do it know?"

Some products need to be smart. The electronic chess master Deep Blue is a case in point, one that has not historically been a comfortable case for its parent, Big Blue, to make. IBM, which took corporate pride in never being afraid of anything, began worrying in the '60s about whether computers could think. Fearing a customer base that feared IBM, the corporation that had plastered the motto THINK on its placards, banners, clocks, and company magazine stressed that the directive was addressed to management rather than product. An advertising campaign was built around the slogan, "People think. Machines work."

That position was hard to sustain. As each generation of computers surpassed its predecessors in seemingly cognitive behavior, the definition of thinking was revised to keep excluding the computer from country clubs and tenure. Like a defense lawyer incrementally admitting a client's guilt, industry spokespersons first asserted, "This is a big dumb tool that can't solve problems." Next they acknowledged, "This big dumb tool can solve problems," pointedly adding, "but only if a human being shows it how." Later the line was modified to, "It's not so big anymore, and it can figure out how to solve problems by itself, but it can't take any interest in the outcome."

All that special pleading led a mathematician at the Rand Corporation to observe, "Saying that a computer can't think because it can't do exactly what we do is like saying that airplanes can't fly because they can't land gracefully in trees."

On the grounds that behavior and results are our only means of knowing whether people think, the English mathematician Alan Turing proposed a charming test, consisting of a dialogue between a person in one room and a computer in another. If, on the basis of a free-wheeling intellectual exchange, the person was unable to tell whether he was communicating with another person or with a computer, then the machine could be said to be thinking.

In time we will learn to design a computer capable of human error. In the meantime, there is relief in knowing that smartness is not the only human attribute our culture confers on designs. The promotional literature of the systems furniture industry, where "smart" workstations abound, is studded with references to "forgiving" and "unforgiving" systems. The latter punish the user for initial mistakes in specification. The design of forgiving systems requires designers who are themselves forgiving, anticipating the possibility of redesign in the future.

But how far can this go? Must graphic designers forgive readers for the sins of inattention, poor vision, and limited literacy? If their priority is communication, they must. "A poor workman blames his tools" is an aphorism balanced by the complementary truth that a poor tool designer blames the maladroit consumer.

An ATM is a forgiving system. If you give it the wrong information, you can press CLEAR and start over. Smarter than the teller it replaces, it is also more polite. And courtesy counts, for one of the problems with smart machines is that they get uppity. Too many products developed to be smart turn out to be smartass—preachy cars, long-winded cameras, self-righteous refrigerator voices to remind dieters when they open the door that they've been there and done that already, show-off watches that say, "Look, no hands." Car alarms, exhibitionist at best, offend everyone but car thieves.

Like people, designs may be smart in some areas and not in others. I wear a watch that is dumb in the same sense that Turing suggested a computer could be called smart: It *acts* dumb. Even though it knows the exact time, it cannot tell it to me, since the face has been designed to reveal only approximate time. It can, however, at least show me that it is getting late. My digital watch on the other hand (pun more or less intended) supplies the precise time on demand, but cannot display a spatial sense of time passing. When we first called objects smart, we meant that they behaved like us. Now we think we're smart if we behave like them. A thermostat was a "smart" product because it operated on the principle engineers call "feedback." Data was sensed and fed back into the operation, changing it in the process. Soon people went around telling each other that *they* needed feedback, as if we were all made by Honeywell. Our electrical devices used to be smart only when turned on. Now we describe each other according to our capacity to turn on, or be turned on by, others. We need input so we can download our ideas and put them on hold. Soon the synthetic lunatics will be running the human asylum. And they'll be laughing all the way to the memory bank.

Any Number Can Play

Cap Palmer, a producer of industrial films, dreamed up the genre "Imagine A World Without X's" to lampoon the industry formula in which a product or material is dramatized by showing what the world would be like without it. A film made for, say, a cutlery manufacturer shows a world where all knives have mysteriously vanished from kitchen drawers, knife racks, Boy Scout sheaths, and pockets. As a result, meat remains uncarved, bread stands unsliced, onions unminced, potatoes unpeeled, fish unscaled. On camping trips, tree trunks are uninitialed and hot dogs and marshmallows unroasted because there is no way to make a pointed stick.

Or a typical film sponsored by a rivet manufacturer might begin with a narrator's voice booming, "Imagine a world without rivets," upon which buildings and bridges on screen fall down, cars fall apart, airplanes lose their wings and drop from the rivetless skies.

The device does dramatize our dependence upon resources we take for granted. Like other marketing stratagems, it is applicable to higher purposes. Our supply of knives and rivets is not seriously threatened. But our supply of natural resources is, and there are probably very few of us who have not in the past few years become keenly aware of how we depend on them for the essentials of life and for thousands of nonessentials. While "Imagine a World Without X's" became a tiresome cliché in sponsored films, it has become a deadly serious game for home use. Any number can play.

Originally published April 1960 in *I.D.* in the article "Industry on the Screen."

Side Effects

I can't remember anything anymore. Lying in bed, I rummage through my unresponsive mind, then ask desperately, "What's her name?"

"Whose name?" my wife answers.

"The woman in the movie. Don't ask me what movie. I can't remember that either."

"It's in there somewhere," she says.

"That reminds me of a story. Hector Berlioz once lost patience with an orchestral brass section that couldn't play a passage from *Symphonie Fantastique* the way he had composed it. He screamed at the musicians, 'The notes are in there somewhere! It's your job to get them out!'"

"It's your job to go back to sleep," she says.

A few hours later I sit up in bed, triumphantly exclaiming "Myrna Loy! *The Best Years of Our Lives.*"

"Thanks for not making me wait until morning to find out," my wife says. "Anyway, I was right. You can remember. It just takes longer now. It's a side effect of aging."

"*Aging* is a side effect," I say.

"What do you mean by that?" she asks, falling asleep again before I can think of an answer. Just as well, for I didn't really mean *anything*. It occurs to me, though, that what I said may have meant something, irrespective of whether I had or not. Namely, that side effects are built into our lives gyroscopically, to keep the world in balance. No gain without pain. The bitter with the sweet. Win some, lose some.

I admit to a lifelong predilection for sides. At a three-ring circus I always ignored the center ring, concentrating on the two at the sides. In fact, I preferred sideshows to main events. I liked carnivals better than circuses, because carnivals were *all* sideshows, pure distraction, unalloyed by anything in particular to be distracted from. Sideshow barkers held an allure no

Originally published February 21, 2005 in VOICE, the online journal of the American Institute of Graphic Arts, as the column "Noah's archives."

ringmaster could match. The high wire act in the big tent carried the suspense of danger. But it lacked the suspense of mystery, the delicious tension in wondering what secrets of flesh and spirit might, as the barker promised, be revealed, if you paid the extra quarter, in the dark of the tent behind the tent.

We are already wearyingly familiar with side effects in a medical context, where federal regulations and the fear of torts force pharmaceutical manufacturers to deliver mandatory admissions posing as voluntary expressions of compassion. After each hyperbolic declaration of miracle cures, the voiceover drops to a softer tone, cooing a litany of hazards so seductively that you're almost charmed to learn that "taking Hypofraudocin may cause nausea, anxiety, behavioral disorders, gastrointestinal bleeding and, in rare cases, death." Then the voice switches to a straight-talk inflection, acknowledging frankly, "Hypofraudocin is not for everybody. Ask your doctor if Hypofraudocin is right for you."

One evening I made a list of eleven different medications advertised that way, and the next morning left a message for my doctor, asking if they were right for me. He has not returned the call.

Nothing we swallow is without side effects. Neither is anything we invent or design. Like cholesterol, side effects come in good versions and bad. They can even be good *and* bad. The introduction of corked wine bottles meant that wine did not have to be drunk immediately upon fermentation. A side effect was the ritual of uncorking, swirling the goblet to boost aeration, studying the color, sniffing, decanting, with the host pouring the first few drops to assure that the guest's glass is free of corkage. True, the excessive show of sniff, study, and swirl threatens to turn a pleasant side effect into a pompous side affectation; but even pretentious ceremony has its place.

Now, however, oenologists have discovered that plastic is superior to cork, and are hinting that screw tops are even better. But the plastic corks don't come out with the same satisfying smooth pop; and opening a bottle of vintage Bordeaux with the same twist one uses to take the cap off a bottle of mouthwash will lift no one's spirit. Although the alcohol is potent as ever, without the side effects we get less kick from champagne.

The more innovative the product, the further removed from previous experience, the more difficult it is to predict side effects. E. B. White suggested that if Alexander Graham Bell had anticipated the trauma of telephone conversation, he might have called the whole thing off. Charles Eames observed that "a plastic cup seems like a very reasonable thing. Who could have guessed that one would actually miss feeling the heat of the coffee or the coldness of the lemonade? Or that the constant neutral temperature of the material would give some of the disoriented feeling of Novocain in the lip? Who would have guessed that one would be disappointed in not hearing it clink when set down, and feel slightly cheated at the thought of its bouncing when dropped?"

Two of my favorite euphemisms for side effects come from the medical profession. *Iatrogenic* illness is illness resulting from a visit to the doctor. *Nosocomial* illness is illness brought about by a stay in the hospital. Both are aplicable to design practice and design programs. Bad side effects are perceived as failure, but they are just as likely to be the product of success. It was the automobile's utility and affordability that led to highway congestion, the computer's limitless adaptability that brought us spam, the cell phone's functional convenience that turns it at times into a public enemy. As architectural planner Jane Thompson says, "Every problem comes from a solution." Or, to put it another way, every silver lining turns out to be under another cloud.

The most memorable side effect in literature is found in

Charles Lamb's *Dissertation on Roast Pig*, the tale of a prehistoric Chinese village where Bo-bo, the teen-aged son of the swine herder Ho-ti, carelessly let his father's cottage burn to the ground with all of the family's pigs inside. As Bo-bo agonized over what to tell his father, "an odor assailed his nostrils, unlike any scent which he had before experienced." Feeling one of the pigs to see if there were any signs of life, he burnt his fingers, stuck them in his mouth and, Lamb tells us, "For the first time in his life (in the world's life indeed...) he tasted—crackling!

"The truth at length broke into his low understanding, that it was the pig that smelt so, and the pig that tasted so delicious; and . . . he fell to tearing whole handfuls of the scorched skin with the flesh next it, and was cramming it down his throat . . . when his sire entered amid the smoking rafters, and finding how affairs stood, began to rain blows upon the young rogue's shoulders."

Bo-bo paid no attention and kept on eating madly while his father beat him. "O father," he cried, "the pig, the pig, do come and taste how the burnt pig eats."

At last his father stopped pummeling Bo-bo long enough to taste the pig. The two then sat down together and devoured the entire litter.

Soon the neighbors observed that Ho-ti's cottage kept burning down with alarming frequency. Once they discovered why, their own cottages began going up in flames repeatedly, until "there was nothing to be seen but fires in every direction." To facilitate the process, people made their rebuilt cottages increasingly frail and flammable, building "slighter and slighter every day, until it was feared that the very science of architecture would be lost to the world."

And that, Lamb tells us, was the origin of cooking. Further development awaited design intelligence. For not until someone saw the possibility of roast pork without the necessity of residential conflagration, could woks and stoves and grills and pots and pans and chafing dishes be conceived and fabricated. Design has always depended on the imaginative reinterpretation of side effects.

For Sale

A standard way of impressing people with the ubiquity of design is to itemize their daily encounters with it. The pitch goes something like this: "You wake up up to a designed alarm clock, brush your teeth with a designed toothbrush, make coffee with a designed coffeemaker, then pour it into a Russel Wright cup, set it on a Noguchi table . . ." And so on through the day or until the listener is bored out of her skull.

Not original, but it makes the point: design is inescapably part of our lives. A complementary point is that all of those objects—even those acquired as gifts—were sold to someone. Selling is also inescapable.

In a little book called *Buying*, the historian Judith Mara Gutman observes, "We reach the shopping center, buy a paper, cigarettes, window shop . . . case the drugstore before it closes . . . the whole process of buying . . . determines our daily pace, dictates our nightly rhythm . . . we buy all the time."

But If we buy all the time it is because we sell all the time. Individually and in corporations, across the counter and over the Internet, through fair means and foul we push and we pitch. The process moves more than goods and services. We buy (or buy into) and sell (or sell out) ideas. We sell plans, wars, rights, images, protection, advice, sizzle. . . . Whether what's offered for sale is a vacuum cleaner or a foreign policy, the warning applies: *Caveat emptor*. Let the buyer beware.

Design, indubitably pervasive in almost every other aspect of our world, is pervasively involved in what we sell each other and how.

Corporate Culture

J Bronowski, the scientist who wrote *The Ascent of Man*, remarked that, "A knife and fork are not merely utensils for eating. They are utensils for eating in a society in which eating is done with a knife and fork. And that is a special kind of society." Design, in other words, is an expression of culture. And since most of the design in our lives is produced by corporations, corporate culture is inevitably reflected in the products we trade in.

When I first heard it, "corporate culture" sounded to me like corporate jargon, but there is such a thing, as TV newscaster Linda Ellerbee acknowledged when she asked, "If men run the world, why can't they stop wearing ties?" In the 70's I read about a musician named Mason Williams who wondered why he couldn't get into a Washington restaurant without a jacket and tie, and concluded it was because the people who owned the restaurants also owned the clothing stores. The power to run the world does not transcend the culture of whatever world it is you're running. A tie is silly and uncomfortable, but no sillier and no more uncomfortable than reading (or writing) a corporate mission statement.

Corporations also have their own individual cultures, and the burgeoning market for company stories suggests that they are attracting their own Margaret Meads. Companies are not as different from each other as Mead's Samoans were from New Englanders, but they are different enough to be recognized as such without anthropological support. At about the time Williams was trying to get his dinner, the design director of a mammoth materials manufacturer was complaining to me that he could not find any graduating design students to hire. That surprised me, for I had just visited a number of design schools and been impressed by the quality of the students.

Originally published November/December 1990 in *I.D.*, as the column "Circumstantial Evidence."

"Oh, they're bright," the director agreed. "And a lot of them are talented."

"Then what's the problem?" I asked.

"They all have beards," he said, spreading his hands to express helplessness in the face of an insurmountable obstacle.

"No one with a beard could design anything," I said sympathetically; but the same corporate culture that resisted beards made him impervious to irony.

"A beard wouldn't necessarily keep them from designing," he replied patiently, "but can you imagine someone with a beard going in to talk to a chief engineer?"

Not only could I imagine it, I could even imagine a bearded chief engineer; but I understood why he could not. There are corporate cultures in which imagination does not run free. Yet something puzzled me. His firm had just won an award for an exciting film on color and texture in materials design—a film I had seen at one of the schools about to send graduates into the world with beards. I happened to knew one of the film makers slightly. She did not have a beard, but she was dating a member of the film crew who did. How had they managed to infiltrate the corporation?

"That was no problem," the design director explained. "They were consultants."

Hiring a consultant is an ingenious mechanism by which a corporation can circumvent the restrictions of its own culture. In fact, a company's going outside itself to effect a violation of its corporate culture may be built into the culture itself. I know a company with a strict policy against alcohol at corporate events that finds co-sponsors to provide the wine, like the orthodox Jews who engage gentiles to turn on lights during the Sabbath.

As a particularly dramatic illustration of how corporate culture transcends a given industry, consider the personal computer as represented by two companies with corporate cultures too widely known to permit anonymity. Even before there were computers in any modern sense, IBM had a reputation for being conservative and looking it. People both inside the corporation and outside it spoke of an "IBM type," uniformly garbed in white shirts and gray suits during all waking hours. The dress code is not as strict today, but still follows a clearly understood, if less explicitly defined, pattern.

The competition was culturally quite different. Visiting the Cupertino, California, headquarters of Apple was like being trapped in a sportswear commercial. To an outsider, one of the striking aspects of IBM's organization was the way in which status was signalled by protocol. You could not hang around the company very long without sensing the distinction between a manager, a director, and a vice-president. And between an ordinary vice-president and a senior vice-president.

At Apple, you couldn't tell a vice president from an intern without a scorecard, and there were no scorecards.

Corporate cultures go deeper than dress and haircuts. I once took part in a presentation to IBM, and nervously asked a colleague, "What do you think Jones will say about our proposal?"

"He won't say anything," I was told. "He's not important enough to speak at a meeting like this."

I set my sights higher and asked, "What do you think Smith will say?"

"He won't say anything," I was told. "He's too important."

Cultural differences are inevitably expressed in design differences. Apple's insouciant logo could not possibly stand for the International Business Machines Company. Nor is it likely that IBM would give one of its products a punning name like Macintosh. (Although one can't be sure. They did name a dictating machine "The Executary," over the designer's protest that it was "like Olivetti's naming the Lettera 22 'O Sole Mio.'")

My first computer was a Macintosh, small, self-contained, and glowing with the promise of user friendliness. When I tried using it, however, it turned, if not user-hostile, at least user-condescending, patronizing me with so-called icons that purported to stand for actions but really stood for words. What was intended as charm, I sourly perceived as cutesy.* To delete a word by pressing a delete command is not an overwhelming burden, and I preferred it to clicking on the word and dragging it into a trash can in the name of simplicity. I resented the mouse (blaming the victim, my son-in-law said I was deficient in mouse skills) and the amount of desk surface it displaced.

After a week I exchanged the Mac for a PC, an efficient instrument that has no personality at all and isn't meant to have. What it has is dignity. The trouble is, it has more dignity than I have. So I may overcome my own cultural bias and go back to the Mac. If I do, I am sure to find that the corporation has met me half way, their culture, and therefore their design, having evolved to accommodate the business side of their business. A living culture resists stereotypes.

In the nineties, I had lunch with Tom Hardy, IBM's Manager of Design Programs. He had a beard.

*This was written before Windows, which has copied everything I objected to in the Macintosh. I am writing this on a Mac.

Cars as Collage

Unquestionably car design is the most widely discussed design of modern times, and without doubt this is because it is the most conspicuously designed. All designers like to think that their contribution determines the success of a product, but only automotive designers know that theirs does. (This has not necessarily enhanced the designer's perceived significance). Marketing people talk as though this were something new, but it was not new even in 1915 when the Barley Motor Car Company of Streator, Illinois, advertised: "There is a point in the production of a motor car where mere utility ceases to signify and beauty becomes the desideratum. The *Roamer* is a splendid car mechanically but its appeal to you is based rather on the unique beauty of its appearance—on its utter distinction of design . . ." It made perfect sense for the copywriter to refer to "a point in the production," for he was aware that the designer's first responsibility was to make a car that would run. Now that the simpler technical problems have been solved, the point-in-production at which appearance becomes a factor in automobile design has been pushed so far forward as to make engineering seem an afterthought. A few years ago a curator at one of the world's most widely publicized art museums explained soberly that automobiles were "hollow rolling sculpture." The British critic Reyner Banham classed them as "pop art," suggesting they could relax and compete with Perry Como rather than with Rodin; but even in that league they were not having a good season.

Perhaps designers, aware that past triumphs like the Cord 810 and the Marmon 16 had been called art, jumped—or were shoved by management—to the conclusion that they were all artists. But designer Gordon Buehrig, discussing the Cord 810

Originally published January/February 1962 in *Canadian Art*.

in an interview with *Time,* explained, "The job was just a job. We worked in a corner of the plant, and none of us thought we were working on a classic."

In 1907 when Henry Ford sat in a rocking chair in a third floor back room while designer Joe Galamb drew Ford's Model T ideas on a blackboard, he did not know that he was creating folk art or even pop art. What he did know was that he had an idea. That idea became so significant in human affairs that it is impossible to appraise it, and quite naturally it became the symbol of industrial civilization, which it epitomized in two ways: the process of its manufacture was the clearest single expression of both the wonder and terror of mass production; and the car itself represented the extent to which our lives could be transformed, and our bodies relocated, by the principle of internal combustion for everyone.

It was not mere satirical invention that made Aldous Huxley deify Our Ford. The car had in fact become a god, powerful and capricious in the best Greek sense. And when it did, designers faced the oldest problem in representational art: what does a god look like?

As is traditional with gods, the car was not always recognized for what it was. It was not nearly so remote or so awe-inspiring to everyone. My father, for example, always took it in his stride, and I cannot think of car design for long without pondering his attitude towards it.

He was not a car buff. Neither was he the average man. Two qualities made it impossible for him to be either: he was unmechanical to an extent that would, by comparison, make Jacques Tati seem like a chief engineer at General Motors, and he had the most admirable values I have ever known.

These qualities had always informed his attitude towards automobiles. Convenience of repair was irrelevant to him, since no repair could be convenient enough for him to manage. His attitude towards design was just as wayward and pragmatic, and, ultimately, aesthetic.

He believed that he did not care about how cars looked. What that meant was that he did not care in the way people normally cared. A man of stature, he never cared about status, and when my uncle once told him he ought to be ashamed of the old hack he drove, he regarded the sentiment with good humored tolerance. He liked to drive old cars, and he liked to look at them. And he formed an attachment for them that went beyond what men can now feel for cars in an age when, to be personally valuable, a car must be either so old as to be eccentric or so new as to establish that the driver's credit is good. In the forties my father drove a Model A to work every day. When some high school students craved it hungrily, he sold it to them for a few dollars, sensing that their affection for it was akin to his own. That night he did not sleep. The following morning he searched for the students, found them, and bought the car back.

Although my father never thought of cars as art, he did *see* them as art. Long before the critics of Detroit identified the "American fat car" my father, who related everything to his wholesale grocery business, observed that Buicks reminded him of swollen cans of spoiled food. And while he resisted buying new cars before he needed them, when he needed them he chose them on aesthetic grounds, as befitted a man who couldn't fix his own flats. Eschewing the motivation to "be the first on your block to own one," he nevertheless was the first on his block to own the Loewy 1946 Studebaker. (Furthermore he was the first on any block to point out that the rearview mirror, which was set on the dashboard that year, afforded an unparalleled view of nothing so much as the heads of the passengers in the back seat.)

So my own orientation to car design was in large measure

sentimental. And I find it hard to be tough about cars now. For what is wrong with the shape of contemporary cars is not that they are ugly, but that they are boring and charmless—characteristics that they share with much modern art, and for the same reasons: they are created directly from fashion and the market, instead of being created from ideas and used for fashion and the market.

The designers and the committees that employ them defend the grossness of our national product with the old chestnut that this is what "the people want." They even have punch-card Rorschachs to prove it. This argument has been dispelled so often that probably even in Detroit no one thinks it is valid.

But one need only look at the futuristic designs periodically done for pop magazines to see that what designers conceive as a dream car, unfettered by the demands of the sales manager, is not markedly different from the cars they now design. And the slight difference is not in the direction of taste. As an avowed sentimentalist of the automotive arts, I can only protest that it is not what I want.

In 1922 it was understood that, in the words of Sinclair Lewis, "to George F. Babbitt, as to most prosperous citizens of Zenith, his motor car was poetry and tragedy, love and heroism." By 1962, to George F. Babbitt it would have been none of those, although by 2002 he would have found his SUV a source of power. There were some outstanding American cars around that time, and some of them live on in "classic" car shows. The 1953 Studebaker hard top, the 1946 Kaiser-Frazer, the original Falcon. But I doubt that any of them meant what the Model A meant to my father.

Essentially the cars of the past were designed in a way that expressed what they did. But this was not because designers were philosophically committed to the honest expression of function; it was because they honestly engaged in the business of making cars and felt that the business was just that: making cars. Manufacturers knew, long before the age of motivational research, that status was important; but they regarded it as ancillary to certain other considerations. People may have bought cars purely for reasons peripheral to the problem of transportation (and we know that they did) but the carmakers did not themselves create cars to appeal to irrational motives.

When Freud reached Detroit—some fifteen years after he reached the drugstore book racks—all of this changed. Car design no longer left consumers free to adapt it to their fantasies. Instead it catered specifically to fantasies they never had. But the designers have had them, and have exploited them, which is how it happens that a small art threatens to come to an end with the emergence of artists. Once cars were sculptural because they were not sculptured—they were the shape of motion as conceived by motion engineers. The result was a large class of patrons concerned with vehicles that they wanted to be beautiful. A later, and decadent, development was the automobile buff whose concern was shape. One reason that the dream cars bubbling up from the psyches of airbrush artists are so often incapable of production is that their creators have no interest in the thing itself. They are like the romantic character in the popular song who wants a paper doll because loving it involves none of the risks of loving real ones. But as the futuristic designers doodled dream cars, scientists and engineers were seriously at work fabricating a technology that makes them possible. The final mocking tragedy of the dream car is that it can be built.

Dream cars tended to be amorphous—an outline, a shape, an effect of line. Today's mass cars find it harder to be sculptural because no one person conceives of the line: the line is not a line anyway, it is a construction done by a committee. It is anonymous assemblage, blurred and indecisive at best, ugly and cumbersome at worst.

If the outline is assemblage, the surface treatment is collage. Surfaces are detailed with masses of chrome, crusts of escutcheon plates, and grilles that have implications of the bedroom, the bathroom, the dentist's office—anyplace but the garage or the road.

Much of this is done in the name of sex. There is nothing startling about relating the automobile to sex. Once every college boy knew the car as both lure and love nest. Traditionally, it attracted girls, and provided a mobile lovers lane with radio, soft upholstery, facilities for a getaway when the campus police appeared, and no mosquitoes. During my sophomore year in college, immediately after World War II, I noticed that couples with wheels were more likely to get married than other couples, the car providing an environment for "getting serious." Indiana winters do not lend themselves to amorous strolling, and the student without a car had nowhere to take a girl but back to the dormitory.

The car as social tool has served us well. But when automobile designers learned that cars were associated with sex, they interpreted this to mean that the automobile was the *object* of sex! Probably it is, but only for those whose tastes are too special to influence mass production.

Perhaps the future of the automobile as art is best expressed in the visual practical jokes of John Chamberlain and Baldacini Cesar, and in the powerful bumper and grille sculpture of Jason Seley. In their work we see cars converted by time and circumstance into scrap, elevated by frivolity or art into something interesting to look at. One need not even go to a museum. For years the monumental roadside scrapyards of northern New Jersey were visually more exciting than any automobile showroom.

This is appropriate and inevitable. The automobile has always been accurately designed—in that it has always been responsive to general prevailing moods: modest and economical in depression; perky during recovery; big and bumptious after the war; and now fragmentary and hysterical. The 1962 Buick LeSabre hardtop in motion, and the 1955 Buick Century in compression both expressed perfectly the spirit of a world in crisis.

The Army Pleads for Survival

Fort Benning, GA. 1960 Lt.-Gen. Arthur G. Trudeau, the Army's Chief of Research and Development, stated a few weeks ago that an army must be able to do three things—"move, shoot, and communicate." The General found it necessary to make the statement because, in the hearts and minds of its members, there is one other thing an army must do: it must exist. And it is no secret that nuclear developments have threatened the existence of the Army by promising to render it obsolete, just as they have threatened the existence of mankind by promising to render it dead. The threat is most palpably evident in the relative prosperity of the Air Force, originally a minor Army branch, and the Navy, which once played the role of a sort of hired carrier. These offspring now flourish like a green bay tree of pre-strontium-90 vintage, while the Mother Service is neglected.

In an ambitious move to dramatize the Army's continuing importance and its increasing needs, the Department of the Army this month conducted Project Man, a three-day conference and demonstration held here "to acquaint key members of the Executive branch of the government, senior commanders, industry . . . and informational media with the needs of a modern Army."

Project Man gets its name from the words Modern Army Needs, but also from a peculiar humanitarian emphasis that finds Man at the core of modern warfare just as he was in the bow-and-arrow days. What is Man that the Army is mindful of him? He is, quite simply, "the ultimate weapon," a definition that found its way into each visitor's night-table literature and out of the mouths of Secretary of the Army Brucker, Chief of Staff Lemnitzer, and even a young Ranger captain I met at the bar.

In his welcoming speech, General Lemnitzer expressed

Originally published May 28, 1960 in *The Nation*.

pleasure at the opportunity to "stress the continued pre-eminence on the military scene of our ultimate weapon, today's soldier." This was the key refrain during Project Man. When the killing power of a nuclear warhead was described, the description was enriched with the warning that we must not become complacent about atomic power: after all, only Man could wage war. (Why, without Man, there was hardly any point in *having* war.)

Another theme without variation had to do with inter-service rivalry. Whenever an Army helicopter or amphibious carrier appeared, someone was on hand to point out that these were not competitive with the more sophisticated equipment of the other services. In discussing the need for new and better air vehicles, General Trudeau modestly explained, "We don't want to fly very high or very fast. But *we would* like to move quietly over the nap of the earth."

For me, Project Man commenced when the Curtiss-Wright company plane in which I was riding descended on Lawson Army Airfield. One of the reporters sitting near a window yelled, "There must be some brass landing. They have an honor guard and a band." Not until we stepped off the plane did we realize the reception was for us. We were the brass! The band played *Semper Fidelis* and a general shook my hand and said, "We're sure glad you could come." "So am I," I said. I was. It was so much like a dreams-of-glory fantasy that all I could think was, "Gee, the kids back home'll never believe this." (Some of them didn't.)

The band swung into the theme from the movie *Bridge on the River Kwai* and we were ushered into buses. We had each been sent a memorandum (in duplicate, naturally) telling what to pack ("Each guest should provide his own sunglasses. . . .") and an itinerary detailed after the manner of armies everywhere:

1530-1550 Open
1550-1600 Load on Buses

1600-1605 Enroute
1605-1610 Unload Buses

All three days' activity was meticulously scheduled this way, and furthermore the schedule was adhered to. Indeed, the entire affair was superbly engineered. It is no easy task to herd some 600 visitors—many of whom outrank you one way or another—around a military base the size of Fort Benning; and the officers in charge did it with the courteous firmness that is the Army at its semi-social best.

We arrived at Building 2756-A, registered, and signed a paper relieving the Army of responsibility for any injuries we might incur. Then a colonel introduced himself and led me to the nearby bar, where we were joined by a Washington reporter who said, "It's about time the Army did a little public relations, and I'm glad to see it happening. The Army's been taking a terrific pasting." Other reporters agreed that the Army had been getting a bad press, and were equally pleased to see that now it was doing some thing about it—courting the press, for one thing.

The Army also purported to be courting industry, although it was not easy to identify the aggressor in that particular romance. Most industry representatives at Project Man were receptive to the Army's case for more and better equipment, because their business is selling the equipment. They were, in effect, co-sponsors—the euphemism in vogue during Project Man was "allies." But they were hardly disinterested allies. It was as though a child were defending his need for an electric train to an adult audience consisting of his parents and three salesmen from F.A.O. Schwartz.

The Army-industry alliance was shaken briefly in a speech by Secretary Brucker, however. Having pointed out that Man was not only a tactical weapon, but actually a strategic-weapons system, Mr. Brucker turned his attention to those weapons that are made and not born. In supplying them, industry "must not allow the desire for profits to assume greater influence in its plans and activities than the desire to serve the nation faithfully and well," he said, adding, "I have always considered any contract between the armed forces and an industrial supplier as a sacred covenant for the good of America." To some industrialists this sounded suspiciously as though the Army thought it deserved weapons whether it could pay for them or not. "We're not buying any of that," one said afterwards. A military writer regarded this as the worst sort of civilian cynicism, and said so. I tried to remember the "true faith of the Armorer" as described by Undershaft, the weapons manufacturer in Shaw's *Major Barbara*. Later I looked it up: "To give arms to all men who offer an honest price for them, without respect of persons or principles."

At the heart of the Army's argument was General Hugh Harris's declaration that, despite the advent of nuclear warfare, "the traditional role of the Army has not changed greatly." His speech was followed by a live firing demonstration, showing how a rifle company might conduct a night defense operation, using artillery, flame tanks, illuminants and rockets with nuclear warheads. Like the other Project Man demonstrations, it was accompanied by a running narration delivered in what I came to think of as The Army Forensic Style—a loud, high-pitched technique somewhere between Oral Roberts and a radio fight announcer. In the narration, as well as on the field, a hypothetical enemy was efficiently beaten. Later on I asked a two-star general what the enemy might have been doing while we were scoring all those direct hits.

"It's a problem," he admitted. "No one has ever hit on a realistic way to simulate war. If you just imagine an enemy, you have to imagine his moves. On the other hand, if you assign a unit to *be* the enemy, you can't use real firepower. Also these things get competitive, and although soldiers are supposed to 'stay dead' once they've been 'killed,' a lot of them keep popping up to score points for their side."

A word about generals. I had never met one before, and here were dozens all about me. As they sat clustered in the bleachers, I watched them, fascinated by how much they looked like generals. Their faces had all the components of virile energy: the tanned leathery skin, the clear eyes, the crisp authoritative mouth, the close-cropped, lead-gray hair. But there was also something disturbing in their faces and in their very presence in the bleachers among the rest of us, something alien and inappropriate: humility. For the duration of Project Man, they had voluntarily subordinated their command to the collective interest. It was not unselfish. It was done in the hope of establishing that theirs was not an outmoded calling. Like the Rangers, who had put on a display of courageous athleticism in hand-to-hand combat, the generals were strong men of proven ability, touchingly gathered in the conviction that no H-bomb could make their ability irrelevant.

Without any question, the most important single contribution to Project Man was the appearance of the President of the United States. He sat thoughtfully with his head cradled in one hand as the latest equipment rolled by. After a demonstration of the speed with which a missile could be set up for firing, the narrator explained that it would not be fired from its present position because "if it were, everyone behind it would be burned to a crisp." The President, who was sitting directly behind it, laughed comfortably. Later, at a firepower and airmobile assault exhibition, he shook his head admiringly as a guided rocket hit the target, and occasionally stuck a protective finger in his ear during explosions.

At the conclusion, Secretary Brucker announced, "The paradox, men—the paradox is that none of this would be possible without Man." It is sobering to think we have a Secretary of the Army who believes this is a paradox. Mr. Brucker gave the President a cast statuette of an infantryman, and promised that we would each get one that evening. Then President Eisenhower—to the apparent surprise of the officials—mounted the rostrum. He gave the best speech I have ever heard him give. Although it was spontaneous, it had none of the embarrassing syntax of his press conference utterances; and although it was not brilliant, the platitudes were clearly from the heart and not ghosted. It was sincere, assured and moving, in much the same way that Project Man itself was moving.

Whenever I am in a strange place I am seized with a compulsion to use facilities simply because they are there; and when we came to a twenty-minute free period I thought of getting a haircut or a shoe shine, or working on one of the typewriters in the press room. Finally I settled for the PX. Wanting to bring home something military, I bought a tube of hair dressing called "Top Brass." I needn't have done it, for when I got back to my room there was a small, white box on my pillow. Inside was my infantryman statuette. The front of it read, "Project Man"; the back of it was an advertisement for the Sperry Gyroscope Company. The next morning I asked whether the President's statuette also carried a commercial, and was told that it did. Well, nobody gets something for nothing anymore, which—any way you look at it—is what Project Man was all about.

Twenty-Five-Year-Old Watchdog

Ideally, the industrial designer is the best friend a consumer ever had. But that ideal has not yet come to pass, and until it does the consumer's best friend is probably Consumer's Union, publishers of a monthly journal of fact and well documented opinion called *Consumer Reports*. Last month both the organization and the magazine were twenty-five years old, and I was glad to salute their sustained service to the cause of an enlightened consumerhood. Walt Whitman claimed that "to have great poets there must be great audiences too," and this month I am claiming that to have good designers there must be good consumers too. (It is demonstrably untrue in both cases; I say it, as Whitman must have, purely for rhetorical purposes).

Consumer's Union is dedicated to the proposition that, in a democracy, anyone has the right to spend money foolishly, but no one should have to spend it ignorantly. To this end—with utter probity—it goes about the business of testing products, comparing them, and telling the world of its subscribers what it has found. Few major manufacturers have been able to get products on the market without coming under CU's righteous scrutiny.

No more interested in the whole product than medical specialists are in the whole body, CU has an almost principled indifference to beauty, and the consumer can expect no esthetic guidance from its editors. This is probably just as well: there is no accounting for tastes, and *Consumer Reports* accounts scrupulously for everything it does. It has not wholly ignored the senses, however. From time to time wines and whiskies are tested, making it possible for people who make fools of themselves on Saturday night to face Sunday morning with the consolation that at least the demon rum was quality controlled, fairly priced, and honestly labeled.

Originally published as an editorial in June 1961 in *I.D.*

In *Pictures From an Institution*, Randall Jarrell describes a couple whose every possession "had been recommended by Consumer's Union—and if you had taken them for a trip on your new yacht, they would have told you how you could have got it at Sears Roebuck under a different brand name and saved four thousand dollars." It is true that *Consumer Reports* appeals strongly to many readers eager to transform the magazine's necessarily restricted editorial approach into a personal way of life. They seem cramped by a kind of Puritan crankiness that renders them unable to make distinctions other than those of price, weight, and repair costs. In pursuit of justice, they apparently cease to value anything else, such as their own time. Recently a subscriber wrote in to boast of having driven for days on a nightmarishly frustrating journey around the countryside looking for a 50-foot clothesline that was not eight inches short.

This spirit is encouraged by the organization's official activity, for CU not only splits hairs—it analyzes them for color fastness and shrinkage. But in the process it has consistently contributed to making consumers more intelligent and manufacturers more responsible.

No other razor blade can make that statement!*

*At the time, "No other razor blade can make that statement" was a slogan used in television commercials for Gillette razor blades.

An Idea Is Not a Three-Piece Suit

There has, during the past two decades, been almost as much written about creativity as about how to lose weight. Perhaps the two subjects have more in common than they appear to: both are processes that come naturally to some people, that others have to learn, and that still others can't ever seem to learn, for all the books, articles, video cassettes, and workshops designed to make it easy.

There is by now a substantial library of materials designed to coax creativity out of its myriad hiding places. Such materials discuss the habits of creative people, the origin of ideas, the events and behavior likely to stimulate creativity. They recommend techniques. They are a rich source of unsubstantiated information about the proclivities of artists and scientists.

I suppose this is all to the good. Far better that we should be looking for easy ways to create than for, say, easy ways to buy handguns. But, like handguns, creativity has consequences. Perhaps because they don't really anticipate successful results, the guides to creativity rarely deal with what happens afterwards. Yet what happens afterwards may present problems as thorny as creativity itself.

One such problem is how to define and protect the rights of the work. After something is created, it takes on a life of its own. At that point, it is reasonable to ask whose life is it anyway? The marketplace of ideas is presumably free in both senses of the word. But since ideas are the currency of creativity, attention must be paid to who, if anybody, owns them.

Consider Saul Steinberg, who is influential both as a cartoonist and a painter. In the seventies, he did a magazine cover for *The New Yorker* in the form of a New Yorker's map of the United States. It is a lovely and hilarious comment on the Manhattanite's distorted perceptions of, and indifference to, the outside world—a peculiarity that makes New Yorkers more

Originally published March/April 1985 in *I.D.*, as the column "Circumstantial Evidence."

provincial than residents of Kansas City. The cover was so popular that *The New Yorker* sold it as a poster.

Naturally the poster was attractive to forgers, and counterfeit copies soon were on sale in Atlantic City, Miami Beach, and Bar Harbor, as well as in New York. I am not concerned here with ripoffs. They come with the territory, and there is not much to say about them. The legal protection afforded us by the state is both complicated and fragile. Designers whose work is forged usually have two alternatives: going to court or deciding to be above it all. Neither recourse is entirely satisfactory.

In the case of a direct copy, both the morality and the legality are fairly easy to establish. Steinberg and *The New Yorker* own the art and anyone who forges it is a thief. Like other thieves, they usually are neither catchable nor worth catching. I am concerned here with something more ambiguous. The Steinberg poster is not only widely copied, it is widely used as a point of departure for new—although not, strictly speaking, original—art. It was perfectly natural for somebody to do a Chicagoan's map of the nation. Then a Texan's. In the beginning these were admiring, parodic allusions—not unlike the homage filmmakers pay to their predecessors. But when Brian De Palma slips a touch of Hitchcock into a movie, he does it because he knows Hitchcock and cares about his work. According to a *Wall Street Journal* article, some of the takeoffs on the Steinberg poster have been perpetrated by people who never even saw the original and who may not have heard of Steinberg, or of Manhattan either, for that matter.

These people are not stealing. They are only using. The trouble is, they are *mis*using. Do they have a right to? After a certain period of time, most published material enters the public domain. Apart from that arbitrary legal state, however, ideas continually enter the public domain on their own, without benefit of counsel. One such idea is Steinberg's inspired cartography. Another, common to newspaper feature columns at the end of every calendar year, is the compilation of what's "in" and what's "out." Robert Benton and David Newman initiated the practice in *Esquire* during the Kennedy administration. Surely they don't own it any more. But did they ever? And what exactly did they own? (A purist might argue that they didn't own it any more than Shakespeare did when he had Lear speak to Cordelia of "who's in and who's out." But while the locution was familiar from Elizabethan court gossip, its application as humor awaited Benton and Newman in the sixties.)

The distinction between influence and plagiarism has usually been a hard one to make. Time helps. If you design a better computer terminal and a competitive company brings the same thing out as soon as they can get it on and off the drawing boards, it is either copying or coincidence. But if, five years later, your terminal remains the best that anyone has been able to come up with, you will have become a legitimate design influence in the industry.

Competition, though, is not the only medium in which ownership is shakily established. What are the rights of a client or customer? The playwright Samuel Beckett protested a production of *Endgame* that did not follow his original stage directions. Do clients buy a piece or a whole? If they buy the whole, does that necessarily include the pieces?

A writer prepares an annual report. The clients are pleased and use the copy, but only *some* of the copy, as an advertisement. The writer argues that they had no right to use it for a purpose he or she had not envisioned, and that in any case they had no right whatever to use fragments. The clients are shocked. "Sure we used your words," they respond, "but those words are precisely what we bought from you."

But was it really words that had been sold? The words themselves, after all, were nothing special—any dictionary provides them all at half the price. What the writer had really sold them were ideas, in the form of words strung together in a certain way for a certain effect.

Beyond the issue of one-purpose use (not to be confused with its close relation, one-time use), there is the issue of fragmentation. A designer I know was dumbfounded when a client asked if they could use one of the wavy lines in a poster made up largely of wavy lines.

"The poster is theirs," she says. "But I told them it was ridiculous to think they could use individual chunks of it."

It does sound ridiculous, even if you remember that Cezanne sold some of the apples from a still life to an art buyer who couldn't afford the entire painting. And yet, is it possible to own a wavy line? If so, the illustrator Robert Blechman has cornered the market for the 21st century.

The rights to commodities are generally beyond dispute. Produce a sales receipt and the goods are demonstrably yours. If you buy a three-piece suit, you can wear the vest or not as you wish. You can wear the jacket with or without the trousers. You can sew a patch on the sleeve or remove one that's already there. And perhaps that is where the confusion originates. Ideas are not commodities.

Outasight Outerwear

My 16-year-old daughter, Leah, came in from the bitter cold protected by the kind of denim jacket Georgia farmers wear in August.

"You need a coat," I said.

"I could use something warm to wear," she agreed.

"That's a coat," I explained. "A coat *is* something warm to wear. That's what I meant."

We went to a department store, where such traditional departments as Junior Miss, Designer Casual, and Budget Shoes had been supplanted by boutiques with names like East of Eden, New Era, and Discoteria. A cul-de-sac called Rising Sun was stocked with an ambiguous collection of what I knew were garments because I couldn't think of anything else that would be hung on hangers.

"I think these are coats," Leah said enthusiastically.

"This is definitely outerwear," the salesperson confirmed, shouting over the same Michael Jackson album Leah had been shouting over when we left home.

"I'm convinced," I said, unconvinced. "But is it outerwear for *her*?" I pointed at Leah, who was examining a mass of woolen tweed partially wrapped in a torn black cotton rag.

"For sure for her. And not just for her, you know what I mean? Everything in this department is specifically unisex." She looked at my own outerwear, a specifically male, tan raincoat. I looked at her innerwear: black leather pants topped by an amorphous expanse of shredded canvas with stenciled shipping instructions: FRAGILE THIS SIDE UP. I would not have known she was a salesperson if she hadn't been chewing gum and wearing a badge. The badge said her name was Kim.

Leah had pulled the tweed apparel from its nest, and I held it uneasily. I have always been clumsy at helping women into their coats and was relieved when the practice was exposed as

Originally published March 18, 1984 in *The New York Times Magazine*.

sexist in violation of civil-rights statutes in 12 states. Even if it were legal, the gesture would have been especially awkward in this case, for the garment had only one sleeve. Or maybe three, depending on how you counted.

"*I'd* better help her into it," Kim said, although what she actually did was to help the fabric onto Leah.

"Does it fit?" I asked irrelevantly.

"It's totally incredible," Leah said.

"Everything here is unisize," Kim said. "Now this," she added, like a television news commentator introducing a commercial break. She held out the black rag, which Leah skillfully attached, shroudlike, to its mate.

"What exactly is that second thing?" I asked, not yet having learned what exactly (or even approximately) the first thing was.

"It's more like a vest," Kim said.

"But doesn't a vest go *under* a coat—I mean, under more like a coat?" I asked.

"Whatever," she said. "There's no one right way. That's the beauty of the style. Also it's warm. Here, feel."

I fondled the fabric. It looked warm, but felt like cold flesh. "It feels like cold flesh," I said.

"Daddy!" Leah said. "You've got your fingers in one of the holes. You're feeling your own thumb."

She was right. The fabric was riddled with holes.

"The holes are Japanese," Kim explained. "Most of your fashion innovations today are Japanese."

I nodded in admiration for the entrepreneurial audacity of a nation that, having captured our steel, electronics, and automotive industries, was now challenging the hegemony of the Swiss in hole production. Protective tariffs would be useless, for the holes—which could hardly be stamped "Made in Japan"—were undetectable by customs officers.

"But, baby, it's cold outside," I protested. "This thing has no buttons, no snaps, no belts or sashes or drawstrings. No zippers. Not even Velcro."

"I can use a safety pin," Leah said.

"We have some fierce ones on the street floor," Kim said. "In 'Uncommon Notions.'"

Beaten, I reached for a credit card. In these postmodern times, when the practical is indiscriminately married to the practical joke in everything from office buildings to novels, why should couture be any different? And who will ever point out that the emperor isn't wearing any closure?

What's New in Deception

The promised production of computers that read cursive script threatens to add yet another item to the list of things my computer can do that I can't. In the meantime, I am the only component of the man-machine interface able, at times, to read my handwritten notes. That doesn't mean I understand them, but then neither does DOS.

On the back of a business card I had been carrying for weeks, I deciphered at last a message so appealingly provocative that I carried the card for several weeks longer: "The subjective is more accurate than the objective by several orders of magnitude." That was said to me not by the person whose card I wrote it on, but by Dr. David Krohn, an ophthalmologist. I think he is saying that even if you can't believe your eyes, you can at least trust them more than you can trust instruments of precision,

It is an idea that perfectly complements another of my notes. This one, written on the Reminders page of my appointment book, reminds me that, "Walt Whitman didn't believe in the curve ball because he thought it was immoral." I have no idea who told me that, but I can't find it anywhere in Whitman. I once knew a botany professor who also didn't believe in the curve ball, but for a different reason. He didn't believe that it could actually happen. What Whitman apparently didn't believe was that it *should*.

To both, the pitch represented deception. The botanist thought the batter was fooled into thinking the ball changed direction when it didn't. Whitman thought the batter was fooled because it did. The same existential enigma animates the story of the man who was asked if he believed in infant baptism.

"Believe in it?" he retorted. "I've seen it done!"

The scientist's disbelief was put to rest by instruments of

Originally published January/February 1993 in *I.D.*, as the column "Counterpoint."

precision showing objectively that the ball does curve. Whitman's concern, being subjective, is not so neatly resolved. So when I was asked last summer for a statement about deception in design, I was ambivalent, uncertain whether to be for or against it. Subjectively, I am repelled by the very idea. Objectively, it comes with the territory. After all, package designers are routinely charged with suggesting the wholesomeness, increased size, and uniqueness of products that are hazardous, smaller, and no different from other brands. Graphic designers are retained to boost the credibility of clients who may be deservedly incredible. Architects design euphemistic artifacts, buildings that—by ignoring the varying abilities of people to walk, see and otherwise negotiate the built environment— make statements to the effect that there are no such people. One of the earliest American product design successes was Henry Dreyfuss's redesign of the Big Ben alarm clock. Dreyfuss had noticed that customers lifted clocks before buying them, evidently equating weight with value. So he cleverly weighted the base of the Big Ben. If illusion is so much a part of design, can deception be far behind?

In Swift's *Gulliver's Travels*, the Houyhnhnms have no word for lying, because they cannot conceive of circumstances under which anyone would do it. What possible motive, they wonder, could there be for saying "that which is not"? We could tell them. Our own vocabulary abounds in synonyms for that which is not, and we need every one of them. Deception is not always a pejorative. In games and sports it is a measure of appropriate skill. The man on first is *supposed* to make the pitcher think he's going to steal when he isn't. Except for Whitman, we all admire the feint in boxing, the fake move in basketball, the quarterback sneak in football.

In school I did not go out for football, a decision ardently supported by the coach. By way of consolation I became a varsity debater. Football is believed to develop character, and it may. Debating is believed to develop reasoning power, but it doesn't. So I left school with no character to speak of and not much capacity for clear thinking either. I was, however, splendidly equipped in the powers of deception, which debating does develop by teaching its practitioners how to argue either side of a proposition and make it seem the better one. Debating saps any character that might have been acquired from football, but it has no immediate effect on the world at large. High school or college debating is not only play, it is *a* play, a performance, deception and counter deception under house rules. The trouble comes when we extend the performance into another house with other rules.

Writing of *Alice in Wonderland*, Bernard DeVoto said, "The reader of fantasy has accepted an open falsehood. We cannot convict Lewis Carroll of . . . victimizing honest burghers. . . . He published legal notice that he was about to practice a deception in the public square and a reader who supposes that the blond is actually being sawed in two is on his own." Deception in the public square is common enough today, but the "legal notice," if published at all, is set in fine print. A viewer can see Oliver Stone's *JFK*, for example, without ever suspecting that, although some of the depicted events are known to have happened (Kennedy really was President and really was assassinated), many are not.

The political scientist Jivan Tabibian speaks of the "susceptibility to persuasion" that characterizes consumers of goods and political services. This is disturbingly close to the "willing suspension of disbelief" that Coleridge said was required for the reading of fiction and poetry. The similarity is disturbing because the ends are so different. When an airline pilot was telling me last summer of his company's high employment standards, I was comforted to hear that flight crews are required to know what they are doing. But it turned out that those were not the standards he was talking about. "We have to hire people with the right image," he said. "The public expects us to look as if we take care of ourselves and are reliable. Disney World is the model. Everyone who works there is clean cut, no long hair, because that's the image the public trusts. It's the same image we're after."

Well, there's nothing wrong with a clean-shaven pilot, but the comparison haunts me. The business of Disney is *only* image, fantasy designed to reflect with meticulous verisimilitude every detail of a world there never was. Flying, however, is real, a circumstance established theoretically by the laws of physics and practically by the fact that sooner or later the plane reaches Cleveland.

Disney World visitors know that and so do airline passengers. The danger is not our difficulty in distinguishing between the real and the fantastic, but our increasing indifference to the distinction. Deception is not new, but our detached acceptance of it is. We have unsubtly shifted from resisting deception and being suspicious of its perpetrators, to embracing it and them. The embrace is mutual and public. There have always been con men and women, but they used to work their craft behind closed doors. Ours is so open a society that the news media that bring candidates to our screen also bring us the specialists who stuff the candidate's head and sleeves. Spin doctoring is not an innovation. The innovation is the willingness of spin doctors to describe their surgical procedures on television, just as the medical doctors on television explain theirs, and on the same shows. Politicians have always hired people to affect perception, but they never before told us about it while they were doing it.

Collusion in our own deception is not new either. But today we go further, demanding to be taken backstage where we can see the mechanics of deception. When Dorothy finally saw what was going on behind the curtain, she fled back to Kansas. Not us. We like it here.

Is it any wonder that when politicians talk about family values they sound sleazy and when Dolly Parton talks about making money she sounds pure in heart? Customer skepticism has given way to soft consumer cynicism. The more sophisticated we become in the mechanics of deception, the less we care about the fact that we are being deceived.

Deception Redux

Somerset Maugham observed that when someone calls and leaves a message instructing you to call back because it is very important, it is invariably important to the caller, rather than to you. That's generally true if the call is important to anyone at all. But it probably isn't. *Important* is part of the inflated linguistic currency we all trade in. Language expands in inverse ratio to the significance of the phenomena it describes. This applies to phone calls and also to a form of communication Maugham doesn't mention: junk mail.

Yesterday, I received a letter with the word URGENT emblazoned on the envelope in crimson caps. Underneath that was a sober warning: AUTHORIZATION REQUIRED BEFORE: And beneath that a blue arrow pointed to a small window in the envelope, where the typed deadline date was visible against a background of highway sign yellow.

In case all those visual cries of alarm did not adequately convey the extreme gravity of this communication, a petition printed in ten point type across the bottom of the envelope read RECIPIENT: PLEASE HAND DELIVER TO ADDRESSEE.

Well, I was the recipient. I was also the addressee. Plainly too hot to handle, the letter was hand delivered by me to myself with a breathless alacrity not tempered by the fact that it had been posted at bulk rate for less than a dime.

We all get mail that looks like this, usually from people telling us we may already have won a million dollars, or offering to make us rich by revealing how to sell real estate without bothering to buy it. What made this piece unusual was its source. When I opened the envelope I found an "executive discount" subscription offer from *Manhattan, inc.*, a magazine about the business world and the personalities in it. Now *Manhattan, inc.*, is not exactly the *American Journal of Physics*, but it

Originally published May/June 1998 in *I.D.*, as the column "Circumstantial Evidence."

isn't the *National Enquirer* either. Its subscription pitch promises such secrets as how Donald Trump makes deals, secrets you couldn't find anywhere else unless you bought Donald Trump's book. Would anyone believe that a bulk mailing piece is so urgent that it requires hand delivery and an immediate response? If the answer is yes, would the kind of person who believed that be capable of putting one over on someone else in a Trump-style deal?

"CONGRATULATIONS! MR. RALPH CAPLAN" is the compelling copy on the cover of a catalog that arrived in the same post. The cover copy goes on to say that "MR. RALPH CAPLAN OF NEW YORK, NY IS A PREFERRED CUS-TOMER and is entitled to a free gift with any order from this catalog. We value your business Mr. Ralph Caplan . . . This is our latest catalog. Every page is packed with exciting new merchandise selected for MR. RALPH CAPLAN."

Although no copy that spells my name right four times can be all bad, I am puzzled. What puzzles me is not the hype but the hope, and the fact that the hope is not unfounded. Just as the URGENT of the *Manhattan, inc.* letter means precisely the opposite—means in fact that hardly anything in the world could be less significant than the material within—so does CONGRATULATIONS state as clearly as anything could that there is nothing to celebrate. Well, almost nothing. I have won a "free gift" (my favorite kind), but to get it I have to order some of the exciting new merchandise selected for me—perhaps the whirlpool foot bath or the New Orleans Ace pistol kit.

The people who prepared and sent this material are con-vinced that it will lure buyers. The funny thing is, they're right. The fact that we get so much highly promissory junk mail is itself a demonstration that it works. If people didn't respond, the stuff would not keep coming.

Why does it keep coming? Why does it work? How could it? A common advertising tactic makes a plus out of a minus, the classic example being the fish packer who labeled his tuna "Guaranteed not to turn white in the can." Variations abound. Luggage advertised as made of "richly grained simulated leather" somehow suggests that simulated leather is the best kind. Pain relievers boast of offering "temporary relief" as if that were preferable to relief that will endure forever. Late-night commercials push the fifty greatest songs of Slim Whitman, an album prized of course for its musical brilliance, but made all the more desirable because it is "not sold in stores." What's wrong with things sold in stores? The same things that are wrong with genuine leather and white tuna, I guess.

Writing in *The New Republic*, P.J. O'Rourke lists all the things he had believed during the sixties. "I believed Bob Dylan was a musician," O'Rourke writes. "I believed I would live forever or until twenty-one, whichever came first. . . . With the exception of anything my parents said, I believed everything."

Such blinding trust is a universal experience. When I was a child I spake as a child. I also believed as a child. I thought cowboy Tom Mix actually ate Ralston Cereal just as surely as Little Orphan Annie drank Ovaltine. My father explained the ways of the world to me, but it was easier for me to believe that my father could be wrong than that Tom Mix could be a hired gun for a cereal manufacturer. By the time I learned about paid endorsements I reasoned that payment did not necessarily invalidate product endorsement. It was perfectly possible that baseball players ate Wheaties, depended on them for strength on the playing field, and just happened to be paid to say so.

That kind of innocence is gone. Maybe James Garner eats red meat, drives a Mazda and takes Polaroid pictures, but I know now that if he does, it is coincidental.

Consider the recent beauty contests in which the winners—women whose beauty and putative talent had been enlisted by dogfood manufacturers and replacement muffler dealers—were stripped of their crowns because they had posed nude or been caught shoplifting. Then, no longer officially the fairest ones of all, they were stripped of their endorsement contracts as well.

That makes a certain marketing sense, even when the information is shared with the market. A network television essay on the 1988 World Skating Championship featured an interview with Debi Thomas's coach. That figures. But it also included an interview with her advertising manager, who explained what his client's endorsement would be worth if she won a gold medal (she didn't). Although advertising managers are not entirely alien to the form of contemporary discourse called hype, his estimate was beyond dispute. In an open society we no longer have to be fooled into thinking something is true in order to act on it. Even if we know that a performer will be asked to endorse products if she wins and not asked to if she loses, and that therefore an endorsement reflects the ability of the endorser but says nothing about the efficacy of the toothpaste or the flashlight batteries, we are still attracted to products that are advertised as if they had something to do with stardom or athletic prowess.

Sometimes "credibility" shrinks with time and overexposure. When the diction and persona used by John Houseman in *The Paper Chase* were recycled to promote the investment house Smith, Barney, the strategy was at first effective. Houseman's old fashioned toughness and character went with the slogan "They make money the old fashioned way. They earn it." It is doubtful that anyone believed Smith, Barney brokers work any harder than anyone else. There is no evidence that they do, and—more important—no evidence that people care whether they do or not, any more than they care whether Houseman actually placed his own orders through Smith, Barney or E.F. Hutton. (Hutton's more meaningful slogan, "When

E.F. Hutton talks, people listen," was fine until the people who listened turned out to be criminal investigators. The slogan was dropped before the indictments were issued.)

There was snake oil before there was Ivan Boesky or Jimmy Swaggart. But you were never allowed to see the con man preparing the snake oil. Imagine the Wizard's career if he had invited the citizens of Oz to come backstage. P.T. Barnum reported that a sucker is born every minute, but he wasn't so much concerned with the birthrate as with the care and feeding of those who had already been produced. He created fantasy but preached reality.

We no longer give much lip service to reality. And the less we talk about it, the more we talk about credibility. It is especially appropriate to think on these things during annual report season, especially *this* annual report season, with reports more elegant than ever refreshing the credibility drained away by last fall's market performance. They may be the only junk mail that wins design awards.

Taking Pleasure Seriously

I cannot imagine a life worth living without fun or without games. Only when combined into a single locution do they appear trivial, the triviality underscored by the use of 'n' as a conjunction, a conceit favored by cute shop names like Books 'n' Things, Art 'n' Stuff, Cats 'n' All That. When applied to design, the term is especially pejorative.

The late Dexter Masters, despite his solemn credentials as director of Consumers Union and editor of *Consumer Reports*, had an exquisite talent for fun. When it came to design, however, he complained of an "excessive inclination to view design in its fun 'n games aspects, or in terms of the useful but limited contribution it can make to an effective promotion of a product that may or may not be really worth the effort of promoting at all."

Are we having fun yet? We are if the satisfaction we get from whatever we're doing is intrinsic, rather than dependent on consequences. Games are often, but not always, fun. Fun may be frivolous; games may be serious business; either may be both. Like play in general they are sometimes enhanced by tools. The tools I coveted as a boy were all available by mail order from a wondrous company in Racine, Wisconsin, called Johnson Smith.

Farmers affectionately referred to the Sears, Roebuck catalog as "the wish book." The Johnson Smith catalog was my wish book. And the prices were so low that what I saw was, sooner or later, what I got. A variety of props and paraphernalia for magic. Texas horned toads and chameleons. Molds for making lead soldiers and cartoon characters. A Kodak Hawkeye camera. Whoopee cushions. Joy buzzers. Handcuffs. A sex indicator consisting of a lead weight at the end of a string that circled the palm of your hand if you were female and swung back and forth if you were male; or vice versa. Itching powder. An X-

Originally published November/December 1992 in *PRINT*, as "But Seriously."

ray tube that purported to reveal the bones in your hands and the lead in a pencil, although the two looked suspiciously alike. The French Viewing Ring with a bathing beauty picture concealed in the shank. Magnets. A printing press. A periscope. Soap that made the user's hands dirty. A kit for reproducing photographs on pillowcases in sepia.

For several years, the cover art included an illustration of a peddler carrying a trunk on his back, from which a voice ballooned desperately, "Let me out, let me out!" The product being advertised was The Ventrilo. A membrane the size of a dime, ringed in tin with a leather border around it, the Ventrilo resembled the Central Operating System of a kazoo. According to the instructions, by placing the device at the back of your tongue you could, with a little practice, throw your voice. Although I swallowed two Ventrilos in rehearsal, I never learned to throw my voice. But I did learn some things from other Johnson Smith merchandise. I learned to make a star printed on a flat wooden wand turn into a moon, or disappear. I learned to play "Swanee River" on a harmonica in the key of C. I learned to analyze the walking patterns of my parents and sister so I could place stink bombs in the precise spots under our living room carpet where they would be stepped on by the family member of my choice. Stink bombs are conceptually vulgar, but their packaging was splendid—three fragile glass globes, glowing with a noxious but lovely yellow liquid, elegantly cradled in a bed of sawdust lining a round wood box that today would be called Shaker-influenced and, for all I know, was.

And there were books. You could do or be anything through Johnson Smith's eclectic library that taught How To: make love, do cowboy rope tricks, tap the age-old secrets of your mind, raise mushrooms in your cellar for big money, build a powerful body, master jiujitsu so you would not need a powerful body, develop your memory, and of course throw your voice. In addition, Johnson Smith was the distributor of the famous E. Haldeman Julius Little Blue Books, an imprint that made Tom Paine, Shakespeare, and Montaigne available for a nickle a book, with discounts on multiple orders. The Little Blue Books were little and the covers were blue and the coarse pages turned yellow while you were reading them. Yet I doubt that anything from the world's finest art presses can provide a more sensuous experience with print. For that matter, neither the Museum of Modern Art gift shop nor the Neiman-Marcus catalog can rival the Johnson Smith inventory for design exhilaration.

The design offices I feel most comfortable in have a certain Johnson Smith flavor, and its appeal is wider than one might think. As a longtime voyeur of client–designer relationships, l have been struck by the extent to which they are cultivated on the designer's turf. Since "Your place or mine?" is a power question in business too, the consultant normally comes to the client. But clients love to go to meetings in a design consultant's office because it is so much more fun than their own.

Surely the paradigmatic palace of fun and games was the Venice, California, office of the celebrated husband and wife team of Charles and Ray Eames. Clients had never seen anything like the Eames office (and it was emphatically called an office, not a studio or atelier) and neither had anyone else. Beyond the visual stimulation you would expect, the space (formerly the Bay Cities fleet garage) throbbed with the unexpected: fish tanks, spinning tops, cakes being baked, organ grinder music, mathematical theories debated—all of it background to the chronically changing display of work in progress.

IBM executives would arrive for sober conferences, loosen

their white collars, and find themselves competing with
Charles at throwing pushpins into the wall. Herman Miller,
Inc.'s former CEO Hugh DePree remembered coming in to
review some new seating, and being put to work as prop man
for a film about toys. The Nobel Prize winning physicist C.C.
Yang came to inspect a science exhibit model and spent so
much time spinning a top (and explaining the physics of it)
that he had to come back the following week to see the model.

In the 1940s, schools and industry united in a crusade to
"make science fun." In the '50s, Eames was producing a series
of exhibits and films designed from the premise that science *is*
fun. In his proposal for the exhibition "Mathematica," Charles
said its purpose was "to let the fun out of the bag. . . . The
excitement, or joke, must be a working part of the idea."

Some of the fun took the form of games. Visitors to the
exhibition called "The Computer Perspective" could play
Twenty Questions on an interactive computer, hardly a big
deal now but pretty advanced for a public space in 1971.

Games matter. To study brain performance recently, University of California scientists used a PET scan to measure the
metabolization of glucose in the brains of volunteers as they
assessed cognitive strategies in a video game called Tetris. John
Von Neumann and Oskar Morgenstern's *Theory of Games and Economic Behavior*, a book intelligible chiefly to mathematicians,
has nevertheless influenced strategic thinking in areas where
mathematicians never wander.

Designers, whose traditional background is art, often turn
out to be astute marketing strategists. Imagination—the ability
to see what's not there yet—can't hurt. It is probably a huge
advantage not to have gone to a business school. More importantly the designer on a strategic planning team is the member
most directly concerned with the end user. But I suspect it also
has to do with a fondness for games that are best played by
people with a strong spatial sense.

Where fun and games in design are concerned, life is not a cabaret but a charrette, with the good times inextricably tied to the good work. How to maintain that connection is not always clear, but there is a clue in what Eames said about pleasure.

He said we have to take it seriously.

Robotic Civility

In Bloomington, Indiana, there was an ugly, comfortable fake-Tudor beer joint called Nick's that was always jammed because it was only steps away from the Indiana University campus. With a location like that, Nick's needed no added attraction, but it had one: a condom vending machine in the men's room that bore the legend, SOLD FOR THE PREVENTION OF DISEASE ONLY. The message was intended to placate anyone offended by contraception, or by sex. No one took it seriously. No one guessed it was ahead of its time.

Today condoms *are* sold, and given away, for the prevention of disease. But Nick's was ahead of its time in another respect as well. The vending machine was an early demonstration of the civility of the man–machine interface. (The times were innocent, but sexist. It *was* a man–machine interface. There was no counterpart in the ladies room.) Actually, not many condoms were sold at Nick's, for the machine was usually out of order or out of stock. Cynics speculated that this was by design, that the empty vending machine was Nick's profit center, and the bar was just a front. The machine had never been filled, they insisted, and never had to be, because none of the students who sacrificed quarters to it would ever complain. That's how innocent the times were. Before drugstores boldly set condom racks out in the aisles as casually as displays of sunglasses, these products were kept under the counter. The trouble was, you had to buy them *over* the counter, waiting until the store was empty, to blurt your incriminating need to the smirking pharmacist. The machine at Nick's cut out the middleman, smirk and all. A civil omission.

Although I am seldom the first on my block to own anything, I was a pioneer in using a telephone answering machine, which I bought because my answering service was expensive, unreliable, and rude. The operators were brusque with callers,

Originally published January/February 1994 in *I.D.*, as the column "Robotic Civility."

got names and numbers wrong, put me on hold when I called in for messages, and seemed to be reveling in my unpopularity when I didn't have any messages. The last may have been more my paranoia than the answering service's behavior, but with Phonemate it wasn't an issue.

I liked the gadget, but other people resented it. "I refuse to talk to a machine," they would say into the machine. Sometimes that was the only message they left. " Don't think of it as talking to a machine," my outgoing message pleaded. "Think of it as cutting a record." Some hung up anyway. Others, stunned by a kind of stage fright, could not leave a coherent message, or recite their own phone numbers, or wait for the beep.

Of course anyone using a phone is already talking into a machine, or listening to one. Somewhere I have read about depressed and lonely people who call the telephone company's time check just to hear a human voice, even if it is digitally produced.

My parents took Phonemate personally. "How can you answer your own mother with a machine?" my father asked.

"At least it tells me when you've called," I said. "Would you rather I didn't know?"

"I think I would," he said.

He meant it. Their habit was to co-phone me, my mother placing the call, my father stationed at the upstairs extension. One day I came home and heard the following dialogue.

My mother's voice: "What did it say?"

My father's voice: "It said to leave a message."

My mother's voice: "Should we do it?

My father's voice: "Of course not!" Click.

Today, however, callers resent it if you don't have a machine. Answering machines have improved conversation, by making a good deal of it unnecessary. I often call people when I expect them to be out, preferring delivery to dialogue.

Two can play at that game, and do. I answer the phone and a disappointed voice says, "Oh. Is that really you? I thought"— i.e., wished—"it was voice mail."

Adjustments take time. Although the first generation of PCs were found deficient in user-friendliness, they were already friendlier than some of their users. Academics scorned early experiments in pedagogical interfaces because they lacked the warmth of the professor–student relationship. But on many campuses there was no discernible warmth, and very little relationship. Computers have from the start been more patient than professors, and, with vastly improved software design, they appear to be more interested in students.

We gravitate increasingly to machines that are nicer to us than the people whose roles they have been programmed to play. A friend and I were splitting the dinner check at a restaurant that doesn't take credit cards. We had cash, but nothing larger than a $20 bill. Neither of us ever has anything larger than a $20, it turns out, because our only source of cash is the automatic teller, which does not traffic in big bucks. That's a small price to pay for lines that are shorter and faster moving, and for interaction that is—if not exactly stimulating—agreeable and cosmopolitan. An ATM is courteous in five languages; a teller is surly in one.

Civil behavior entails a certain respect for privacy. When the onset of supermarket design raised concerns about the disappearance of service, the trade magazine *Chain Store Age* investigated the dynamics of grocery shopping. Self-service, one of the researchers concluded, was a "higher form of service." Now, more than 30 years later, a Japanese whiskey vending machine, the Toshiba One-Shot, is promoted with a brochure proclaiming that "Not forcing service is the highest form of service." That philosophy may help explain why Japan leads the world in vending machines per capita.

What was going on back then in Bloomington? What's

going on in Osaka now? Do-it-yourself means no questions asked, a principle exemplified at Nick's at about the same time it was being scientifically validated at Safeway and A&P. Less expensive cuts of meat sold better in self-service meat departments than they did in stores that had clerks behind counters. And the class of meat known in the trade as "offal" sold *only* when there was self service, because consumers who were willing to pull it off a shelf were ashamed to ask for it by name. If you are concerned about your weight, you might find it inhibiting to ask a clerk for Twinkies, but have no problem tossing the offending item into the shopping cart yourself. True, you still have to present your weakness at the checkout counter. But the checkout clerk is not selling, merely counting; and is likely to be so unobserving and so coldly indifferent as to allay even the most neurotic fear of censure.

Machines, forgiving our neurotic impulses, treat us better; but they cannot impose civility on an environment that is itself brutish. New York subway stations used to be lined with small vending machines that dropped chocolate bars down the chute with a thump that could be heard over the screech of trains, and that somehow seemed to enrich the flavor. They vanished years ago, victims of theft, vandalism, and the city's inability to maintain amenities underground. Aboveground, machines in private spaces still work, but they cannot work magic. A Manhattan office had coffee available round the clock, the quality varying according to who made it and how long ago. Last year they replaced the automatic-drip unit with a highly sophisticated coffee vending machine that brews each cup on demand to the cup size and strength specified. This is a machine so self-consciously state-of-the-art that it invites you to look into its innards at what your button-pushing has wrought. PRODUCT BEING PREPARED. WATCH! Actually there is not much to see, but it makes a satisfying hum. And that's where the satisfaction stops, for the coffee, being vending-machine coffee, tastes like vending-machine coffee. As computer scientists warned us from the beginning, garbage in/garbage out.

Liquor is not the only solace vended by machine in Japan, where vending machines, like 7-Elevens here, are ubiquitously at your service day and night. Fried foods, neckties, cut flowers, pantyhose, software, and bags of rice are purveyed from machines designed to be placed in shops or in front of them, where they free the shopkeeper to concentrate on larger sales, just as the ATM frees bankers to concentrate on high-interest loans. The most characteristically Japanese vending machine in Japan, however, is imported from France, and what it sells is not a convenience, but a national necessity. Described as a cross between an ATM and a word processor, the machine asks you to type your name, affiliation, title, address, phone, fax, and e-mail address, and choose from an assortment of 18 layout and type styles. Thirty seconds and ¥1000 later, the machine pays off with an emergency supply of what in Japan is a mandatory instrument of civility: business cards.

Pitching Machines

W
hen Ron Mace, the architect who pioneered barrier-free design and was one of its most widely known advocates, died, I was asked by a magazine to comment on his life and work. I said I knew him only slightly, admired him enormously, and had been impressed with his resistance, despite his own severe disability and his earned access to media, to letting himself become a poster boy for universal design. As soon as I said it, I anxiously tempered my remark with the recurring caveat from the late sitcom *Seinfeld*, "Not that there's anything wrong with that."

Poster children, like posters, can be crucial to the awareness of important enterprises. But, like posters, they have limited efficacy. What our most important causes require are not images to dramatize them but leaders who can design ways to carry them forward. This Ron Mace did, with students and colleagues, throughout his career.

As an architect, he was trained for the job, but many of his most effective fellow advocates are informed amateurs whose personal disabilities led them to discover the possibilities of design. Aimee Mullin is a double-amputee track star and *I.D.* cover girl whose qualifications for posterdom are formidable. Young, intelligent, accomplished, articulate, funny, and photogenic, Mullin could easily let her advocacy rest on those attributes. She won't. Like other disabled high achievers I have known, Mullin cringes (or at least laughs) when someone calls her inspirational, knowing that, however sincere, it leads away from the contribution she can make to the arts of living.

That people are inspired by her has made her a poster girl by default. She has no intention of stopping there, but why do we need anyone in that role at all? I think it is because buying and selling have become our principal form of interaction. There are poster children for Gap stores and for milk mus-

Originally published July/August 1998 in *PRINT*, as the column "Peripheral Vision."

taches and Calvin Klein, paid endorsers of products that have nothing to do with their success or their radiance. The non-profit poster child is another breed, often including people who suffer from a condition the cause is meant to alleviate. What they endorse matters so much to them that they are driven to proclaim its feasibility and, in the case of universal design, even its profitability. Ron Mace, generally credited with having coined the term, explained, "Universal design is as much a marketing idea as a design concept," since improved access creates increased sales opportunity.

Our cultural addiction to buying and selling is not to be confused with the search for excellence, or quality. It is not a quest for a better mousetrap, or even a nicer one. While junk surfing the other night, I switched directly from an evangelist selling prosperity to Marie Osmond selling Marie Osmond dolls. What surprised me was how unsurprising this was. Here was one half of a lapsed television act back on the screen peddling *tchotchkes*. A curious turn of events? Not at all. Nothing had changed. Ms. Osmond was doing exactly what she did as a performer. Years of using her persona to sell goods had positioned her to sell the persona itself as goods.

Television is the ultimate pitching machine for both profit and good works. Whatever advantages public broadcasting has, freedom from commercials is not one of them. To begin with, there is PBS's incessant peddling of itself. Pledge Week, once an annual affliction, seems to come hourly now, with hectoring messages far more repetitive and far less entertaining than the commercial ones.

If pledge drives weary us, what saddens us is the introduction into public broadcasting of real commercials—*commercial* commercials. Corporate sponsorship, perceived as a necessary evil, was initially less evil than boring. Little more than vehicles for dragging the sponsor's name through the viewer's head, the messages were blandly self-serving but mercifully brief, as parodied in the 1950s by Mike Nichols when he reduced them all to "DuPont Owns Everything." Those innocuous blurbs have been replaced by video clips almost as hard-sell as the ones for pet foods and cereals. At the same time, the commercial network advertising for cars, investment houses, and Archer Daniels Midland has become indistinguishable from the grandiose old sponsor statements on public television.

Jim Lehrer and Charlie Rose at least don't have to make the pitch themselves. On National Public Radio, however, the message from the sponsor is increasingly read by the talent. My local NPR outlet was enriched for years by a traffic reporter named Lorie Jordan, whose mellifluous accounts of morning delays on the inbound Gowanus made commuting a pleasure, especially if, like me, you were still in bed and didn't know where or what the inbound Gowanus was. Her curious combination of melodic voice and ultra-high-speed delivery, which brought romance and clarity to rubbernecking on the Cross Bronx Expressway, was later required to plug Chrysler Plymouth dealers and a soporific called (honest) "Night Night Plus Melatonin." Then she was gone, but the plugs stay on.

Where will it end, and when? It won't, of course. When *The New York Times* asked people to identify the most useless concept of the 20th century, modernism made the list and so did postmodernism. No one asked me, but if anyone ever does, I'm ready: *closure*.

The trouble with closure is that it invariably opens something, usually a can of worms. Our processes are, like housework, never done. I resolve, for example, to get caught up with my correspondence. It cannot be done. The people I owe letters to are, by definition, the kind of people who write letters. That means they will answer letters, including the one that I finally write in response to the dozen of theirs that have piled up over the months or years. Their immediate reply puts me in the position of owing them a letter, which is where I was in the first place.

That's the way with friends, but now it is the way with marketers, too, and they are harder to lose. After you have made the call, surrendered the card number, mailed the check, you are not through with them. With each first invoice for a magazine subscription comes a letter urging you to renew at a discount. No sooner do you fulfill a pledge to PBS or NPR than you receive mail repeating in print the harangue that irritated you for weeks, and asking for more.

Selling is as close to a perpetual motion device as we have yet devised, for it is self-regenerating through advertising. Junk mail breeds junk mail. To buy something, or even to inquire about it, is to be put on a list, which itself is advertised, bought, and sold. American Airlines, which tries to sell me flowers, insurance, and cocktail glasses bearing its logo, would, if I ordered any, sell me to other companies who want to sell me flowers.

And the selling of products brings new products into being. We have all been in places to which we vow never to return. I have also been in places to which returning is so manifestly unthinkable that no vow is necessary. Last spring, I found myself headed for one of them, a blisteringly hot cow town where 30 years ago I had spent a night in a hotel that had as its single amenity a homemade cooling system consisting of a *Casablanca* fan whirring loudly over a cake of ice.

There have been some changes made. The hotel is air-conditioned and landmarked. The lobby has an espresso bar. The western apparel store I remembered still has Stetsons, boots, and bolo ties, but also stocks baseball caps and Nike cross trainers. A rack of Birkenstock socks is described on a placard as "exclusively designed to look and feel great with Birkenstock footwear."

My daughter the retailing consultant calls this "product

extension." My daughter-in-law the poet calls it absurd, insisting that whatever freedom is gained by wearing sandals is lost in wearing socks with them. They both miss the point. Whether product extension or silly excess, is there any need for such highly specialized socks? There must be. Why else would I have bought them?

Omission

When product competition was an additive process, manufacturers promised more—more features, more weight, more life-sustaining calories, more nutrients, more cleaning power—although the claims themselves may have been spurious. In John P. Marquand's novel *H.M. Pulham Esquire*, Pulham is an advertising copywriter assigned to a soap account. He consults an encyclopedia, where he learns that soap cleans by emulsifying fats. From this slender factoid the agency develops a campaign claiming that their client's chemists "have evolved a soap of a new high emulsifying power based on a secret property they call EMUL." Sales climb to the wild skies. "To sell soap," the hero concludes, "it was necessary to endow it with some unique quality which would appeal to the consumer."

That was then. Now to sell soap it is necessary to take something away from it, to endow it with a uniquely appealing lack. The "secret ingredient" that was a staple of advertising hype has been replaced by a kind of Swiss water method of leaching everything out of everything. Just as all soap had emulsifiers, all potato chips have no cholesterol, a minus used by advertisers to suggest that vigilant chemists in the potato chip factory have filtered out a cardiac hazard.

In an economy of abundance, omission is salable, and one of the most compelling reasons for buying anything is the appeal of what it has not got: calories, lead, asbestos, caffeine, meat, milk, sugar, salt, eggs, antibiotics, high fructose corn syrup. Doing without has become a luxury of sorts. It costs extra to have an unlisted telephone number; and the chief selling point of a very expensive piece of luggage is that it doesn't carry the designer's initials.

From Notes on Omission, a notebook published in 1979 by Herman Miller, Inc.

4

Being There

The psychologist Jon Kabat-Zinn writes, "Wherever you go, there you are." Well, yes, but where exactly? As I have noted earlier, almost everyone, whether they've heard of her or not, can quote Gertrude Stein's famous remark, "When you go there, there isn't any there there." She was talking about Oakland, but the observation is becoming universally applicable.

Assuming there *were* a there there, how would we get to it? If I knew I wouldn't tell you—traffic is bad enough without you. The congestion of roads and ramps loaded with outsized vehicles is compounded by the confusion of signs misdirecting us to airports, on and off highways, and through towns and cities. Designing better ones is harder than ever, for the designs must compete with each other and with advertisements. Even those that are clear and well designed deliver information that is unreliable and subject to change without notice and frequently without reason.

Lewis Mumford wrote about such matters for more than 50 years in books that remain as enlightening as they were prescient when written. More recently, William H. Whyte, Jane Jacobs, Christopher Alexander and Tony Hiss have contributed sigificantly to what has been called "the science of place"; but that is so far more literature than science.

A science of place—even a *sense* of place—requires the restoration and refreshment of more than amenities. The relentless proliferation of Starbucks, for example, may soon reach every corner and shopping mall of our lives. But as the Mastercard commercial might say: "Small cup of drinkable coffee, $1.90. Regional flavor, priceless."

The Poetry of Pasta

Italian has been "in" for so long I have to remind myself that for me it wasn't always. I grew up in a steel-producing town that was "ethnically diverse," although none of us knew enough to call it that. All we knew was that there were a lot of Poles, Czechs, Ukranians, Croatians, Russians, Greeks. And Italians. With the exception of a handful of peripheral Jewish merchants, whoever was left was "American." That is what we called them: Americans. There were not many of them and they were the elite. All of us kids knew there was a difference between people with names like Pugliano, Montagna, Mancini, Ciano, Tucci and people with names with Arnold, Caldwell, Hamilton, and Bradley

At twelve I read *Puddinhead Wilson*, Mark Twain's novel about a small town in Missouri brought to fever pitch by the arrival of a pair of Italian twins. The heroine is atwitter with the prospect. "Italians! How romantic! . . . Luigi—Angelo. They're lovely names; and so grand and foreign—not like Jones and Robinson and such."

I couldn't believe what I was reading. *Romantic?* Luigi and Angelo were the names of kids I played with and fought with every day. In our town it was Jones and Robinson that were exotic. People with names like that worked in offices. The fathers of my Italian friends worked in the mill. Today the mill is closed.

Incredible as it seems to my children, pizza was unknown in my childhood, as carbon paper was in theirs. We *had*, however, heard of spaghetti. It was canned under the Franco-American label and tasted like wet worms. We ate it often at our house, because my father sold it in his grocery store. He also sold genuine pasta, which I sometimes tasted raw, brittle, and dry, straight out of the box. (Even that way it tasted better than Franco-American.)

Originally published May/June 1994 in *I.D.*, as the column "Circumstantial Evidence."

Uncooked pasta was the first glimmer I had of the aesthetic richness of Italian design. This had nothing to do with gustatory sensation, it had to do with poetry. The pasta my father sold came packed in rectangular wooden crates, weighing, I think, about 25 pounds each. One of my jobs after school was to unload the truck and pile the crates according to their contents. Two of us did this. It was not pleasant work because, although the crates were light, the rough wood scraped the skin off our bare forearms. Yet we welcomed the macaroni assignment because as we stacked the crates into wooden columns we would call out the product names. We loved saying them. *Fettucini, fettuce, linguini* rolled off the tongue in joyous liquidity. And there were images to go with them, provided in the graphically splendid macaroni chart published by the San Giorgio Macaroni Company.

Such experiences were undeniably special, but seemed to have nothing to do with what was thought of as "Italian."

How, then, did Italian design come to seem not only lovelier than our own but more authentic? Sports cars helped. But the real force was a design product more hugely appealing even than fine cars: fine films. Films that made our own appear like rigid imitations of life. American films were about people who purported to be "just like us," but who were recognizably nothing like us. But in *La Strada* and *Open City* and *Bicycle Thief* we began to see people whose lives and language were foreign, but who nevertheless represented us more deeply than the inhabitants of Hollywood films ever did. We also began to understand the design of popular films as the control—and therefore the liberation—of writing, acting, camera work, and sets. Postwar Italian films illuminated those aspects of the Italian character that are now so highly prized in clothing and machinery, in lighting and in graphics. Those moving pictures moved differently. American filmgoers experienced a dramatic reality heretofore confined to the stage.

Is this an exaggeration? Of course it is, but who cares? You can't think about Italian design without hyperbole. Why would you even want to? It is a series of passionate contradictions. For the tension of design in Italian everyday life comes on the one hand from the nonjerkiness, the limpidity that lends an unbroken line to every art endeavor, including conversation; and on the other hand from the volatility that breaks up almost every experience into a series of furious (but essentially harmless and even healing) explosions. How does one incorporate these aspects of the national character into the design of buildings and products and spaces?

There may be a clue in Sergio Pininfarinas' contention that in order to understand Italian design, one has to understand the cultural dualism rooted in the Catholic church and the national political system. I don't know what he means, but it suggests a willingness to eschew purism and exploit whatever opportunities present themselves. (How else could anyone have been inspired to make sauce out of ortica?) When polypropylenes first appeared in the technical press, it was unsurprising that the new family of versatile plastics came largely from the work of Giulio Natta of the Polytechnic Institute in Milan, and that they were produced by Montecatini. The Italians had taken the leadership in developing petroleum-based synthetic materials, and even more strikingly in designing with them. In the United States "plastics" was a pejorative. (Even their limitless promise was the subject of parody: in the 1967 film *The Graduate*, an avuncular businessman whispers into Dustin Hoffman's ear, "I want to say one word to you. Just one word . . . 'Plastics!'" a line of career advice that became as well known as the film.) For all their advantages and promise, plastics were downscale, perceived as cheap and tawdry. Designers objected that plastics—unlike, say, wood—could not be "understood."

At least they could not be understood by us. But Italian

designers understood them and were using them to make marvelous, shiny, synthetic looking products that were—as if to confirm their design integrity—expensive. It cannot be just a semantic coincidence that the Italians were better than anyone else at using plastics sensitively, and that Italian design itself was plastic. Fluid, resilient, and malleable, with components flowing into each other, whatever the material, like Fred Astaire dancing, whoever the partner.

Ups and Downs in NYC

September 11 showed us much that we don't yet understand. One of the things we understand better than ever is that New York City is a vertical concept. Yesterday's hole in the ground is tomorrow's office tower and, tragically now vice versa.

New York, having more than its share of life, has more than its share of ups and downs. From Dow Jones averages to the Mohawk construction worker climbing to and dropping from the workaday sky, the constant juxtaposition of highs and lows is woven into Manhattan's history. In E.B. White's words, this fluctuating city "managed to reach the highest point in the sky at the lowest moment of the Depression."

Verticality might appear to be more an urban phenomenon than a regional one. After all, most American cities have *some* tall buildings. But Manhattan is a small island with an enormous number of people and activities demanding vertical accommodation. The very sky is parceled off in the form of air rights and the sewers charged with rumors of baby alligators flushed into the system and grown to dragonhood down there.

Middle America is situated differently, with space and time for lateral motion. People in Omaha check out the environment by looking left and right, like spectators at a slow tennis match. When they come here they bring unused muscles into play, trying to watch this enchanted yo-yo of a city as it soars and plunges, sometimes tangled in the spinning of its own string.

New York has never caught up with itself. The City's intense building activity is chronic and cyclical: construction and demolition go on like a kind of purposeful pillowpunching. Whenever something is razed, something is raised in its place. All that action calls for a lot of actors. New York is peopled largely

Originally published 1982 in *Up and Down*. Designed and created by Chermayeff & Geismar Associates.

by those who tear the City apart and make it over again; and by those who stand by and watch them do it. Riveters, utility repairmen, demolition crews, helicopter pilots, cherry picker operators, designers who decorate the construction barriers, graffiti artists and poster installers who also decorate the construction barriers—all contribute to our daily rebuilding.

If the volume of the construction industry describes the City's momentum, construction workers describe part of its character. Stereotypically, they have supplanted the New York cab driver as fountain of conventional wisdom, dispenser of unsolicited opinions, defender of the national honor, whistler at passing women, and backbone of a back-breaking town.

Some years ago, wherever the Consolidated Edison Company tore up the streets to lay cable, they erected a semi-apologetic sign reading: Dig We Must for a Better New York. Not all disruption is so candidly signed. New York Telephone also has to tear up streets, but prefers to do it under the cover of a wholly owned subsidiary, The Empire City Subway Co., Ltd. Empire City collects no fares and operates no trains, but discreetly does the parent company's underground work.

"Dig we must" became a local catch phrase, partly because the solemn inversion of subject and verb sounded funny, but also perhaps because it expressed a truth of New York living. Dig we indeed must to install underground the energy that supports us, but more significantly to plant the roots of high buildings and, as urban archaeologists, to discover roots already in place.

This is a basic life process not precisely synonymous with excavation, which construction crews and dentists perform with elaborate equipment. Digging is more nearly an animal activity. We dig to bury treasure and to find it. The New Yorker, like any other human survivor, digs for sustenance and shelter. The paradox is that the higher we aim, the further down we have to go in search of a foundation.

Urban construction conjures up images of heavy equipment and gigantic, unfeeling machines. But the human body remains central to the mission. If we, like the ancient Egyptians, have not finally escaped the drudgery of tired muscle and bone, neither have we entirely lost the lyricism of a body bending or the aesthetic pull of broken earth waiting to be occupied. As the architect George Nelson once asked, "Has anyone ever seen a building that looked as good as a hole in the ground?"

Next to, "It's a nice place to visit, but I wouldn't want to live there," the best known cliché about New York is, "It's for the very rich or the very poor." That isn't exactly true (New York has a huge middle class) but more people here are required to live beyond their means than elsewhere, and New York contains more of the spectacularly wealthy and more of the truly needy than, say, Grand Rapids or Bakersfield. Moreover, in New York the two classes are far more likely to be neighbors than they are in Grand Rapids or Bakersfield. (This is not new: Sidney Kingsley's *Dead End*, a play about Manhattan in the thirties, dramatizes the discrepant proximity of a slum and a luxury apartment house.)

This physical closeness and the fact that in New York people do rather unremarkably shift positions (your waitress today may be nominated for an Academy Award next year) makes for a juxtaposition of high life and low that is as interesting for similarities as for differences.

Figurative height almost immediately becomes literal in New York City, and perhaps that has been true since the twenties, when high steppers got high and went off to watch high kickers. It persists in the dream of one's name in legendary (and high) lights, in the gaiety of a champagne fueled cabaret girl commanding the shining expanse below, in the association of "the top of the city" with "making it." Maybe all that glitters is not gold, but at 50 stories it can pass.

Manhattan is an island that feels landlocked, perhaps

because so few pedestrian vistas include water. Up high the experience is different, and river views are prized. But everyone can take pleasure in a first-rate second-best view, also involving water: the earth-toned tanks that crown the City's rooftops.

Resembling nothing so much as a dispersed African village, these hut-like forms are a design response to problems of the urban North. The conical tops keep the snow off and provide space for heating coils. Not all tanks look like huts. Some reflect a prepostmodernist tendency to hide the shape under architectural enclosures posing as towers or penthouses.

The water tanks point up the fact that, in vertical New York *all* life forces travel up and down. To live here is to defy gravity with every breath, but there is a point at which the defiance of gravity is not cost effective. That point seems to be eight stories—as high as City water mains can pump water directly as tapped.

For years the only Jewish delicatessen in Indianapolis was called Sam's Subway, because it was a few steps below sidewalk level and served a New York cuisine. Indianapolitans could never decide which was more exotic, the high cholesterol ethnicity of corned beef and pastrami or the locally unique experience of going down into a basement for any reason other than to check the furnace.

Significant stuff is lodged underground all over the world—cables, gas mains, sewer pipes, and missiles. On special occasions scenes are played out below the surface, like the chase through the Paris sewers in *Les Miserables*. What is astonishing about underground New York is not that our support systems are down there, but that for so much of the time so many of us are down there with them.

New York, like Indianapolis, offers subterranean corned beef (although you have to go deeper to get it), but more: pizza, souvlaki, calzone, salted pretzels, corn bread, kielbase, crunchy granola, and oysters. You can also buy fresh flowers, Danish modern furniture, authentic kilts, fake furs, rare books, CD's, Ipods, money market funds, and investment advice. You can buy a knish, a digital camera, or a hundred shares of IBM. You can bank, get business cards printed, have your hair cut, your nails trimmed, your blood pressure taken, your fortune told, and your passport photo taken. A New Yorker is someone who knows how to walk from Fifth Avenue and 50th Street to Sixth Avenue and 47th Street in a heavy rainstorm without getting wet. A rich fantasy can be sustained around the notion that almost anything one wants to do can be done in New York without going out of doors. Someone born in a subway-serviced hotel could conceivably live a full (and even useful) life getting fed, cared for, dressed, educated, employed and wed; join a library, swim, work out in a gymnasium, study yoga, have clothing altered, consciousness raised, and soul saved—all without ever coming up for air.

Zoned for Weird

Eccentricity makes life rich, and is not just for the eccentric. Anyone enamored of the solid beauty of ordinary things, cannot ignore what the nineteenth-century poet-priest Gerard Manley Hopkins called the "pied beauty" of "all things counter, original, spare, strange." True eccentricity is a by-product of paying attention to what matters. (Andy Warhol seemed like an exception but wasn't; for him, eccentricity *was* what mattered, especially when it could be cloaked in the routine.) When she was in the convent, the printer, designer, and calligrapher Sister Mary Corita relished the freedom of not having to decide what to wear or eat, or where to go. Mufti opened up a world of distractions for her. Appearances are designed to be protective as well as deceiving. The writer John Cheever wore a suit and hat to the office, even when his office was in the basement of the building he lived in.

Asked by a psychiatrist if he ever had bizarre thoughts, a character in an E.B. White short story wonders, "Ever have any bizarre thoughts? What kind of thoughts except bizarre had he had since the age of two?"

I know the feeling, and wouldn't trust anyone who didn't. So it didn't hurt (for long) when Peter Bradford, a designer no one has ever accused of normalcy, observed that the area in which I had bought a house was "zoned for weird." The phrase is charming, and now that I think of it, where except in places "zoned for weird" had I been since the age of two? Every town I've lived in, every school or camp I've gone to, every place I've worked, every team, department, squad, company, battery, club I've belonged to has seemed strange.

My high school was so far removed from reality that innocent practical jokes were grounds for expulsion, a circumstance that propelled me to a private school, where a ramrod-rigid retired Army colonel assigned us Macaulay's essay on the

Originally published 1989 in *The AIGA Journal*.

behavioral peculiarities of Samuel Johnson. Despite his prodigious accomplishments, Johnson was plagued, Macaulay wrote, by "a morbid propensity to sloth and procrastination. . . . Eccentricities less strange than his have often been thought grounds sufficient for absolving felons and for setting aside wills. . . . He would conceive an unintelligible aversion to a particular alley, and perform a great circuit rather than see the hateful place. He would set his heart on touching every post in the streets through which he walked. If by any chance he missed a post, he would go back a hundred yards and repair the omission."

To students of our generation, and of our ilk, such practices made Johnson an object of derision. But the colonel, with the military's empathy for the obsessive compulsive, ordered us to tolerate.

"When I walk," he confessed defiantly, "I take care to step over the cracks in the sidewalk." Sternly, his eyes scanned the classroom. "Why do I do it?" he demanded.

No hands went up, so he appointed a volunteer. "Why do I do it, Caplan?"

"I guess it's superstition, sir," I said.

"It's just a game!" he thundered. "Everybody plays games."

At the time, I thought the colonel was telling us that, if everybody did it, it was not eccentric. Now I understand that he was telling us it was eccentric, but no less normal for that. Until then I had thought of all adults not in my immediate family as normal, but had no idea how they got that way, or even what it consisted of. Jerry Seinfeld in an interview admitted, "I don't know what people do who go in and out of buildings." That was exactly what I didn't know then. At the time I believed in the supremacy of bell curves. Now I feel perfectly at home in Garrison Keillor's Lake Wobegon, "where all the children are above average."

Designer Teachers

I was reared near Pittsburgh, popularly known at the time as Iron City. The rearing didn't come easy. Frustrated by my inability to learn addition and subtraction, my parents and my fourth grade teacher conspired to send me to the Iron City Normal School (as teachers' colleges were called then) to find out why I wasn't. After a battery of tests, the house psychologist concluded that, for reasons unknown and best kept that way, numbers were so abhorrent to me that whenever I saw any I took refuge in daydreaming.

The psychologist was right about the daydreaming—I was a pioneer in attention deficit. But I was not daydreaming to *escape* numbers. I was daydreaming *about* them. While the teacher was doing her thing, I was doing mine: staging dramas in my head, where a stellar numerical repertoire company performed daily. I don't remember any of the scenarios, but the players are fixed in my mind. Number 5 was the hero in every production. 2 was the woman in his life. 8 was an *older* woman. 7 was a wise guy, buddy of the protagonist. 9, my favorite, was a con man. I can't explain why, but if I were a casting director I would put them all in the same roles today.

I couldn't tell anyone about it, because they would think I was crazy. I couldn't tell anyone because I was afraid they would be right. So I went on, more audience than pupil, eschewing arithmetic in favor of dramatic fantasy. Once in junior high school, as I stood before a blackboard full of figures I could not decipher, Mr. Burns grabbed my collar and slammed my head into the blackboard so violently that when I think of it now I see the flashing colors I saw then. A man given to rage and, it was rumored, to afternoon drinking, he had lost control. Or he may have hoped that the intelligence on the board would penetrate my skull and lodge in my other-

Originally published February 21, 2005 in *VOICE*, the online journal of the American Institute of Graphic Arts, as the column "Noah's Archive."

wise unreachable brain. It did not; but it gave me a lump, a headache, and a chalky brow.

Those memories were pulled from the depth by an invitation to participate in the 2004 Summer Design Institute organized by the education department of the Smithsonian Cooper-Hewitt National Design Museum. The Institute brings educators and designers together to develop techniques for teaching design in, as they say in the trade, grades K through 12.

When I mentioned the program to a friend, he asked skeptically, "Why would teachers want to get involved in design?"

"I guess it's because they are already involved in design," I said.

They are. Classrooms are designed, as are the furniture, books, and computers used in them. So are the two activities classrooms are intended to support—teaching and learning. Teachers routinely design courses, lesson plans, lab experiments, and field trips. Although the Institute's purpose is to foster design as curricular content, the design process is at least equally germane as a vehicle of instruction. At best, the two are inseparable.

Exhibition design, for example, has been a teaching resource since the first science fair, perhaps since the first blackboard. *Show and tell* is intrinsic to the schoolroom. Even in this digital age, designers instinctively take everything at hand—pictures, ideas, data—and stick it up on a wall, where it can be seen, discussed and organized. Teachers do the same thing. As a pedagogical tool, exhibition offers visible participation and visible correction to students who learn design while they learn the subject of the course. In helping to create instructional exhibitions, students confront such design issues as color, scale, logical connections, and legibility—both visual and verbal. They do product design, set design, interior design, and editing.

Because every exhibition yields more material than it is possible to display, design firms become repositories of information and ideas about a staggering range of subjects—computers, American history, the Holocaust, Native American tribal rituals, solar energy, productivity, weather. Designers always learn more in creating an exhibition than visitors learn from attending it. That comes as no surprise to teachers, who invariably learn more from preparing a course than students do from taking it.

If education is design, what is the product? Not students, although principals and headmasters speak pridefully of the students they "turn out." The only educational product that schools can be reasonably charged with designing is the educational environment—including not only classrooms and laboratories, but the situations in which students interact with each other and with faculty members. If educational environment is the product, teachers have got to be among the designers. Instructional design is surely a more rewarding use of their talents than the present tasks of disciplinarian, scorekeeper, monitor, scapegoat, and supervisor of tests.

The 19th Century educator Mark Hopkins inspired the claim, "all that's needed for a good education is Mark Hopkins sitting on one end of a log and a boy sitting on the other." It was quoted approvingly for decades in a simpler time. Since then, girls campaigned victoriously for a piece of the log, and the log itself was soon supplanted by technology. Closed-circuit TV, film, computer-assisted instruction, and programmed teaching materials were heralded as the antibiotics of education, promising to be, like penicillin, indiscriminately applicable to every ill. By the time I finally learned to add and subtract (although not to do long division), calculators and PC's were already on the horizon, promising to free me from arithmetic chores forever.

They did. But they did not relieve me of the arithmetically

induced fear of discovery. That had to wait until October of 1962, when *The New Yorker* appeared with, for me, a truly liberating cover by Saul Steinberg . A couple of numerals—5 and 2 of course—were seated across from each other at a table, having a drink! It could have been a promotion still from one of my interior films. I felt elated and redeemed. True, the drawing didn't necessarily mean I wasn't crazy. But if I *was*, so was Saul Steinberg. As good company goes, that's good enough for me.

Cleveland?

Sorry, I can't be there," I said. "I'll be out of town."

"Where are you going?"

"Cleveland."

"Cleveland?" she said. "Why Cleveland?"

"I'm giving a talk there."

"What are you going to talk about?"

"Cleveland," I said.

That was not exactly true. It was not exactly false either. Cleveland was not the subject of my lecture, but its launching pad, for I started off with the following story.

One of my prized New York relationships was a slight acquaintance with Rocky Graziano, the former world middleweight boxing champion who had become a popular television comedian. The essence of Rocky's comedy was a punch drunk persona, which he incorporated into his off-screen demeanor as well. Incredibly shrewd and sharp, he took a mischievous pleasure in acting punchy. When we were introduced, Rocky took my hand in his—the same right that had stopped Tony Zale in six of the most brutal rounds in boxing history—and squinted dubiously, as if he vaguely remembered meeting me before and hadn't especially liked it. At last he said, in the blurred delivery of a man who has been hit in the head too often, "Didn' I fi' you in Clevelan'?"

It was a perfect line, and I laughed whenever I thought about it; but I did not understand it until I told the story to the late art director, graphic designer, and photographer Henry Wolf.

"That's very funny," Henry said.

"I know it is," I said. "But I don't know why."

"It's Cleveland," Henry told me.

"What do you mean?"

"I mean, since you're obviously in no shape to get into a

Originally published October 1998 in *PRINT*, as the column "Peripheral Vision."

ring, and never were, 'Didn't I fight you?' could be amusing in itself. But not hilarious. 'Didn't I fight you in New York?' would not have been funny either. London, Paris, Los Angeles, Rome—none of those would work. Making it Ashtabula or Kalamazoo or Punxsutawney or Slippery Rock might be funny, but only because the names are funny themselves. For that joke to work, it has to be a second class city."

That hurt. Did he mean that the Cleveland Museum of Art, Jacobs Field, and the Rock and Roll Hall of Fame count for nothing? My mother was from Cleveland, and I logged a lot of pleasant time there as a child. Henry's notorious elitism made his view of cities suspect. But about jokes I trusted him absolutely. The creator of some of the wittiest magazine covers ever published, he understood the anatomy of humor. His book *Visual Thinking*, both a compendium of his own best work and a provocative guide to imagery in design and advertising, includes the most convincing (and, come to think of it, the only) explanation I have ever seen of the psychology of sight gags on the stage and on the page.

Henry had the rare ability to analyze humor without taking the fun out of it. He approached the subject warily, for he knew that, as Mark Twain said, a sense of humor is the one thing no one will admit not having. This is why so many people equip themselves with the exterior components of humor: they are like the people who, unable to afford a television set when the medium was new, installed antennas on the roofs of their houses anyway, as a status symbol. People who are constantly laughing, or who keep a disconnected smile nervously within reach at all times, are, in my experience, likely to be humorless. They *may* have a sense of humor, but more often they merely believe that they *should* have one. I have noticed too that people armed with enormous funds of jokes that they draw upon continually are frequently unable to recognize humor in any other form.

There are exceptions, of course: a friend of mine who made a subcareer of collecting and publishing tasteless jokes is one of the most genuinely funny women I know. But in general, joke mongering has no more to do with a sense of humor than identifying canned foods by their labels has to do with a sense of taste. A genuine sense of humor implies the personal perception of what is funny in situations, including one's own.

That's what Rocky Graziano was demonstrating when we shook hands. He was not joking about Cleveland, but about his own stereotype. In Cleveland, I was not joking about Cleveland either, but using Rocky's Cleveland shtick to make a point about design. Designers are necessarily generalists, but their work is best understood in the particulars. House Speaker Tip O'Neill famously instructed the nation that "all politics is local." So, in a sense, is all design. We speak of it in grand terms and supplant them with even grander terms. International design gave way to global design, and universal design is even more comprehensive. But what makes design universally valid is that it responds to the local needs of our families, our friends, and ourselves. Design, like humor, always comes down in the end to Cleveland or equivalent.

I Wish I Were McGaffegan

A discouraging feature of campaign planning today is the speculation by both politicians and pundits on how a given position will "play in Peoria." I doubt that there still is a Peoria in the sense that gave rise to the expression. I have never been there, but I am confident that contemporary Peoria has a Starbucks, a unisex hair styling salon with a cute name, an outlet for DKNY, and a store that sells what a designer I know calls "things that are black or gray."

In *The Accidental Tourist*, Anne Tyler described a travel guide for people who want wherever they go to be as much as possible like wherever they come from. Alas, it already is. I think of the time I woke early one morning in a Japanese mountain resort and decided to take a walk. The woods gave off a smoky autumnal smell, enriched by alien food smells as I approached the edge of a village, where households were already at morning chores. In the village, produce and fish merchants, their shops marked by signs I would never understand, were arranging food I probably also would never understand. No matter. Unfamiliarity intensified the heady feeling of walking alone through The Real Japan—a feeling that persisted until I turned a corner and found myself facing a Benetton shop window.

I have been thinking about this in airports, which are the best possible environments for the purpose. After flying to Seattle recently, I flew on (because the ferry stops running in October) to Vancouver, British Columbia, where I had been invited to speak about design as an instrument of regional development. I don't know much about western Canada, but I know something about regions, having spent several years searching for enough particularity, enough flavor to define a region in any terms other than geographic. The moment the plane landed I stood up in eager anticipation. Vancouver is an

Originally published January/February 1989 in *I.D.*, as the column "Circumstantial Evidence."

attractive city, but I would have stood up anyway. I always do, springing from my seat with relief as soon as the captain instructs the flight attendants to prepare for arrival. I am not relieved that we made it. I expect to make it. I am relieved to be someplace after being noplace.

But that sense of relief is always premature. It vanishes in the airport, because when you're in an airport, you're still noplace. All airports—at least all metropolitan airports—have a transitory character that is perfectly appropriate to the fact that the business they are in is transit. Whether anxious about schedules, or bored with killing time, the people you see in airports look temporary. Like you, they *feel* temporary. There is a sense in which—just as when you're between jobs, you're not working—when you're between flights, you're not quite living. What you are doing instead is waiting, a tourist in a country with no culture of its own, no ruins to examine, no idiosyncrasies to learn, no language or even dialect, no regional cuisine.

Airports, for me at least, quicken the desire to belong to something or someone or someplace. Even when no one is meeting me—even when no one even knows I'm coming!—as I roll my carry-on through the platoon of limo drivers holding up shirt cardboard signage inviting JOHNSON or GOLD-BERG or MR. PHELPS OF AMALGAMATED MISSIONS to make themselves known, I search for my own name. Last month in St. Louis a driver holding up the name McGAFFE-GAN noticed that I was staring longingly at his sign. "Mr. McGaffegan?" he asked tentatively.

I thought it over, finally admitting to him that I was not McGaffegan while admitting to myself that, for a moment, I wished I were.

In Seattle and Vancouver, of course, the feeling of nowhere-ness is dissipated during the drive into town, but that is not true everywhere. We are increasingly building cities that have no more sense of place than airports do. The people who live in them look as if *they're* waiting for a boarding announcement.

And the most public design element—the architecture—confirms this lack of place. Joseph Conrad once described the orchestra in a third-rate hotel by observing, "The musicians were not making music, they were murdering silence." In the same sense we have architects who are not creating architecture, they are murdering space.

The Intentional Tourist

How many tourists does it take to change a lightbulb? One, and I'm married to her. But this is not about marriage or wattage, but about tourists and redesign.

"There is no such thing as writing," an editor once told me. "There is only rewriting." It made a kind of harsh sense, and at the time I saw no reason to limit it to a single craft. "There is no such thing as design," I told a group of students. "There is only redesign." But, as I hope they realized before I did, that isn't true. Rewriting is a prepublication activity. Redesigning is more often done to change an already existing design. Manuscripts are rewritten. Magazines, like toasters and interiors, are redesigned.

Not all redesign is performed by professional designers. Travel makes redesigners of us all, which is why airport gift shops sell so many gadgets for overcoming the inadequacies of artifact and environment. Because design for travel—from luggage to accommodations—has to address highly personal needs with impersonal amenities, we need wheels to make luggage portable and marking devices to identify it at the carousel, inflatable cushions for making airplane and car seats bearable, mattress stiffeners to support the bed that won't support your back, masks for bringing darkness on, and reading lights for dispelling it.

The redesign of accommodations is as often reductive as additive. The first thing I do upon entering a hotel room is to take down all the standing signboards advertising restaurants, health club, bars, and room service. These I stuff into the bottom dresser drawer, weighing them down with the massive looseleaf book of services, regulations, churches, synagogues, and dentists, and the various publications hyping local shops. Once the surfaces are pristine, I can unpack. If meddlesome

Originally published March/April 1997 in *PRINT*, as the column "Peripheral Vision."

maids reinstall the stuff I have hidden, or bring replacements, I repeat the procedure, but that is as far as I go.

Not my wife, who routinely takes down pictures, moves furniture, and even buys her own supplies. Last spring, while I cursed the darkness in our room, she drove to the nearest Piggly Wiggly and came back with a package of 100-watt bulbs.

The change brightened the room (and gave me a lightbulb joke) but it did not brighten my day. I was suffering from the dissipation of self-esteem that comes with being a tourist. I am deeply intolerant of tourists, and if I have to be one I choose to do it in denial, with vacations tied to speaking gigs or other business, so I can rationalize that wherever I am, I am not there just because it is a nice place to be.

Now, however, I was in one of the nicest places to be, Charleston, South Carolina, for no reason except to enjoy it. Well, not exactly in Charleston, but on one of the barrier islands near it. No one had told us we would arrive the day of the annual Cooper River Bridge Run and Walk, an event that brings 30,000 runners and walkers into town, along with about twice that many watchers and well-wishers. A tired but cheery voice at the fifth bed and breakfast we called said, "Are we fully booked? Honey, *Charleston* is fully booked. You might try the Isle of Palms."

We did try, but at first did not succeed. Having learned early on that things are not what they seem, I never seem to remember that they are not even what they are called. Show me a tourist, and I'll show you a victim of signage.

The principal instrument for getting to Isle of Palms from Charleston and back again is a bridge called the Isle of Palms Connector, or the IOP Connector, or just the Connector. But it is called that only by residents and mapmakers. The signage calls it Route 517 or the Clyde Dangerfield Bridge or, most of the time, nothing, since once you know where it is, there is not much to say about it. In the meantime, as tourists, we deserved to be lost.

My prejudice in this matter has not gone unpunished. At a pre-Expo '67 design conference in Montreal, I decided to go on to Quebec City afterwards. The conference was sponsored by the National Design Council of Canada, and Henry Strub, one of the conference organizers, volunteered to make reservations for me.

"The Chateau Frontenac is where all the American tourists stay," he said. "But If we're lucky we can get you into a real European hotel overlooking the most charming waterfront square in Quebec City." I congratulated myself on having friends in high places.

Henry had not exaggerated. The square *was* charming and the hotel did have a flavor I guess you could call European. My reservations were in order. Actually they were the object of some local curiosity, for this was the sort of hotel whose guests ordinarily did not know very far in advance where they were spending the night or with whom. Nor were they necessarily expected to stay the entire night. I learned later that most of the conference organizers had been in on the joke.

Well, it served me right, but my aversion to being a tourist is not snobbery, but a symptom of an oscillating boredom threshold. It is a legacy from my father, who could not abide organized sightseeing. When a tour guide begins to talk, my eyes glaze over. My father simply closed his. When some Ohio relatives trapped him into visiting the childhood home of William McKinley, he went grudgingly, responding to the docent's historical pitch with body language legible to the most insensitive observer. Challenged, the docent tried to disarm my father with a friendly word, asking him where he was from and what he did.

"I have a grocery store in Pennsylvania," my father said.

"This glimpse into our nation's history doesn't exactly fascinate you, does it?" he said.

"No," my father agreed.

"Do you mind telling me just what kind of thing *would* interest you?"

"Ketchup," my father replied.

He was, I suppose, an accidental tourist. In Anne Tyler's novel *The Accidental Tourist* the protagonist, who hates to travel, writes popular travel guides for people who hate to travel. His readers are business travelers in search of American amenities abroad: "What hotels in Madrid boasted king-sized Beautyrest mattresses? What restaurants in Tokyo offered Sweet n' Low? . . . Did Mexico City have a Taco Bell? Did any place in Rome serve Chef Boyardee ravioli?"

The book is funny and wise, but misleading in respect to business travelers, who, in a global economy, cannot afford to be xenophobic, and aren't. Like other accidental tourists, they may come for profit but often stay for adventure. It is the *deliberate* tourists, the passengers on cruise ships and tour buses, who want tips on how never to have left home.

My daughter worked for awhile in a restaurant on the Piazza Santa Croce in Florence that catered to Americans who found the native dishes hard to order and hard to eat. They were thrilled to find food they could identify with in an environment they considered foreign. And it was foreign in all the ways that mattered to them: it was foreignly photogenic, you had to travel a long way to get to it, and the natives talked funny. One day a woman wandered in from a tour bus and was so thrilled by the menu that she telephoned her husband to come meet her at once. "They have Cokes and cheeseburgers, Stan," she told him, "and it's easy to find. It's right by Santa Croce—that's what *they* call Holy Cross."

Intentional tourists want no part of the reality they pass through, unless that reality is certifiably virtual. I know a man who takes his family to Disneyworld because it satisfies any urge he or they might otherwise have to visit Europe. "It's got all the same stuff, and it's cleaner and easier to get to," he says.

More user-friendly too.

Native Tourists

A dentist's chair is not the environment of choice for meditation. Simultaneously stirred by the prospect of pain and blunted by nitrous oxide, the escaping mind scurries fearfully from image to image. Mine began with a trip to the zoo and ended with the design of stay-at-home tourism. There's no such thing as a free lunch or a free association.

"I've been to the zoo," is the opening line in Edward Albee's play *Zoo Story*, a line undiminished in poignance in the years since playwright and play were first acclaimed as American eruptions of the theatre of the absurd. As the zoo itself, located in New York's Central Park, grew seedier and the animals grew shabbier, it became far better to have been to the zoo than to be there. It closed in the eighties for reasons both humane and aesthetic, reopening years later, in a triumph of redesign.

I've been to the dentist. Not much poignance in that line, but dentists can teach us something about absurdity, and they might as well since you can't talk back while they're working anyway. No other profession has so sure a hold on a captive audience.

Dental office captivity has its uses, even its pleasures. I once went to an exodontist who, as soon as I was chair bound, papered over and anesthetized, showed me his Safari slides; they were surprisingly good. The inventor Alan Murray was sitting in a dentist's chair when his big idea struck: teeth fit because they are molded to fit the mouth; shoes do not fit because they are designed as if feet differ in size but not in shape. On the basis of that insight he made a fortune with the Murray Molded Space Shoe, almost before the Novocaine wore off.

I was not making a fortune in the dentist's chair; I was spending one. In preparation for a root canal, a cap had been

Originally published September/October 1991 in *I.D.* as the column "Circumstantial Evidence."

removed and replaced with a temporary, which fell out the night before a business trip. Anxious about traveling to the Midwest with an exposed molar, I made a nervous call to the root canalist. No problem. "Your tooth has been sealed against the environment," I was told. I envied it.

After the next root canal installment, the temporary cap fell out again. This time I knew not to worry, and didn't—not even when the bill for the cap specified an amount that once would have covered major surgery and a postoperative vacation on the Riviera. But I did begin to brood. I was still brooding when I went back to my dentist.

I handed him the temporary cap. "Does this have any resale value?" I asked.

"You'd have done better leaving it for the tooth fairy," he said.

"It fell out twice," I told him. "The first time it happened I was alarmed because I was going out of town. I was afraid of infection."

"You didn't have to be," he said.

"So its falling out made no difference?"

"Not really."

"Then why on earth did you put it in?"

"Cosmetic reasons," he said.

"Cosmetic reasons!" The tooth is so remotely positioned in my upper left jaw that even I have never seen it except in X-rays. "It isn't visible to anyone but you and the specialist you sent me to."

"With eight out of ten people, that tooth is visible from certain angles when they smile," he said.

"I never smile," I reminded him. "Even if I did, according to your own actuarial statistics, I'm one of the two out of eight for whom it doesn't matter. What are you anyway, a cosmetician of the unseen?"

"I'm a perfectionist," he said.

"I've never heard of anything so ridiculous," I said. Actually I had. You can't hang out with designers without noticing the hegemony of the cosmetic. Sometimes what you see is all you get.

And sometimes the more there is to look at, the less there is to see. It was tiresome when everyone quoted Marshall McLuhan every time a conversation touched on sight or sound, but McLuhan knew things. One thing he knew was that radio was visually rich precisely because it gave us nothing to look at. That's why Joe Louis remains a more vivid image to me than Madonna, although her dressing room repartee is snappier.

As McLuhan was the first to perceive, the trouble with television is that you can see it. This does not make commentary unnecessary (there are far more TV announcers covering any given event than there ever were in radio) but it makes it different. Because the audience sees what's going on—sometimes better than the referee does—it is redundant to give a running account of what's happening. So what announcers provide is "color."

My father enjoyed watching fights on TV with the sound turned off and the radio turned on. He delighted in the extravagant disparity between what the radio announcers claimed they saw and what, if anything, was really happening. A colorful announcer like Bill Stern could charge the air with an electric account of pinpoint jabs, savage uppercuts, devastating left hooks, and brutal right crosses, while the fighters were either embracing each other or resting in their corners.

TV announcers, however, are less likely to exaggerate what's happening than to ignore it. I remember watching the 1992 NCAA final between Duke and Kansas. The announcers set up a backdrop of praise for Kansas's rebound mastery, their control of the court, their superior polish. Against it, they painted a despairing view of Duke's problems in getting the ball, keeping the ball, sinking the ball—problems tragically compounded by Duke forward Christian Laettner's numbing fatigue, and the coach's incomprehensible error in keeping him in the game when he was so obviously ready to drop at any moment.

While that was being fed into the viewer's ears, their eyes couldn't help noticing that Duke was ahead, stayed ahead, and won the game. The announcers, with an admirable disdain for bottom-line thinking, explained everything about the game except the score.

When you can see for yourself what's happening, score-board reportage is subordinated to "color." The same phenomenon occurs in design and marketing: when design features are plain to see, products are described in terms of lifestyle changes and (after the fact) trends, rather than in terms of how they work and what they do.

Of course some design is visual, its only purpose to be seen. When preparing a talk for a group of designers who specialize in "signage," I thought of dramatizing their significance in the cosmic scheme of things by envisioning a world without signs. But as soon as I envisioned a world without signs, it looked like Paradise and I wondered whether the absence of signs was what made it Paradise. It may have been Lost, but no one was lost in it. The inhabitants were confused about consequences, but never about directions; when Adam and Eve were banished they didn't ask the Archangel which way to the exit ramp. Eden, then, was defined not by what was in it but by what was left out. So, it wasn't just a rumor—God had read Mies!

Now, unsure whether it was Mies, God, or the nitrous oxide talking, I tried to imagine what else had been omitted from Paradise and noticed that it had no tourist industry. That figures. Tourists are the principal consumers of signage, people who don't know where to go because they can't imagine what to do when they get there. A tourist is the person not working when everyone else is. The person in search of someone else's life. The person without mission or purpose or reason for being. Because there were no tourists in Paradise, no signage was required until The Fall. Ever since, the world has needed directions, and designers to fashion them. The best directional designs help us find home, wherever we are. The worst make us tourists in our own countries.

World's Fair

When I was in college I was invited to a dinner party at the home of a professor who believed in faculty–student fraternization. I believed in it too; I had a crush on a biology lab instructor who had red hair and a fiancé in Des Moines. After dinner, as we sat awkwardly around the living room the host proposed that we take turns answering the question, "What first comes to mind when you think of the British Museum?"

Nothing did. I had never thought about the British Museum. I doubt that I had heard of it before. I sat in terror, waiting to be revealed as the world class ignoramus I plainly was.

The host began with the claim that what came to his mind was Karl Marx writing *Das Kapital* in the Museum library. An English major came up with the Elgin Marbles. My biologist friend recalled a display of stone scarab beetles from Egypt. And so it went until a professor of political science said, "This will classify me as a lowbrow, but what I thought of instantly was the sign over the sink in the main men's room, which reads 'For Minor Ablutions Only.'" The ensuing laughter, followed by speculation as to what behavior exactly was forbidden by the sign—shaving? hip baths? infant baptisms?—stopped the game before I was called on. I almost changed my major to political science on the spot, out of gratitude for the save.

There is something compelling in the juxtaposition of lowbrow associations and highbrow environments, like the romantic incongruity of all the scenes (there may be only one but it feels like dozens) in which Carole Lombard, dressed in a ball gown, has her limousine pull up at a diner where she orders a hamburger and an extra side of onions. So when I think, as I have a right to do at my age, of the 1939 New York World's Fair, my most vivid Fair grounds memory is of seeing, and actually talking to, Jack Johnson, who had been one of the great heavy-

Originally published May/June 1989 in *I.D.*, as the column "Circumstantial Evidence."

220 • Being There

weight boxing champions of the world. As conversations go, it was not world-shaking (I asked him for his autograph and he said no). I have a friend who believes that everyone should be permitted one ecologically unsound personal practice—like the use of an aerosol can, whether it's hair spray, fake whipped cream, or Mace. I don't know about that, but I believe that to be fully human everyone needs a strong attachment to one activity that is socially indefensible. Mine is boxing.

The last day we were in New York I asked my parents if I could be excused from the fair to spend a day at Stillman's Gym on Eighth Avenue. Stillman's was more seductive than Flushing Meadows, and the twenty-five cent admission fee was good for all day. At Stillman's a kindly fight photographer introduced me to a down-and-out fighter who was hustling for a sandwich. His name was Lew Jenkins. Within the year he was a contender for the lightweight boxing championship, which the following year he won. How could a World's Fair compete with a World's Champion?

The fair's theme was The World of Tomorrow, with various components of that world on display, each as The Something of Tomorrow—house, kitchen, car, shaver. These were created by such stellar designers as Raymond Loewy, Gilbert Rohde, John Vassos, Russel Wright, Donald Deskey, and Norman Bel Geddes, whose Futurama revealed Tomorrow as a massive intercontinental highway system.

One could argue gloomily that Bel Geddes was right, but he thought civilization-as-freeway would be a desirable way of life, and at the fair it looked that way. I have seen Futurama, and it worked—but only because it was a model, with 50,000 cars, but no gridlock, smog, or urban crises. The most widely publicized fair designs were post-Depression fantasies, grounded quite realistically in technological possibilities. But while celebrating technological potential, they didn't reckon with the technological consequences: that a world in which all kinds of marvelous things could happen was a world in which all kinds of terrible things could happen at an unprecedented scale and pace. The wonders of technology were, if anything, understated by the fair's designers. Except for a robot or two, nothing in their wildest renderings presaged the ubiquity or power of the computer.

My personal World of Tomorrow was most successful when it evoked yesterday, as Billy Rose's Aquacade did, with ex-Olympic swimmers Johnny Weismuller and Eleanor Holm Jarrett paddling lethargically in a pool while a crooner sang of her dismissal from the U.S. team for drinking wine. I came home with a Trylon and Perisphere paperweight and with thoughts of Jack Johnson knocking out Stanley Ketchell thirty years before with a right so powerful that two of Ketchell's teeth were later found embedded in Johnson's glove.

Then, as now, the so-called design impact of World's Fairs was exaggerated. The House of Tomorrow was a nice place to visit, but you wouldn't want to live there and nobody does. True, the Barcelona Chair was commissioned for the Barcelona Exposition, but Mies could as easily have done it for a Chicago bank. World's Fair designs are rarely meaningfully influential or accurately predictive.

Why, in an age of satellites and modems and fax machines in every garage, do we go on having Fairs anyway? They made sense when the only way to see the other products of other countries (or other counties) was to gather them in one place. Now Fairs make sense because we want them. They were never intended to illuminate social issues or even to acknowledge them, but invariably they do. With their celebratory design mandates, Fairs may be dedicated to our most irresponsible dreams but, against their will, they provide occasions for seeing where genuine vision is most needed. Jack Johnson was not just heavyweight champion of the world. He was the man whose invincibility gave rise to the cruelly desperate need for a "Great White Hope" to beat him. I thought of that the morning the 1964 Fair opened, with Lyndon Johnson (no relation) inside the gates, talking about the Great Society, while black activist James Farmer stood outside the gates, protesting that it wasn't great yet.

The Grinning Quaker

When the subject is design, the audience is usually made up of designers. This should not surprise anyone, and it never does. It should not discourage anyone either, but it almost always does.

"We're preaching to the converted again," is a lament heard at design conferences from coast to coast and from year to year.

But consider the source. I don't mean the complaining designers; I mean the source of the analogy, which is, I suppose, the Protestant ministry, since there is relatively little preaching in Moslem, Buddhist, Jewish, and Catholic services.

Good preaching holds a fascination for me that has nothing to do with Biblical accuracy or the winning of souls. I am probably the only one on my block who keeps a copy of *The Real Billy Sunday* close at hand for periodic refreshment. I am certainly the only one who ever played Aimee Semple McPherson tapes at parties. Once in Indianapolis, when friends went to the Indy 500 I went instead to the Cadle Tabernacle, where the threat of hellfire and damnation was more exciting and just as loud. I followed Jim Bakker and Jimmy Swaggart before they were sex objects, and bought a special antenna to pick up Ernest Angley's healings live from Akron, Ohio.

Television ministry, to be sure, has more in common with the rest of television than it has with the rest of the ministry. But it has even more in common with the itinerant evangelism that flourished here as the century turned. From Billy Sunday through early Billy Graham, evangelists had been suspect among the pastorate. They were charismatic figures whose glamour and energy obscured the village minister who, in addition to his own weekly sermon, had to meet the daily needs of a congregation. Visiting evangelists tried to win over

Originally published September/October 1988 in *I.D.*, as the column "Circumstantial Evidence."

local pastors by arguing that, although they left town richer in dollars, they left the town richer in souls ripe for church affiliation. Theirs was the homiletics of awareness. Saving souls was their specialty. As Sunday said in 1912: "This is a day of specialists. . . . I couldn't be a pastor, and many a pastor cannot be an evangelist." Evangelists preached to the unconverted and converted them.

Most church preaching, on the other hand, is necessarily preaching to the converted, since no one else comes to church. Ministers do not find this peculiar, for they understand preaching as a means to sustain the faith as well as to save sinners. I have never heard a pastor complain that the members of his congregation were true believers.

But when designers protest that they are not the most appropriate audience for sermons on design, they are right. Not, however, because designers are the wrong audience, but because sermons are the wrong medium. Something quite different is called for. Namely, the exchange of ideas about design at a level that goes beyond the insistence that it is important. Design *is* important, but it is not as important to keep saying so as it is to make the importance self-evident.

One common designer sermon likely to resonate with the general public concerns the loss of flavor in contemporary life. Flavor has been seeping out of our GNP for some time now. The other day I heard a commercial for Quaker Oats, not advertising the cereal directly, but advertising the Quaker on the box. "We've been waking up to his reassuring smile for over one hundred years," the voiceover said reassuringly.

No we haven't. The Quaker, chosen not for his good humor but for the association of probity, didn't start smiling, as I recall, until the late fifties, when a package designer named Jim Nash wiped the smile onto his face out of fear that his stern expression would frighten consumers into buying some other brand.

Of course the logos and symbols are merely symptomatic. Flavor is identity. The real corporate identity crisis is not that designers have eliminated personality, but that so few companies and brands have any, largely because they are owned by other companies in other businesses. For years I have been carrying a pocket organizer called Day-Timer. The graphics are reassuringly homely. It will never compete for cachet with Palm Pilot or Blackberry, but it doesn't break when dropped and is friendly in a way that became less convincing once I learned that it comes from the kitchens (or at least under the aegis) of Beatrice Foods. In our own kitchen we have a package of Fattorie & Pandea breadsticks. They were baked in Italy, and they taste good. But not as good as they would taste if the package didn't carry a picture of that same Quaker, multinational now, but still grinning his designer grin.

Graphics and Graffiti

Environmental graphic design has intrigued me since early childhood. In the western Pennsylvania town where I grew up, a highway was cut through the hills above the Ohio River, leaving an expanse of naked cliff that served as a backdrop for official messages and graffiti. The warning to "Watch Out for Falling Rock," was well intentioned but, as with Magenta Alert, or whatever the coded warning this week, it was hard to guess what you were supposed to do if you saw any, other than drive into the river or the wrong traffic lane. What it meant, I guess, was "Watch out for *fallen* rock."

Much clearer, but just as mysterious, was the declaration, "Jesus Saves." No ambiguity about what it meant, but who put it there? Have *you* ever seen anybody paint "Jesus Saves" or "He's coming soon" on the side of a cliff? Neither have I. Neither has anyone else.

My mother's interest in roadside signs was confined to their absence. Whenever we drove past a building that wasn't plainly identified as a college or a church or corporate headquarters, she complained, "They never tell you what it is."

She was right about them. They often didn't. But now that they do, we discover that it isn't enough. Paradoxically, we also discover that it's too much. The results can be confusing and unlovely, as Ogden Nash noted when he wrote:

I think that I shall never see

A billboard lovely as a tree.

In fact until the billboards fall

I'll never see a tree at all.

The settlers who brought the public sign to the West were only following an Old Testament injunction: "Write the vision, and make it plain . . . that he may run who readeth it." Now *that* was signage! And when running ceased to be the fastest

Based on a speech given at Cranbrook Academy, August 1982, to the Society of Environmental Graphic Designers.

available means of locomotion, the message still had to be legible to people on the move. With the advent of the automobile came the sophistication of the highway sign.

The literary use of highway signage did not stop with the Bible. The optometrist's sign in *The Great Gatsby* is the book's basic metaphor. In *The Grapes of Wrath*, John Steinbeck juxtaposes the promises of a highway Coca-Cola sign with the promises that feed the spirit of the Okies precariously and thirstily passing by. Nelson Algren called his book on Chicago *The Neon Wilderness*. But it was the Burma Shave Company that created signs that *became* literature. If they were not high art, they were as close to it as you were likely to come en transit. They informed, entertained, reminded you of the product. Nothing is more poignantly nostalgic to people of a certain generation than the Burma Shave quatrains narratively lining the highways of our childhood.

I never understood how the sign makers figured out the placement of each sign. Computers do this now. But how did the Burma Shave copy writers pace their rhymes so precisely to the speed at which my father happened to drive?

From the Biblical marks on doorposts to the mandatory theater exits, much of our important information has always come from signs. Yet designers over the years have displayed an intense ambivalence toward commercial signs. On the one hand, they worry about "visual litter," which they think most signs are. On the other hand, they must know they often are designing signs even when they are not specifically designing *signage*.

When the Boston Architectural Center mounted an exhibit of signs and lights, Peter Blake, who was then the director, noted, "Architects have fought against these aspects of the modern American scene in part because they have never learned how to use them to their own advantage." So one of the purposes of that exhibit was "to encourage architects and designers to use these devices instead of attempting to defeat them." Yet architects realize that most buildings are, in their way, signs as well. The Eiffel Tower and the Transamerica building say things to millions who have never been in, or even seen, them. In Detroit, the Renaissance Center is not the center of anything, but a sign that says, "Look, even in Detroit you can be safe from Detroit."

People learn quickly to read the body language of a building or a city and always have. As architectural historian James Ackerman said, "The powerful Greeks did not need architects to shelter them but to communicate their messages."

What the Greeks did not foresee was the proliferation of messages, or a landscape loaded with environmental graphics that communicate messages not intended for most people who encounter them. I am thinking of the unintelligible road signs meant only for road repair people or telephone crews or surveyors. What they say is usually none of our business, although that is not why we don't read them. Rather, their meaning is withheld by specialization.

Yet some of them are lovely, and to look at them is to confront a rich visual landscape that yields secrets to the trained eye. To someone who can read it—an Indian scout or a naturalist—every forest is dense with coded messages: where insects live, where eggs are hidden, predictions of weather, records of meals eaten and battles fought. The same kind of informed reading is necessary in our own urban forests, which makes the environmental graphic designer an important figure in forest management.

If the Greeks did not foresee the multitudes of messages to come, and if they did not foresee the environmental chaos compounded by the signs using public space to communicate private messages, there is no way they—or we—could have imagined the extent to which public and private communication would merge. People say things to Oprah and to the vast unseen audience of television viewers that in the nineteenth century they would never have told their spouses or closest friends. Celebrities are not the only ones empowered to spill their guts. In what has been called an age of narcissism, inhabited by what has been called the "me generation," there seems to be an intense urge for a sign of one's own. The personal sign always seemed a wild luxury, like hiring a hall to share your fantasies with the world. In one of her last films, Judy Holliday played a secretary who used her entire savings to rent a massive billboard that carried nothing but her own name. The same theme appears in a Mary Tyler Moore sequence in which a flamboyant suitor rents a billboard to declare his love for Mary.

Today, however, personal messages need not be fantasized. They are affordable in the form of bumper stickers and imprinted tee shirts that lay on innocent people the stressful burden of assimilating information we didn't ask for, don't want, and can't do anything with. "I'd rather be sailing." Who asked you, and who cares? "Nurses have more fun." More fun than whom? And what am I supposed to do about it? Or my favorite: "Caution: I brake for animals." This sanctimonious announcement does at least tell you what to do about it. It is in this sense like the driving school car with a big sign saying "student driver," meaning, "Watch out, because this vehicle is driven by someone who hasn't yet learned how to do it." "I brake for animals" means, "Watch out, because I have such a saintly respect for wildlife that if a rabbit leaps in front of my car I am perfectly willing to risk slaughtering a dozen people in a five-car pile up." The odds are that very few people are individually self-righteous enough to make that declaration on their own. Have you ever heard anyone say, "You know, I hate to brag, but I brake for animals"? These messages are fabricated by companies that sell them to people with no statements of their own to make—people who probably once bought pet rocks for their own use.

In fiction, personal signs are not always personally financed or self-imposed. *The Scarlet Letter* was nothing more than a sign designed by the community to force a woman to advertise to them what they had decided she was. What is peculiar to our time is the number of messages that *are* personally financed but are imposed by manufacturers and by advertising agencies. During the Depression—and you see this in pictures from the Bettman Archive and old magazine cartoons—a common advertising vehicle was the sandwich man. This was cheap advertising, using an occupation of last resort at a time when last resort was often all there was. No mother hoped that her child would grow up to be a sandwich man. But, as a matter of fact, he probably has and so has his sister. For we have become a nation of voluntary, unpaid, amateur sandwich advertisements perfectly willing to use our bodies to plug Tommy Hilfiger, Fila, Nike, Calvin Klein, DKNY, and the neighborhood garage, ice cream parlor, or Broadway show. Not only are we unpaid, we *pay* for the privilege. In New York it is possible to spend $75 on an orchestra seat to a show, then spend an additional $25 for a tee shirt that turns you into a walking advertisement for the same show.

As with any other kind of barter, there is a quid pro quo. Why is anyone willing to wear a label on the outside of his clothing? Because, while it does a selling job for the advertiser, it simultaneously advertises the kind of person the wearer wishes to come across as being. Consequently, you don't have to go through the agonizing process of becoming a real person. You can buy a personality and, because of our mass-market distribution, you can buy the same personality at Target as you can at Bloomingdale's, and for less.

The consumer is going public, the designer is turning pro. There is a professional mystique in this country that may be as close as we come to a genuine class consciousness. Everybody wants to be a professional. Hairdressers are professionals. Air traffic controllers got the designation "professional" included as part of their union title, so they wouldn't be confused with hobbyists. The shampoo I use happens to be marked "for professional use only," not because I need specialized training to wash my hair—sadly, that gets easier every year—but to carry the suggestion that this is potent stuff that experts use. Dating services advertise that they are professional. Furthermore, their clients are professional singles—a marvelous marketing gambit because they have it both ways. Professionals sign up to meet people just like themselves. Nonprofessionals sign up to meet people classier than they are.

What is a professional anyway? Minimally, a professional is paid, which raises expectations of a certain level of competence. When a boxer turns pro, it not only means that he gets money for fighting; it means he has to be prepared to fight longer bouts, with lighter, less protective gloves, against competitors picked from a much more highly selective pool. But that is purely a technical designation.

A professional is supposed to have basic skills plus a basic education, an education comparable to that of his fellow professionals. But no such education is possible unless there is a codified body of knowledge.

In addition to the codified body of knowledge, there must be acknowledged standards.

Related to the professional standards there is some describable professional conduct. This may include a dress code, although increasingly today it does not. It may include such things as an injunction against advertising, although increasingly it does not. It may include membership in an organization presumably designed to enforce standards and codes of conduct. It invariably includes jargon such as "signage," specialized language designed to exclude outsiders.

If I were asked which of those criteria is the most important professional criterion, I would reply, "None of the above." The salient criterion is quite simply that professionals profess something that has importance. They take a stand rooted in what they know and think from having studied, apprenticed, done research, worked, learned, made mistakes, and otherwise qualified themselves through experience. But that stand also represents the moral position without which ethical codes are both unenforceable and meaningless.

For designers, the urge to be professional tends to take the form of a lust for professional trappings rather than a commitment to professional values. If designers have no counterpart to the Oath of Hippocrates, they have many counterparts to the American Medical Association.

The search for professional status has led designers down some strange corridors. One of these is licensing. The license to design would, in the minds of some, endow designers with the recognition that doctors, lawyers, and architects have, or had. But they are not licensed because they are professionals, but because their reprehensible or inept practice would, and frequently does, create a public hazard. Exterminators, security guards, chiropractors, barbers, cab drivers, and street vendors are licensed for the same reason.

What makes medicine a profession is not that doctors are paid or licensed, but that they are presumed to know the science, and pledge to practice it responsibly. This is not to say that any given doctor *does* know the requisite medical science or that doctors as a rule *are* faithful to the Oath of Hippocrates—only that those standards exist. Lawyers are professionals for the same reasons—which is, again, not to say that any given lawyer knows law at all or that lawyers as a whole behave as Blackstone or Oliver Wendell Holmes would have them behave, only that the standards are there.

Finding the Way

Graphic design hardly seems the therapy of choice for our battered environment. But if environmental graphic designers cannot restore our lakes and rain forests, maybe they can help us negotiate the built, and largely urban, environment in which we live. One of the field's principal concerns is "wayfinding," a term that, after years of professional service, has not yet been emptied of charm or meaning. Jargon aside, graphics are the means by which we find our way through cities, onto and off highways, into and around malls, shops, prisons, nail salons, zoos, theme parks, bowling alleys, cathedrals, factories, bars, and public events.

The content is not usually difficult in itself. A four-year-old child can grasp most of it without help of parent or teacher. For that matter, a four year-old child could have written most of the messages. STOP DON'T WALK MEN WOMEN NO RIGHT TURN WRONG WAY HILTON HOTEL WELCOME TO NEBRASKA SLOW GAS FOOD LODGING DANGER FOUR SEASONS EAT Sometimes there is no information, the banner or sign or display saying nothing explicit because the purpose is purely celebratory: to make nice. The process is intricate, the technology is sophisticated. A massive signage system for Euro Disney or O'Hare Airport is staggeringly complex in development and specification and fabrication; but not in the message content of most units.

DON'T WALK is an injunction anyone can comprehend. In New York the problem is not to make it clear and inviting, but to make it convincing to a pedestrian determined to get across the street before the blinking red words are replaced by a steady red light that ends the cessation of hostilities and releases the nervous vehicles from the starting gate.

The unwillingness of either pedestrians or drivers to believe the signs they see, and to comply with their directions,

Originally published November/December 1992 in *I.D.*, as the column "Counterpoint."

accounts for the city's pedestrian fatality average of one per day. In response, the Department of Transportation commissioned a new series of signs to instruct pedestrians in safety measures (HOLD YOUR ARM UP HIGH WHEN CROSSING) or at least scare them into thinking it over (A PEDESTRIAN WAS KILLED HERE).

The first 1,000 signs were to be placed at the most lethal locations throughout New York City, such as Houston and Allen streets, where, the previous year people were killed while standing on the Houston Street median. A department spokesman explained that they were "run over by large trucks turning left from Allen onto Houston," adding that, "often the rear wheels of these trucks roll up over the curb and intersect with pedestrians."

On our streets, vehicular components intersect with pedestrians. On our highways, they intersect with each other. In neither case is it because the safety messages are complex. Approaching the city on Route 684, a motorist is warned that the lane she occupies will vanish in a quarter of a mile. That is not complicated information. But the driver reading it, and trying to factor its content into the act of changing lanes, may be going 60 MPH while chattering on her cellphone, switching radio stations, adjusting the sun visor or the air-conditioning, wondering where the Saw Mill River Parkway turnoff is and worrying about finding a place to park, should she ever reach the city. All that *is* complicated, which is why only the simplest messages can be assimilated under the circumstances. The designer's task is to steer through the traffic congestion in the driver's head.

Environmental graphics have to be made simple to help us navigate through labyrinthine urban space. But, paradoxically, space is our primary resource for the metaphors that make language graphic and clear. If you listen to what people say in meetings (not a practice I would ordinarily urge on anyone), you notice how much of it is spatial in derivation. I told you that *going in*. We have been totally *up front* with you. This is the *cutting edge*. *Moving right along* now. Do you see *where I'm coming from?* Let me tell you what I see *coming down the pike*. Right now we're *in a pretty good place*. (Or a *tough spot*. Or *backed into a corner*. Or *against a wall*.)

Metaphors are instruments of simplification, which makes them useful to teachers and politicians. They are also instruments of complexity, which makes them crucial to art. In design they serve both purposes. Although schooled in the organization of materials and space, designers are alive to the pleasure of surprise. Is there anyone with soul so dead that he would not prefer the chaos of an open-air market in the Caribbean or in Spanish Harlem to the meticulous grid of a supermarket in any suburb?

The Enchanted Tub

I once participated in a "symposium" on the design of bathrooms. The event was held in Toronto, which explains why I was invited. As the author of a book with a subtitle (*Why there are no locks on the bathroom doors in the Hotel Louis XIV and other object lessons*) alluding to both bathrooms and a Canadian hotel, I must have looked like a natural choice.

Actually I have no special knowledge of either bathrooms or Canada, although I frequently visit both. Nevertheless I was not wholly unprepared for such a seminar. In a sense I have been preparing for it ever since I was old enough to take baths alone and unsupervised which, if you have a Jewish mother, could be early adolescence. That was when I began the series of experiences I call "the enchanted tub."

I would take the Sunday comics, which were in color, into the bathtub with me, read them, then tear them apart into single frames. I would then moisten any frames that still needed moistening, and stick them to the sides of the bathtub. Lined with comic-book art, the tub was transformed into a museum—one of the few I have ever entirely enjoyed. It was marvelously satisfying to combine something done on command—take a bath—with something done for its own self-satisfying sake: displaying images of Dick Tracy, Maggie and Jiggs, Barney Google, Snuffy Smith, and Steve Roper. For all I know, I may have invented Roy Lichtenstein.

Bathrooms, of all spaces, ought to be designed with equal respect for function and aesthetics, for they simultaneously serve animal necessities and human glories. The bath is a medium—although not always a happy one—for cleansing, grooming, thinking, relaxation, hydrotherapy, medication, stimulation, ritual, escape. In anticipation of the Canadian adventure I began making the following notes.

Originally published July/August 1984 in *I.D.*, as the column "Circumstantial Evidence."

#1   The Louis XIV, no longer in operation, was a Quebec waterfront hotel that boasted of private baths. The boast was valid but exaggerated. The private bath was private in the sense that your room opened onto it. But so did someone else's on the other side. If there were no interior locks, there was no privacy. But if there were locks, one guest would be certain to lock the other out.

Well, there were no locks on the bathroom doors of the Louis XIV. But, tied to each inside doorknob was a length of leather thong with a hook attached. You simply closed both doors and attached the hooks. If you were short, you could strangle yourself brushing your teeth, but there was no way to get back into your room without giving the other person access to the bathroom. This was the perfect fusion of product and circumstance, and a demonstration of the design process at its best.

#2   In 1969 the National Commission on the Causes and Prevention of Violence issued its report to the American people. Headed by Milton Eisenhower, at the direction of President Lyndon Johnson, the commission consisted of some two dozen task forces. It is difficult now to see any effect that the reports have had on violence. Somewhat earlier, in 1966, Alexander Kira issued the first edition of his massive study on the bath, conducted at Cornell University. In the seventies an expanded second edition appeared. Unlike the study of violence, it actually told us things that no one had known before. Yet, like them, it seems to have had no effect on the way we bathe or the way we design equipment and environments for bathing.

#3   Question: behind the walls and under the sinks, plumbers practice a craft of mind-boggling complexity. But where it shows, on the faucet handles, they have only one installation

detail to keep straight: the distinction between hot and cold—
H and C. How do they manage to get it wrong so often?

#4   Milton Glaser has identified a category of design he calls
"the Devil's Workshop." Included in this category are all the
objects we live with that must have been designed with malice
in mind because ineptness alone could not have done the job.
Milton cites the can opener with the cork screw inside the
handle that rips your palm to shreds every time you open a
can. Another: the shoelaces that have built-in untying memory.
Every block and a half, without any coaching, they remember
what it was like to be untied and reproduce that state. In the
bathroom, a contender for the Devil's Workshop would be the
material used for hotel counter surfaces that causes water to
gather in little pools in which your toilet articles sit all day.

#5   In the movie *If I Had a Million*, which can still be seen on
late television, the comedian Edward Everett Horton has a
recurring comic scene in which he ends arguments with his
wife by going into the bathroom and closing the door. In many
households the bathroom is indeed the sole hideaway, the only
retreat, the one place where locking a door from the inside is
socially permissible.

#6   Technically the bathroom is a room where bathing is done.
But, in the U.S. and Canada, the bathroom is almost always
synonymous with *water closet*, where something else is done.
And in fact, the bathroom is so closely identified with the
water closet that, not only is it a euphemism for the place to
go when you have to urinate or defecate, it is a euphemism
once removed. That is to say, it has a euphemism of its own—
"restroom," where nobody goes to rest, but which means *bathroom*, where nobody goes to bathe but to. . . .
    In any case, it's difficult to think of the bath without think-

ing of the *whole* bathroom as Alexander Kira did. Dr. Ivan Popov, a specialist in longevity, performed very detailed studies comparing the amount of excrement left in the bowel after using a standard toilet and the amount left after squatting, streetstyle. He found that squatting permits, and in fact encourages, almost total elimination and that American toilets inhibit it. For health and longevity Popov recommends the installation of metal footplates in all bathrooms.

#7   On a visit to a southern textile factory, an industrial reporter I know noticed that the toilets had unusually wide and curiously shaped bowls. The plant manager explained that cotton was delivered to the factory wrapped around paperboard spools, which—as an economy measure—were put in the water closets for use as toilet paper. The workers, being human, had to adapt to this. The toilet and plumbing, being mechanical, could not adapt to it, and regularly became clogged. So a special bowl had to be designed. The history of product design is packed with examples of our willingness to pay more attention to the needs of machines than to the needs of people.

#8   A friend says he shaves in the shower. When I told him I couldn't imagine shaving without a mirror, he replied that he couldn't imagine why anyone needed a mirror when the face was the same, morning after morning.

#9   My immediate neighborhood in New York City has three shops specializing in bathroom accessories. Like the shops that specialize in automobile accessories, this is a business based on the inadequacies of standard products. If the things were designed right in the first place, one wouldn't have to buy mats to keep people from slipping in the tub, or massive handles to give them a chance for survival when they do slip, or special liners to keep the soap from turning into gelatin in the soap dish, or extra racks and hooks and rods, and special shower heads to make up for the fact that the ones installed in the first place don't work well. We buy shower heads from WaterPic, as we buy wheat germ from Kretschmer: to supply what could as easily have been there from the start.

#10 Question: Is there any compound that dissolves bathtub ring without making the tub unpleasantly and dangerously slippery?

#11 Famous bathers in history: Cleopatra; Sarah Bernhardt, who used milk; Mary Martin in *South Pacific*; Doris Day, who, after bathing, encased her entire body in Vaseline, then wrapped it in plastic and went to bed; Marat, who was murdered in his bath; Archimedes, who discovered in his tub the relationship between buoyant force and fluid displacement; John Lilly, who popularized—if that can possibly be the word—the isolation tank. Lyndon Johnson reputedly conducted meetings in the bathroom, but I have found no evidence that he bathed while they were going on.

And yet the concept of a social bathroom, a place in which friends and colleagues can congregate as they now do in kitchens, is fascinating. I am not thinking of a shared bathing experience, such as Japanese baths or hot tubs. I am thinking of a bather's being joined by others who keep him or her company in the way that a cook is joined in the kitchen by dinner guests.

Armed with those notes I boarded a plane for Toronto. Upon arriving I did the most appropriate thing I could think of: I took a shower. After toweling myself dry I tried to hang the towel on a hook. I couldn't, for there was no hook. Speculation on the terrifying prospect of having to stand there with a damp towel in my hands until a carpenter came gave way to speculation about the meaning of a hookless bathroom.

The most obvious meaning was negligence. Somebody goofed. Either the designer forgot to specify hooks or the contractor forgot to have them installed or the installers skipped a room now and then. That seems unlikely for so routine a requirement, but the more you hang out with designers, the more likely it becomes.

That is a plausible reason, but not a very interesting one. A meatier reason would go like this: This is a classy hotel; we don't cater to a clientele that would use the same towel twice; forget about the hook, you hick! Toss the towel on the floor and the maid will remove it when she comes in to put a mint on your pillow after you've brushed your teeth. (Of course, a really classy hotel would have said all that with a basket labeled Used Towels.)

An experience like that can drive you to drink, which is not irrelevant. Consider.

We take alcohol for relaxation, although in fact it heightens tension; we drink it for warmth after skiing, although it really drives the body's temperature down; we use it to induce sleep, which it brings on unreliably and at great penalty in the morning; we drink it for courage, although its long-run effect is the reinforcement of cowardice. Alcohol, as it turns out, is not very good for any of the things we want to use it for. So we might as well drink it for pleasure.

The bathroom tends to be something like that. We use it for elimination, although the American toilet requires a posture that inhibits healthy elimination; we use it to shave, although the height of the sink causes back strain; we get into a tub to relax, although neither its form nor its dimensions make this possible; we retreat to the bathroom for privacy, but since its water closet and bathing functions are incorporated into the same space, the privacy is, in most families, short-lived. When you go in there for some reason, somebody else needs to get in for another reason: it is like trying to use the corkscrew on a Swiss army knife only to have your roommate interrupt because of an urgent need for the nail file. The bathroom is the locus for cleanliness, which we are told is adjacent to godliness, but the room and its equipment are difficult to keep clean. With the advent of television and hard rock, the bathroom is, for many families, the only room in the house where reading can take place, but it is badly lit and furnished for the purpose. Although it is where medicine is stored and taken, it is generally not equipped with such accessories as spoons, glasses, measuring instruments, prescriptions, and instructions. The bathroom is an environment designed for two sexes, though it does not serve them equally.

Like alcohol, the bathroom is not much good for most of the uses we put it to. But unlike alcohol, it is not optional in our lives. It is, in a sense, the only game in town.

Another Trip to the Bathroom

Shaving, unlike most other forms of punishment, is usually self-inflicted. (Barbers can no longer perform the service affordably and, in any case, are no longer trained to do it. Morticians still shave their customers, but not daily, death being inevitable but not habitual.) Perhaps because this form of ritualistic torture is invariably a do-it-yourself enterprise, men who shave each morning are ambivalent: we are willing to perform the ceremony for whatever dark Jungian reasons, but we would like it to become as nearly painless as possible.

This is not another example of a nation growing soft. Men have always sought to minimize the damage and danger of shaving, a circumstance that made King Camp Gillette one of the major inventors of the twentieth century. Shaving today, like things in Kansas City, may have gone about as far as it can go. Friction-reducing chemicals have made comfortable shaves routine. Silicon—the lubricant, not the valley—gave us what product designers could not: it made shaving less of a drag.

Before that happened, genuine improvement was so hard to come by that marketing wizards in the shaving products industry were dreaming up claims to a dazzling but irrelevant ergonomic specificity. (Long before MBA's began talking about segmentation, shrewd manufacturers were looking for ways to divide and conquer.) I remember being sorely tempted by a series of advertisements describing a razor specially designed to meet the needs of men cursed with "heavy beards and sensitive skin."

Well, that didn't describe me exactly. I have a heavy beard, but my skin has been described as preternaturally thick. Did that exclude me from the category of users? I wondered. Wouldn't such a razor be even more effective on a heavy beard with normal skin? What about men who had light beards and sensitive skin? Wouldn't it give them an even closer shave?

Originally published March/April 1986 in *I.D.*, as the column "Circumstantial Evidence."

The questions, of course, were hypersensitive, because the ad itself was hype. Distinctions in user needs are not necessarily spurious; there are special needs and one of our healthiest design impulses is to design for them. But when the design is successful, it almost invariably turns out to be nonexclusive: we can all use it. My wife has the same kind of razor I have. Her shaving needs are, to be sure, different from mine, but that difference does not require a different design or a different instrument.

I was thinking on these things recently in Milan where, for the second time in an otherwise uneventful life, I found myself in a seminar on the design of bathrooms.

One of the emphases of the seminar was on "the aging and the handicapped." But it is redundant to speak of "the aging and the handicapped." For design purposes, elderly people *are* handicapped, and their special needs are not defined by the number of years they have lived, but by the number of things they can no longer do. The redundancy is useful, however, for it reminds us that the handicapped are not an alien species: they are us. Being handicapped, after all, is a state most of us pass through sometime—look around you at any ski resort. And apart from the short-term handicaps we may acquire, there is the almost inevitable handicap to come. If we live long enough, we will be old and will be politely referred to as "aging," although there is no one alive who isn't.

Well, bathrooms can help. Both literally and metaphorically, water is our most enduring antidote to aging. Ponce de Leon searched for the fountain of youth. The wrinkles of age are treated with moisturizers and emollients. We go to spas to take the waters. Fluidity is a sign of youth. Baptism, I have been reliably informed, is the medium of eternal life.

Is this line of argument all wet? Maybe. Nevertheless water and the artifacts we make to manage it have particular urgency for those who are no longer young. Therapy carries danger, in this case far more than it needs to. It is by now no secret that most serious accidents happen in the home. Nor is it a secret where in the home they are likely to happen. The bathroom is wryly described as the safest room in which to smoke. It is also the place where the odds of slipping, cracking your head on a hard surface, drowning, or cutting yourself are highest.

But those are undesirable activities at any age. We all want to avoid them. And if someone can design a way around them, it is likely to be the way of choice for all of us.

None of this, of course, has any more to do with bathrooms specifically, than ease of cleaning has to do with the elderly, specifically. Responsible design is not a medical specialty, nor any other kind; it's something we all need.

Why do we have to be old to appreciate convenience? We don't. Why do we have to be old to need safety? We don't. Why do we have to be old to deserve comfort? We don't. Why do we have to be old at all?

I don't know. I'm a stranger here myself.

Attention

Designers complain that people who are truly unable to see are required to make decisions based upon visual information. Well, tough. The rest of us struggle with people who do not know how to listen but are required to make decisions based upon what is said. The inability to see and to listen really are aspects of the same problem—and the problem doesn't stop with seeing and listening. Among the more significant findings of the widely publicized Masters-Johnson research was the discovery that large numbers of adults had never discovered how to touch. This inadequacy was responsible in large measure for the development of sensitivity training as a growth industry.

The real problem, it seems to me, does not have to do particularly with the eye, the ear, or the fingertips—or with any or all of the senses as such. It has to do with attention. The ability to pay attention, to focus, to concentrate, to resist distractions, is as essential to the design process as it is to successful life generally. It is the quality of attention that distinguishes design detail, that enables an architect to design a building that belongs where it is. For attention to detail does not mean fussiness, but an appropriate locating of energies.

In the end, it is something very close to grace.

From Notes on *Attention*, a notebook published in 1978 by Herman Miller, Inc.

5

Now and Then and Next

D on't look back," Satchel Paige famously warned, "something may be gaining on you." On the other hand, George Santayana even more famously said, "If you don't know history, you will be condemned to repeat it." One of the promised uses of the past is to show us what to avoid in the future, but when it comes to the things that really matter—war and peace, relationships—that rarely works.

We try to honor the past, believing it may inform what comes next. But it is hard not to wonder, like the protagonist of W.G. Sebald's novel *Vertigo*, "what relation was there between the so-called monuments of the past and the vague longing, propagated through our bodies, to people the dust-blown expanses and tidal plains of the future."

In 1849 a journalist named Alphonse Karr wrote "plus ça change, plus c'est meme chose"—the more things change, the more they stay the same. The observation is as recognizably valid as ever, and as frustrating. Every day brings new evidence that what's gone around has come around—the fear of attack with weapons of mass destruction prompts a boom in protective technology sales, accompanied by guidelines without guidance; new research reveals that smoking is unhealthy, as old research had revealed decades ago; the low carbohydrate diet introduced in 1863 is rediscovered and becomes controversial once again. Pundits proclaim the end of history, the end of irony, the end of print, the end of whatever you name "as we know it."

But not the end of reporting on the future before it gets here.

End in View

"he world won't stop," Mary Chapin Carpenter insists
on one of her earlier CDs. Her claim is backed up by
paleontologist Stephen Jay Gould, who said "apocalyp-
tic predictions always fail!" Certainly they have failed so far.
The world has not ended; but, its component parts have been
slipping away so steadily that each day brings the prospect of a
new singular cessation. We are threatened regularly with the
end of such prized chunks of experience as arable land,
breathable air, art, lobsters, parking spaces, and film.

"Cinema is dying. Cinema is being reborn," the film critic
Molly Haskell writes mockingly. Well, Tibetan Buddhists have
always known that was the way it works.

A friend of mine takes comfort in reflecting that even if
print were to disappear, words would not. Words on a screen,
he maintains, are as good as they are on a page. I'm not sure
they are, and the idea sends chills up my spine and along my
thumb, which would rather caress a book than a mouse.
Words on a screen are less palpable than on a page, not subject
to the same level of ownership. Words on a screen do not
belong to anyone. They are there on sufferance; renters of electronic space, they can be evicted without notice. I know,
books can be burned; but that is not the same. In such cases, it
is the artifact that is destroyed. Words on a screen, like vam-
pires, depend for their survival on fuel from the outside, and
at the turn of a switch or the failure of a generator they drop
away into darkness.

The schism between word and picture, between "visuals"
and "copy," is artificial and blinds us to the fact that words *are*
visual—not just in the typefaces that contain them, but in
themselves, before a serif is added or taken away. In the beginning was the word because without it there would have been
nothing on which to base the image of creation. Some of the

Originally published November/December 1997 in *PRINT*, as the column "Peripheral Vision."

most intensely visual words designers work with are pre-design, when thinking is a landscape where images reside until you figure out how to put them into someone else's head. This does not necessarily entail putting them on a page first. It may be better not to. Prose is never so prosaic as when it has been hammered out by wordsmiths.

On the other hand, words themselves may be so highly charged with visual metaphor that no further imagery is needed. I have always admired Muhammad Ali's right more than I admired his rhymes. The doggerel with which he predicted knockout rounds ("If he's still alive/I'll deck him in five") was amusing but betokened no great mastery of the craft of poetry. Or so I thought until I saw the documentary *When We Were Kings*, in which Ali is seen delivering this paean to his own toughness:

> I murdered a rock!
> I hospitalized a brick!
> I'm so bad I make medicine sick.

The sentiment, poetic imagination, and humor of those lines call up Bessie Smith's "Black Mountain Blues," a town so mean that:

> Down in Black Mountain
> A chile will smack your face.
> Babies cryin' for liquor,
> And all the birds sing bass.

With outsider poets like these, there is no end in sight.

The Past and the Pendulum

I don't know or care much about professional figure skating, but I am certain that, as a radio commentator warns grimly, "the problems of professional figure skating are not going to go away." We have been told the same thing about the religious right, the irreligious middle, the homeless, crime, and the San Francisco pass receivers. They are not going to go away either.

What people mean by that, I guess, is that we have to face reality and its persistent problems. But problems do not persist because we have not faced them, rather they persist because we have not solved them. The few that go away unsolved would probably have gone away unfaced. One way of facing reality is to acknowledge how little of anything ever truly goes away. Experience is a resource to be recycled, just like paper and plastic. This too will pass, whatever it is; the present vanishes, even as we are experiencing it. But it is instantly converted into the past, where we can observe it with hindsight, if not with clarity.

When a friend recommended a book called *The Past is a Foreign Country*, I got the title wrong and asked for *The Past is Another Country*, which, as it turns out, is another book. My bookstore has both on order. In the meantime, the titles alone are eloquent reminders that the past is inhabited by people whose language we do not speak.

Coming to terms with the past is an aspect of coming of age in design. At the School of Visual Arts in New York, Steven Heller wrapped up his eighth annual seminar in graphic design history, just as the American Center for Design in Chicago was launching its own symposium on "Making History in Design." Not all designers find it necessary to "make history," since, like timber, so much of it is already there for the chopping. In the *New York Times*, Patricia Leigh Brown

Originally published May/June 1995 in *I.D.*, as the column "Counterpoint."

writes, "Let history record that the Young Turks of American architecture are really old fogies." On the other side of the page a report from a Paris furniture show tells us that as "furniture designers bored with the present rummaged through the colorful past" the fervor of their rummaging caused the general merchandise manager of the Japanese department store Takashimaya to caution that "the pendulum has swung too far into the past too quickly."

How far is too far, and how quickly is too quickly, and is that what really happens anyway? The pendulum is an important mechanical device, and a graphic metaphor for describing the back-and-forth swings of fashion and manic depression. Design, however, is driven more by need and talent than by gravity and momentum. Of course, a lot of design is fashion, and some may even be manic depressive; but movement in design is rarely a fixed arc.

In our discomfort with the past, we accuse each other at every turn of "rewriting history," as if that were fraudulent in itself. As far as I can tell, rewriting history is the only thing historians do for a living. They hope one day to get it right.

So do designers. Modernism at its most extreme was an assertion that if the past did not go away it could be stripped away, column by column, ornament by ornament. When Gordon Bunshaft was the genius of record at Skidmore Owings Merrill, someone asked him if SOM was going to go on making those sterile glass boxes. "Yes," Bunshaft said, "and we're going to keep doing it until we get it right." Postmodernists explained that you could never get it right, because the premise in itself was wrong. But if the worst of Modernism rejected the past, the worst of Postmodernism swallowed it in discrete doses, like a homeopathic pill. The poet Stanley Kunitz scolded MoMA for what he called its "rapacious historicity" in turning every trend into a legend. It is equally rapacious to turn classics into novelties. Both attitudes betoken disrespect.

During a gig at the Boston Children's Museum, I got a fresh look at what respect for the past entails. The occasion was a stump-the-experts evening hosted by the museum's departing director, Kenneth Brecher. A childlike anthropologist who can turn any venue into a playing field, Brecher knows that playing fields are more fun when they are not level. So the panel of experts included a nonexpert ringer: me. The real experts were Susan Vogel, founder and then-director of the Museum of African Art in New York; and the writer Henry Louis Gates, head of African American Studies and Professor of Humanities at Harvard. Vogel and Gates were there because they know things. I was there because I pretended to know things; it was not a posture I could sustain for the entire evening.

The museum has a collection of some 50,000 objects—some of them precious, some of them legacies they did not know how to turn down, many of them bizarre, many of them obscure, many of them unidentified. Curators presented selected artifacts to individual panelists (the audience saw the things projected onto a screen) and we were challenged to say what the objects were, where they came from, and when.

Exercises like this are not ordinarily my idea of a good time. I have always avoided the scripted and costumed docents who staff places like Sturbridge Village in Massachusetts, Conner Prairie in Indianapolis, Economy in Pennsylvania, and Williamsburg in Virginia, and who relieve their own boredom by pointing to arcane gadgets and asking unsuspecting tourists to guess what they are. I refuse to play, although once I did and scored. Asked to classify a pair of minuscule red plastic chips held together with wire, I said sarcastically that they were sunglasses for chickens. That, it turns out, was too close for comfort. Seems that chickens bred for medical experimentation are shipped to biology laboratories in crowded cars and would tear each other to bits at the sight of blood. The red plastic lenses kept them from seeing it.

No such luck in Boston, where I got nothing right; but being there was an instructive pleasure. Among the objects presented at the museum were a beaded Native American pouch containing an umbilical cord (which Vogel correctly identified), some stuffed dolls (which Gates was asked to comment on), and a caned wooden ball in a caned wooden cage, which I was invited to explain if I could. I recognized it instantly as a turn-of-the-century Belgian birth-control device that, based on the rhythm method, was disastrously ineffective because turn-of-the-century Belgians had no sense of rhythm. (No one else knew what the thing was either). Another device awaiting my authentication was a glass goblet that had no orifice into which wine could be poured or from which it could be drunk, although there was a small hole in the stem. Dismissing my first thought (that it was used for toasting celebrants at abstinence meetings), I described it as a cooking implement for a northern Chinese regional cuisine consisting of dumplings too fragile to be shaped by hand or stamped with wooden or ceramic molds. In fact, it was Japanese and, when the stem was blown into, produced a sound that I will not try to represent on the printed page.

However obscure these objects may have seemed to us, once their purpose was explained, it became visible in their shape. I do not think that will be true of our contemporary artifacts, which would offer up to future panelists a bewildering array of nearly identical cases housing software and chips for sending messages, playing games, waging war, writing novels, reckoning profits and losses, or analyzing the strength of building materials. Future panelists may know or guess what the artifacts are, but they will not find much confirmation in form.

There is something else that they may not find, although I hope they will. The most moving, and most instructive, point in the evening came after Gates was asked to interpret some black-faced rag dolls clothed as farm workers. He examined them carefully and concluded that the intentions were honorable. "I do not think these are stereotypes," he said. "If they were meant to be cruel caricatures, they would look different, particular features would have been exaggerated." To Gates they appeared to be people—as in the phrase he pulled out of the past for the title of his book *Colored People*. "I regard them as positive," he said.

The dolls had an austerity that made them more like soft statuary than children's playthings. Being able to handle them, look at them closely, the three of us could see details that were not visible on the screen, like an elegantly stitched patch on the back of the man's trouser legs. Susan Vogel drove the point home. "You wouldn't put this much craft into something," she said, "if you did not love the people you were representing."

An Ideal Whose Time Has Come

Industrial espionage looks as boring as any other kind, so I don't mind agreeing not to do it. Still, whenever I am asked to sign a nondisclosure agreement, I am afflicted with subclinical paranoia. What if—after promising, upon penalty of prison or penury, never to tell what I am shown—I am shown something I already knew about?

It's been known to happen. The shock of the new is continually diffused by the persistence of the old. As Aldous Huxley observes, certain of life's lessons are perennials. That is, they keep coming up for relearning. What goes around, comes around. What's more, it keeps coming around like the brass ring in a carousel—predictable, but hard to grasp. "I know what I ought to do," Huxley complained, "but I go on doing what I know I ought not to do." Me too. You too. Combining new knowledge with the vivid recollection of what we have always known is an ideal whose time has come and seems destined to come again.

Every day we learn all over again that smoking is unhealthy; that war is hell; that there is no free lunch. And that opening junk mail is usually as much a mistake as eating junk food. If you receive an envelope postmarked Paramus, New Jersey, and bearing 16-cents worth of metered smudge and no return address, you know better than to open it. So did I. But I opened it anyway. The letter inside posed a brutally direct question: DO YOU FIND THE THOUGHT OF BEING BURIED UNDERGROUND DISTURBING?

Actually, I find it less disturbing than the thought of being buried under the defensive line of the Philadelphia Eagles. Although the prospect of death is annoying, the prospect of getting cold and damp afterwards seems unterrifyingly anticlimactic. I have always thought it would be nice to have my bones sunk in, or ashes scattered over, a corner of a tree-lined

Originally published May/June 1994 in *I.D.*, as the column "Counterpoint."

college campus, but that is not a preference I can account for rationally. I don't believe it represents a craving for youth, for I have never wanted to be young while dead.

So I was not lured by the accompanying brochure extolling the consumer benefits of "above ground (*sic*) burial" (in crypts that are "clean, dry, and ventilated, and offer protection from the unfriendly elements of the weather and ground.") Nor was I swayed by copy urging me to "consider that the cost is less than in ground burial, since there is no care to pay for and no monuments to buy," and calling attention to a bonus benefit: "Think about visiting your loved ones in a climate-controlled environment!"

Well, if I were installed in it, I wouldn't be visiting my loved ones, they would be visiting me. And high time, too. By way of visual aid, the brochure depicts a typical crypt in a typical designer's rendering. A couple of visitors, in the mode of the well behaved figures that lend scale and verisimilitude to interior architecture models, are standing in front of an arrangement of file drawers, reading the labels or locker numbers of the loved ones within. This is systems furniture for the dead. Except for such refinements as fancy trim and carpeting, it looks very much like an array of rental storage lockers—not inappropriate, since storage lockers have long been the repositories of choice for bodies not meant to be retrieved or discovered. I have seen the future, and it sucks.

Against the Wall

The first time I saw New Canaan, Connecticut's famous-architect houses, I was with Lisa Ponti, then editor of the influential Italian magazine *Domus*. It was her first visit too, and her response after visiting Philip Johnson in his glass house was as dramatic as the architecture.

"I can't believe it!" she said.

"You can't believe *what*?" I finally asked.

"I can't believe that all these great buildings we publish really exist."

I knew what she meant. As the then editor of a design magazine, I was painfully aware that most of the work we published was judged on the basis of photographs, as it is in design competitions. For practical reasons, this was the only way it *could* be judged.

John Ciardi has written, "The camera always lies." Well, maybe not always. And maybe it doesn't necessarily lie. But the camera misleads at least as much as any other instrument of perception. In certain kinds of photography this is its principal function. You don't need to be a phenomenologist to count the number of ways in which pictures do not resemble what they purport to be pictures of.

I bring this up because I once wrote about the disparity between the two distinctly different Vietnam War memorials on the Mall in Washington, D.C. A few months later I went to Washington to take another look. In fact it was my first look; but it engendered a second opinion.

On the basis of the many photographs I had seen of Frederick Hart's bronze statues, commissioned and installed to appease the veterans groups and others who believed that Maya Lin's black granite wall of names was not heroic enough, I had called the statues "memorial business as usual." On the basis of finally seeing them, I need to qualify that statement.

Originally published January/February in *I.D.*, as the column "Circumstantial Evidence."

Surely they do not invite celebration for their sculptural originality. They look pretty much like the kind of thing seen in small town squares since World War I. Except—and this is a major exception—for the faces, which are uncommonly sensitive to the ambiguities of the particular war they commemorate. These are not square-jawed, clear eyed expressions of the superior character of the average American. Rather, each of the three soldiers looks pained and confused—caught in a trap he neither made nor understood—which is a pretty accurate expression of the way the war is registered with many of us. Hart's figures do not in any respect dominate the memorial site. The scale is reasonable, and the soldiers look toward the wall from a distance, detached from it and from its complex of meanings.

This statuary has its own constituency, for reasons that designers are rarely willing to take seriously. As stunning as Maya Lin's design is—and it is more than stunning; it may very well be the best memorial ever made—there are great numbers of people who seem to need something more literal.

Is the contradiction on the Mall the same one that gave post-Modernism its initial thrust? No, although it looks that way at first. When Robert Venturi published and praised gaudy roadside attractions that we had all been taught to despise, no one could dispute that they had more warmth and vitality than any comparable stretch of, say, Sixth Avenue in New York, just as in graphics it was hard to resist seeing that any issue of the *National Enquirer* was likely to be more interesting to both eye and mind than a prize-winning corporate brochure. In graphic design, there is a simple reason for this: the designers of corporate brochures may know what the client wants to say and what they themselves want to do formally, but have very little understanding of the reader. This becomes self-justifying, for corporate literature frequently *has* no genuine readers.

The same sort of design statement at the expense of use

occurs in product design, even when the product's purpose includes the expression of the vernacular. As a small girl, my daughter desperately wanted a dollhouse. As an indulgent father, I bought her one. And because I was a design-conscious father as well, the one I bought her was manufactured by Creative Playthings and approved by numerous agencies of good taste and good intentions. Leah smiled bravely and pretended to like it, but she never played with it. What she had wanted was a *doll* house—with a peaked roof and colors and curtained windows and rooms instead of areas.

What I had brought home was a dollhouse designed for sophisticated adults who had read Le Corbusier, or read about him. A flat box made of unpainted hardwood, it looked very much like the structures featured in design magazines in those days. The resemblance included lack of occupancy: it would have been almost an outrage to have put a doll into it—unless the doll were an unadorned mannequin bought at an art supply store. I seem to recall that the promotional literature did show a doll nearby but, as with people shown in architectural magazines, it was there to illustrate scale.

Frederick Hart's representational memorial provides for its solemn purpose what a real dollhouse would have provided: emotional recognition. Maya Lin's wall is an abstraction; but it is an abstraction of human experience, not of design theory. Consequently, there really is no contradiction on the Mall. Without Hart's figures, the wall would apparently have been psychologically inaccessible to many of the people it was designed to serve. Without the wall, the statues would remind us only of how little we have learned.

The wall reminds us of far more, for its significance lies, significantly, less in how it looks than in what it does, which is to incite deep participation. Writing about architecture recently, Maya Lin alluded to "post-Modern skyscrapers that make countless references to man's past, but cannot seem to bother with man's presence." Her memorial is a study in man's presence. The siting and choice of material are subordinate to Lin's prophetic understanding of the power of a personal name. Visitors are movingly driven to search out names they know, and to reinvest them with meaning.

Not every visitor has names to look for. My wife and I were shocked to realize that neither of us had personally known anyone who had been killed in Vietnam. My wife remembered that the fiancé of an old college friend was a Vietnam casualty. She had never met him and didn't remember his last name or the year in which he had been killed. But she did know his first name, and we spent half an hour looking for Thomases. We never found the name, or if we did she did not recognize it. But the searching made us more than spectators, which is precisely what the design of the wall encourages and the design of the statues does not even expect.

Real Worlds

W hat kind of girl are you, anyway?" I asked.
"What kinds of girls are there?" she answered—a smartass response I deserved.

I remember asking the question, but cannot remember who answered. It must have happened at a time when calling a woman a girl was accepted, if not acceptable, usage. Why does that fragment of dialogue float through my head now, I wonder. Suddenly I know. I had picked up the cadence of TV anchors asking "What kind of world will the next century bring?"

Well, what kinds of worlds are there? My friend Robert Gersin had an idea about that. Like many other successful design office heads, Bob had become impatient with what he regarded as the inadequacies of design school graduates. In 1970 he seriously proposed starting a school of his own, to be called The Real World School of Design. I mentioned that another designer, Victor Papanek, was just about to publish a book called *Design for the Real World*. Bob was alarmed. "My lawyer has already arranged to protect the name," he said. He needn't have worried. Victor's book and Bob's proposed school were real worlds apart.

Surfing now I see a Prudential-Bache television commercial that plants the firm squarely in "the real world." On another channel a Jesuit activist is described as "a real world priest." Later a commentator speculates on how the concept of glasnost and perestroika have fit into "the real world of revolution."

Although it is remotely and beautifully set in the hills above Pasadena, the Art Center College of Design is a college that makes most corporations look like ivory towers. I have been looking through a handsome brochure entitled "Why Art Center?" Here are a few of the answers:

"I call customer driven total design 'the real world

Originally published March/April 1990 in *I.D.*, as the column "Circumstantial Evidence."

approach.' I could just as easily call it the 'Art Center College of Design' approach." Jack Telnack, chief design executive of Ford Motor Co., and a 1958 Art Center graduate in transportation design.

"Art Center has managed to bridge the traditional gulf between education and the real world." Industrialist Sherman Fairchild, Art Center's former chairman of the board.

"All of the hard work I experienced here definitely gave me an edge in the real working world." Graphic designer John Casado, who graduated from Art Center in advertising design in 1966.

When design offices—independent or corporate—complain that design school graduates are not sufficiently acquainted with the real world, they usually mean—to substitute one cliché for another—that they do not sufficiently appreciate the supremacy of the bottom line. At bottom the real world is tough. There are payrolls to meet, vendors to pay, customers to satisfy, prospective customers to pursue. It may be market driven or customer driven or technology driven, but it is in any case driven, and by someone else. Leave the driving to them. It is a world, above all, of other people's expectations.

That world is real enough, I guess, but it is not the only one that is. There is another, with quite different criteria for reality. Call it the Realer World. In that world the bottom line is important, but so are all the other lines, the ones that represent the experience of getting to the bottom line. If all that mattered were the bottom line, corporations could send their stockholders fortune cookies instead of annual reports. That might turn Chinese bakeries into a growth industry but would have devastating consequences for the graphic design community, which has a certain stake in the production of four-color solid waste.

Design evangelists talk about the role of design in the real world, but the news of the day—of any day—makes clear that the role of design depends on which real world we cast it in. On a CBS program called *The Wall Street Journal Report* one Sunday an automotive industry expert is asked by the program's astute anchor, Consuela Mack, to comment on Detroit's loss of market share.

Quality, he explains, was the challenge the Japanese gave us in the eighties, but we've now put that behind us. "I think the Japanese have changed the whole automobile industry," he says. "Today, the story is design. The consumer wants a new car, a fresh car in design rather than quality."

That answer says more about the loss of market share—as well as the loss of face and of reason—than you'd find in a bound volume of industry analysis. In the Real World, design is divorced from quality, and the divorce is blamed on the consumer. But in the Realer World design is understood to be an instrument for investing the product with quality from the start. Why do we have to learn that from the Japanese, and why does it take so long to learn it from anybody?

A headline in *The New York Times* on the same Sunday: WINNING BY DESIGN: SYSTEM PUTS 49ERS ON TOP. Another headline, a few days earlier: DESIGN FLAW IS CITED IN SCHOOL COLLAPSE. Both news flashes come from the Realer World, a world where design really matters. It's not how the game looks, but how it's planned to be played. If you don't design them right, buildings fall down.

Everyone preoccupied with what they call the Real World agrees about where it is located: *outside*. Just as 14th century theologians had no doubt that Heaven was Up There, design schools have no doubt that the Real World their students graduate into is Out There, and that college therefore is only a preparation for something else. That is an attitude perfectly appropriate to a world in which the only values are someone else's. In the Realer World, however, you do something because it is worth doing. College is not preparation for life. While you're there, it is life. People ask jokingly, Is there life after thirty? Is there life after therapy? "There's life after the Mets," Mookie Wilson said and proved when he was traded to Toronto. Is there life after design school? Don't ask. Better to ask: Is there life during design school?

As a reality check, consider the case of Vincent van Gogh, who was during his entire lifetime regarded as totally out of touch with the real world. His brother Theo supported him financially, morally, and emotionally. And Vincent's letters to Theo describe a world far different from the one in which a single van Gogh painting is expected to fetch between $40 million and $50 million. But which is more real—the world of a painter in the agony of creation or the world of an auction house in the ecstasy of inflation?

Not all design schools are equal, but all of them house the same conflict. To concentrate on the Realer World is to be accused by design offices of not teaching the skills young designers (and the offices that hire them) need. To concentrate on the Real World is to run the risk of developing graduates with magnificent portfolios but no inner resources. When faced with a contradiction, William James instructed us, you have to make a distinction. If we make a distinction between skills at one end of the learning spectrum and wisdom at the other, we begin to distinguish between training and education. Training imparts skills. Education does not in itself impart wisdom, but it can at least help us move in that direction. Is it possible that training prepares people for the Real World, which is its purpose, and that education prepares people for the Realer World, although that is not necessarily its purpose?

In general, education implies values and training does not— it doesn't matter to the word processor which words are processed. This aspect of the difference between training and education is illustrated by all the courses available on audio, video, and even in print, purporting to teach skills that never were even considered skills before—how to speak to interviewers, how to buy airline tickets, how to ask for a raise. The utilitarian *Sunday Times* again, from a piece on the use of private coaching in intrapersonal management skills:

"One 38-year-old management consultant recently hired a coach to help him win the attention of the firm's partners. In 10 meetings, complete with videotaped role playing sessions, he and the coach worked on making him appear more self-confident.

"It worked—he recently negotiated a hefty raise and bonus. 'Before I asked for it, she and I role-played it, practically scripted the conversation, put the body language together with the content,' he said. 'I asked for the money with a level of self confidence that communicated that I deserved it.'"

Did he deserve it? The reporter didn't ask, and I can't see why the coach would either. Her mission was accomplished.

But there are other missions. A college administrator raises the question, "What is our product—the graduate or the work that he or she does here?"

The answer is neither. Student work, however excellent, is not the product; it is just a by-product of the process by which students learn to do work. But the graduate isn't the product either, however proudly institutions boast of the designers they "turn out." The only product that an institution of learning creates is the learning environment. That's what design schools provide to the students inside and the world outside. In that context, education and training can't possibly be in conflict, although not every institution is prepared to offer both. "I am in it with all my heart," Vincent van Gogh writes in a letter to his brother. Well, we knew that. But he adds, "I must become more skilled than I am before I can be ever so slightly satisfied with myself." For all of van Gogh's genius in seeing, and in being, he still had to learn to draw.

Clearly we live in both worlds, and that's where real designers work their craft. To do it, they need training to survive and education to make survival worthwhile; they still need skill to ride on when they're in it with all their heart.

Virtual Reality

I f it was eavesdropping, it was inadvertent. They *made* me do it. I was in Denver to give a speech I had planned to work on in the hotel room, but when I came back from breakfast two cleaning women were already there.

"Will it bother you if I work?" I asked.

"No," one of them said. "Will it bother you if we talk?"

"No," I said. But it did. Their conversation was more interesting than the speech I was writing. Here is what I heard.

"You know, Margo lost her baby."

"Yeah, I know. She had an abortion."

"It shook me up. I never thought she'd go through with it."

"Oh, you could tell. I figured all along that's what she was going to do."

Well, that shook *me* up. Only a few years ago, I was certain, women would not have had that exchange while a stranger, much less a strange man, was within earshot. A few years before that, the conversation would have been describing a criminal act. I knew times had changed. But that much?

Yes, that much. But not exactly in the way I had thought. The maids left the room and I was, as flight attendants love to say, free to move about. I did move about, into the area where they had been standing. I stared at the Spanish Colonial TV cabinet they had been dusting. Idly I wiped some dust off it with a shoe mitt, and was struck by a sudden suspicion that would drive me crazy if it were not confirmed. I had to know.

I dashed out of the room and pursued the chambermaids through the corridor (NEW YORK MAN CHASES MAIDS IN LOCAL HOSTELRY the headlines would say, but I didn't worry about that at the time). I caught up with them at the service elevator. Their names were neatly revealed on white badges as Edna and Gail.

"I don't mean to intrude," I said (Why was I so diffident?

Originally published January/February 1999 in *PRINT*, as the column "Peripheral Vision."

Hadn't they intruded in imposing Margo's affairs on me?). "I don't mean to be personal, but I couldn't help overhearing. Was she a friend of yours? Maybe someone who worked in the hotel?"

"Who?" Edna asked.

"The woman who had the abortion. You know, Margo."

"Margo!" They laughed loudly and good naturedly. "She don't work here," Edna said. "Margo is *Margo*—you know, on *As the World Turns*."

So I was right in my suspicion, which somehow rattled me as much as being wrong would have.

"I can see why you were confused," Gail said to comfort me. "When we talk about the soaps it's like talking about family."

Much of the debate about the effects of television on children has focused on whether young children confuse the screen with the world. They must at least do it emotionally, because adults do, and for the same reason: emotionally, the people on the screen and people off it have comparable vital signs. Margo wasn't real to Edna and Gail; but she was at least as real as the folks next door.

A poster I saw in a Toronto exhibition consists of two elements: a drawing of a bugle and the following copy:

Is this a bugle?

If not, why not?

If it is, blow it.

I don't know a more charming expression of the perennial conflict between representational art and objective reality.

Bishop Berkeley, in *Principles of Human Knowledge*, argued that, since representation was all we had to go on, matter does not really exist. This led James Boswell to observe that while Berkeley's position was plainly nonsense, it was just as plainly irrefutable. To which Samuel Johnson replied by kicking a stone in the road and declaring, "Thus I refute Berkeley."

But the dramatic validity of Johnson's demonstration that the stone was real rested on the premise that his foot was real, a proposition easy to believe but difficult to prove to the satisfaction of Berkeley, who remained preposterous but unrefuted.

They cared about such things in the 18th century. Do we still? Marshall McLuhan told the story of a woman sitting on a park bench while her children played in the sandbox. A man sitting next to her remarked, "You have such beautiful children." Waving the compliment away disparagingly, she opened her purse and said, "Wait till you see their pictures!"

Wallet-sized and suitable for framing, pictures are always easier to handle than reality, which is messy even when we can't identify it.

Joan Brady's novel *Émigré*, begins, "Reality? What's so good about it? Where's the structure in it? Nobody wants it. Nobody buys it."

Well, I'd buy it, if I could afford it. To eschew reality carries the penalty of never fully coming to life. Consider Dan Quayle, whose presidential campaign boasted, "He was right about Murphy Brown. Family values do matter." Since families matter and values do too, of course he was right, but the slogan misses the point. Quayle was not lampooned for being wrong in defending the sanctity of families. He was lampooned for picking a fight without noticing (or, since he admitted he had never seen the show in question, without having been told by his sound-bite writers) that his chosen antagonist was a fictional character, while he himself was being presented to the public as a real one. The Reverend Jerry Falwell, on the other hand, having become a fictional character himself in *The People vs. Larry Flynt*, was fully qualified to attack the Teletubbies on their own turf.

Lately my interest in reality has been stirred if not shaken by an encounter with the startlingly prosaic sculpture of Duane Hanson. On the way home from the dentist, I passed the Whitney Museum, where a Hanson retrospective was on view. I have always found his work fascinating for what I assumed were the usual reasons: admiration for photorealistic achievements that, like the J. Seward Johnson sculptures in front of urban buildings around the country, are more real than photos because, being three-dimensional, they can be walked around and bumped into. As with a magician's performance, you know there is a trick to it, but it is no less intriguing for that. Figures like this, I figured, were to be enjoyed one at a time and briefly. It had not occurred to me that a retrospective would heighten their effect, and I had not planned to see the show.

Yet here I was and here they were. I went in. And came out prepared to eat crow. There is more to Hanson than meets the I. A Hanson standing alone is too fleshy to look like sculpture exactly, and too inelegant to pass as the higher form of life that once inspired the dreams our stuff was made on. In *The Tempest*, Miranda, seeing for the first time a man who was neither her father nor a beast, cries "Oh, brave new world, that hath such people in't." Could such a response be elicited by a piece of sculpture? Adonis or David maybe, but never the schlumpy denizens of Hanson's universe. Whatever his creations evoke, it is not the Pygmalion impulse, although that impulse lives on. Open a fashion magazine—and they are almost all fashion magazines—and you see portfolios of people who want to look like mannequins and do. Readers in their turn want to look like the models who look like mannequins. But no one wants to look like a Duane Hanson. His predilection for blue collar subjects has been called patronizing (he has been called much worse) on the grounds that he caricatures people who are safely mocked because they are not the kind of people who go to art museums. Don't bet on it. At the Whitney, at least when I was there, the visitors looked unnervingly like the show. So much so in one case that I mistook a man for a work of art.

He was, to be sure, an unprepossessing person, and he was standing still in a roomful of what I think were Hansons.

The roomful makes a difference. However individual they seem, these are not representations of particular persons. They are abstractions, just as George Segal's people are. But instead of taking what is there and reducing it by the selective removal of individual attributes as Segal seems to, Hanson reduces the way a chef does, by intensifying essence until nothing is left but the eerily recognizable. If, as has been said, Segal's figures look like ghosts, Hanson's look like ghosts who have retained color and flavor, and are thereby able to show us something about ourselves. His artistry is not in the verisimilitude but in the shared depth of observation.

Once, in the Nelson Atkins Gallery Museum in Kansas City, I mistook a Hanson for a janitor—but only for a moment. That is apparently so common an experience there is no point in remarking on it, except that at the Whitney I made the same mistake, but stayed with it more rewardingly. A wall caption designated a piece entitled "Policeman," but there was no policeman in place. Usually in such cases, a curatorial apology explains that the captioned art object has been temporarily removed. As there was no such notice on display, I turned to the guard and asked when the sculpture would be restored. He did not answer. He was not a guard. He was "Policeman."

As I turned away in embarrassment from the art cop I had thought was a guard, the man I had thought was a work of art came into the gallery. I was equally embarrassed to see him, although he could not have known I had thought him unreal any more than "Policeman" could have known I had thought he was a Whitney guard. The man, who was lethargic at best, stood still again. I looked from one to the other. Clearly there was a difference between them, but I could not have said what it was. I had gone through something like this before, and suddenly I remembered where and when.

During my sophomore year in college I lived and worked in the Klute Funeral Home in Richmond, Indiana. For the most part, living there was the work—someone had to be on hand at all times because either state regulations or industry ethics precluded leaving a corpse unattended. As college jobs went, mine was considered a plum. It was better than waiting on tables, and there was plenty of quiet time for study and contemplation. What I studied and contemplated was the corpse in the next room. I had seen dead bodies before but had never had any of them all to myself. They were unlike anyone else I knew, but how exactly? Anyone could see that they were not alive, not asleep, not unconscious, not faking. Something had gone out of them, but what?

I didn't know and still don't. There is an enormous difference between the quick and the dead. Hansons, neither one nor the other, never having lost what was never theirs to lose, may, in time, help illuminate the difference. But I'm not going to hold my breath. They don't hold theirs.

Looking (But Not Far) Ahead

Petit St. Vincent is a tiny, enchanted island resort in the Grenadines, with amenities in abundance but very little outdoor lighting. That is by design, for there is nowhere to go at night except the dining pavillion. To make getting there possible, each cottage is equipped with a powerful flashlight. There is no more peaceful place on earth than Petit St. Vincent, but the walk to the dining room invariably engenders bickering. My wife complains that I throw the light beam so far ahead she can't see where she is walking. Well, that's the way I was taught to do it in summer camp. I have no macho attachment to flashlight dominance and would be perfectly willing to leave the lighting to her. But she directs the beam straight to our feet like a traveling spotlight on Fred Astaire and Ginger Rogers, whom we resemble in no other way. I can't see where I'm going, although I can see very well where I am.

Clearly we need help, but what kind? A lighting engineer would provide outdoor lights. A marriage counselor might reveal the flashlights as battery-powered symbols of hostility. A good designer would solve the problem by putting two flashlights in every cottage. But this is not a lighting problem or a marriage problem. It is a difference in attitudes towards the future. She knows where it is and takes it for granted; I have to keep reassuring myself.

This came to mind several weeks ago when I was asked to speak to the Professional Members Forum of the World Future Society. The program chairman described the audience as "people who earn their living as futurists." I replied that I was not one of them.

"No problem," he said. "What we're looking for is a 'consumer of futurism.'" That didn't sound like me either. When I tried to figure out who it did sound like, the only image I

Originally published September/October 1986 in *I.D.*, as the column "Circumstantial Evidence."

could come up with was someone eating a scenario, and I am uncomfortable when people talk about scenarios, unless they are in the film industry.

Nevertheless, I went. I had never seen an assembly of futurists before and thought it might be something like a trip through time. It wasn't. It was very much like other meetings of other professional groups. I had never even thought of futurism as a profession. Oh, I knew there were people called futurists, but I had assumed their actual work lay in more conventional disciplines. Nostradamus was a doctor; Alvin Toffler, a journalist; Herman Kahn, a social scientist; Arthur Clarke, a science fiction writer.

As it turns out, professional futurists have the same problems other professionals have and worry about them in the same way. They discuss such topics as: What is a futurist? Is forecasting useful? Has futurism a future? As I came into the auditorium, a speaker was calling for Renaissance Men, as speakers do routinely at conferences. Incidentally, in his fascinating study of the history of the future, *The Pattern of Expectation*, I.F. Clarke claims that during the only period in history when any Renaissance men were actually sighted—namely, the Renaissance—there was no future as we know it. He places the emergence of the future in the mid-18th century, in which case Nostradamus was doubly prophetic, having foretold both the future and the fact that there would be one.

President Eisenhower once electrified the nation by announcing, "The future lies ahead." This was taken up by the press as a hilarious gaffe, and was used as a title by satirist Mort Sahl, but it was as reasonable a statement as anyone else has made on the subject.

The design process always has to do with the future, since there is nothing else to design. But designers rarely look beyond the millennium, where futurists have been operating for a great many years now. The futures we work with are relatively short-term. Once I was driving through farm country listening to a radio report on pork belly futures, and I recall thinking that hog bellies were closer to our kind of future than trend line analysis was. So were jam sessions.

I doubted that I could hold the attention of futurists with either hog bellies or jazz, but I remembered a passage in a lecture by the physicist Richard Feynman that I thought might move futurists as it had me. I called the American Institute of Physics, where a researcher found the lecture for me, and I read:

"For some reason, the universe at one time had a very low entropy for its energy content, and since then the entropy has increased. So that is the way toward the future. That is the origin of all irreversibility . . . that is what makes us remember the past and not the future, remember the things which are closer to that moment in the history of the universe when the order was higher than now, and why we are not able to remember things where the disorder is higher than now, which we call the future. . . ."

That, as it happens, was not the passage I was looking for, but it seemed to be something futurists ought to take into account, so I read it to them. Also I had a dim hope (unfulfilled) that one of them might be able to tell me what it means. It comes from a lecture called "Ratchet and Pawl."

The ratchet and pawl, Feynman explained is "a very simple device which allows a shaft to turn only one way." His entire lecture explores this phenomenon, concluding with the passage that I *had* been looking for and that was as moving as when I first read it.

"The ratchet and pawl works only in one direction because it has some ultimate contact with the rest of the universe. . . . It is part of the universe not only in the sense that it obeys the physical laws of the universe, but its one-way behavior is tied to the one-way behavior of the entire universe."

The one-way behavior of the universe! At a time when designed objects are praised for the statements they make, it is enlightening to be told how much an object can say—and mean—just in the process of doing what it's supposed to do.

INDEX

A-bomb, 78, 110, 111. *See also* nuclear weapons
"aboutness," 31–33
The Accidental Tourist (Tyler), 207, 213
Ackerman, James, 229
Adams, Henry, 58
Addams, Charles, 15
advertisements, 53, 109, 149, 182, 244–45; for cars, 137; for clothing, 84–85, 231; deception in, 165–66; endorsements and, 166–68, 179–80; omission in, 184; promotional literature, 87–88; sandwich man, 231; "suitable for framing," 88; TV commercials, 180–81
African Americans, 24
aging, memory and, 124. *See also* senior citizens
AIDS and its Metaphors (Sontag), 42
airlines, 75, 161–62, 182; delays and, 35–36
airports, 74, 207, 208–9, 210
Albee, Edward, 215
alcohol, 126, 134, 150, 242, 243
Alexander, Christopher, 187
Alfred University, 63
Algren, Nelson, 228
Ali, Muhammad, 254

Alice in Wonderland (Carrol), 161
Allen, Herbert, 84
alphabet, computerized, 107, 108
Alpha Romeo (car), 116
American Airlines, 75, 182
American Center for Design (Chicago), 255
American Design Ethic (Pulos), 67
American Institute of Graphic Arts Journal, 49
American Institute of Physics, 280
American Society of Composers, Authors and Publishers (ASCAP), 22–23
Apple computers, 45, 134–35
Archimedes, 241
architects, 19, 160, 262
architecture, 209, 228–29; skyscrapers, 193, 264–65
Aristotle, 42, 77
Army, Project Man and, 144–49
Art Center College of Design (Pasadena), 266–67
art direction, 49. *See also* painting; sculpture
Artschwager, Richard, 113
The Art of Computer Interface Design (Nelson), 45

ASCAP. *See* American Society of Composers, Authors and Publishers
The Ascent of Man (Bronowski), 133
Aspen Music Festival concert hall, 43
ATM (automated teller machine), 121, 176
attention, 247
automobile design, 50, 116, 119, 137–43, 268; ads, 137; dream cars, 140–41; sex and, 142

Babbit (Lewis), 140
Bad: The Dumbing of America (Fussell), 69
Baker, Nicholson, 101, 105
Baldwin, James, 11
Banham, Reiner, 79, 137
bar design, 115–16
Barley Motor Car Company, 137
Barney Greenglass the Sturgeon King (store), 100
Barnum, P. T., 168
baseball: curve ball in, 159–60; fantasy in, 91–92
bathroom design, 237–46; accessories, 240–41; door locks in, 238; for elderly and handicapped, 95–96, 245–46; famous bathers, 241; multiple functions in, 242–43; shaving and, 240, 244–45; toilet in, 239–40
Beatrice Foods, 226
Beckett, Samuel, 154
Becoming a Writer (Brandes), 40
Bedford, Robert Q., 41
Bel Geddes, Norman, 221
Bell, Alexander Graham, 126
Bennet, Arnold, 103

Benton, Robert, 154
Berkeley, Bishop, 273–74
Berlioz, Hector, 124
Big Ben alarm clock, 160
"Black Mountain Blues" (song), 254
Blake, Peter, 228
Blechman, Robert, 155
books: eclectic, 170–71; ownership of, 103, 253; tactility of, 114–15
Boston Architectural Center, 228
Boston Children's Museum event, 257–59
Boswell, James, 273
bottom line, 91, 218, 267
boxers and boxing, 27, 220–21, 222–23, 232, 254; Rocky Graziano, 204–5, 206
Bradford, Peter, 198
Brady, Joan, 274
Brandes, Dorothea, 40
Brecher, Kenneth, 257
Bring in 'da Noise, Bring in 'da Funk (musical), 27
British Museum, 220
Bronowski, Jacob, 133
Brown, Patricia Leigh, 255–56
Brucker, Secretary of Army, 144, 146–47, 148–49
Buddhists, 13, 253
Buehring, Gordon, 137–38
Buick (car) design, 139, 143
Bunshaft, Gordon, 256
Burma Shave Company, 228
Burton, Richard, 7
business, 119; education and, 70; good design and, 50; naming of, 7. *See also under* corporate
business cards, Japanese and, 12, 178

button pushing, 100–101
Buying (Gutman), 131
Byrd, Robert (Senator), 43

calligraphers, 106–7, 108
Cambridge, Godfrey, 97
Caplan, Leah, 156–58, 264
car design. *See* automobile design
Carmichael, Dennis, 83–84
Carpenter, Mary Chapin, 253
Carrol, Lewis, 161
Carson Roberts (design firm), 74–75
Casado, John, 267
catalogue shopping, 71, 165
CBS network, 20, 119, 268
Central Park zoo (NYC), 215
ceramics, 69
Cesar, Baldacini, 142
Cezanne, Paul, 155
Chain Store Age (magazine), 176
chair design, 80, 98, 119, 222; Eames chair, 48, 75
Chamberlain, John, 142
Charleston, South Carolina, 211
Cheever, John, 198
chess master (IBM Deep Blue), 120
Chicago Merchandise Mart, 10
childhood innocence, 166
Ciardi, John, 97, 262
The Cider House Rules (Irving), 31
circus side shows, 124–25
Clarke, Arthur, 279
Clarke, I. F., 279
"clean design look," 71–72
Cleveland, 204–5, 206
client-designer relationships, 171–73
Clinton, Hillary, 31

closure, 181
clothing: advertising, 84–85, 231; corporate dress codes, 135; fashion outerwear, 156–58
CNN (Cable News Network), 37
Coleridge, Samuel Taylor, 161
college clothing ad, 84–85
Colored People (Gates), 259
"the comma poet," 107
commodities, ideas as, 24, 152–55
communication, 80; obscure language in, 27–30, 35. *See also* language
complexity and theory, 79
computer graphics, 114
computerized alphabet, 107, 108
computers, 54, 110–11, 115, 159, 222; corporate culture and, 134–36; Eames's exhibition, 172; metaphor and, 44–45; paperless revolution and, 35; personal, 107, 134–36, 176, 202; thinking by, 120–22
"The Computer Perspective" (exhibition), 172
condom vending machine, 174
Conrad, Joseph, 209
conscience, 65
constraints in design, 34, 79, 90–94
consultants, 134, 171
consumer cynicism, 163, 174
Consumer Reports, 150–51
Consumer Union (CU), 150–51
Container Corporation, 88
cooking, invention of, 127–28
Cooper Union design symposium, 29
copyright, 23–25. *See also* intellectual property
Cord 810 (automobile), 137–38

corkscrew design, 84, 97, 239
Cornell University, 238
corporate brochures, 260–61, 263
corporate culture, 133–36
corporate identity, 5, 226
corporate sponsorship, 180–81
corporation, role of, 83
cosmetic design, 216–17
Covington, George, 29, 97
craft and design, 63–69
Cralle, Bob, 114, 116
Creative Playthings, 264
creativity, 152
credibility, 54–55, 78, 160, 168
credit, assignment of, 18–21
cross-over designers, 13–16. *See also* nondesigners
cultural bias, 136. *See also* corporate culture
cultural workers, 66
culture, small talk and, 35
cummings, e. e., 106–7

Davis, Ossie, 81
Day, Doris, 241
daydreaming, 200. *See also* imagination
Dead End (Kingsley), 195
Dean, Abner, 12
death, 277; burial and, 260–61
Death of a Salesman (Miller), 22
deception, 159–68; credibility and, 160, 168; in debate, 160–61; endorsements and, 166–68; image and, 161–62; in junk mail, 164–65
Dee, Ruby, 81
Deep Blue (chess-playing computer), 120

dentist office visit, 215–16
DePree, Hugh, 172
Descent into Hell (Williams), 24
design: consequences of, 43, 73–77; constraints in, 34, 79, 90–94; cosmetic in, 216–17; craft and, 63–69; expectations of, 40–41; influence of, 154; risk-free, 83; smart, 118–22; theory of, 78–81; trickery in, 90; ubiquity of, 131. *See also* automobile design; bathroom design; flatware design; graphic design
designers: client and, 171–73; as conscience of industry, 65; as consumer, 88; expectations of, 40–41; industrial, 80, 86, 107–8, 116; nondesigners and, 13–16, 38–39, 84; parallel universe and, 33–34; professionalism and, 233. *See also* graphic designers
Design for Human Scale (Papanek), 72
Design for the Real World (Papanek), 266
"Designing Facilities to Survive Terrorist Attack," 84
Design (magazine), 71
Design Management Conference, 50
design museums, 61–62
design schools, real worlds and, 266–71
design sermons, 224, 225
design shows, 64, 91
design teaching, 201–3. *See also* teaching
Design Within Reach, 61
Deskey, Donald, 221
Devil's Workshop, 239
DeVoto, Bernard, 161
Diffrient, Niels, 75

Jarrell, Randall, 151
Jarrett, Eleanor Holm, 222
Jenkins, Lew, 221
Jenny Craig (weight-loss company), 31
JFK (film), 161
Johnson, J. Seward, 275
Johnson, Jack, 220–21, 222–23
Johnson, Lyndon, 223, 238, 241
Johnson, Philip, 262
Johnson, Samuel, 53–54, 62, 199, 273–74
Johnson and Johnson bandaids, 96
Johnson Smith, 169–71
Johnston, Edward, 107
Jordan, Lorie, 181
junk mail, 88–89, 164–65, 182, 260–61
juried design shows, 64, 91

Kabat-Zinn, Jon, 187
Kahn, Herman, 279
Karr, Alphonse, 251
Kauffmann, Edgar, Jr., 68
Kaye, Danny, 17
Keillor, Garrison, 199
Kennedy, John F., 19, 161
Kennedy, John F., Jr., 37–38
Kent, Corita, 66, 107, 198
Ketchell, Stanley, 222
Kettering, Charles F., 79
Kingsley, Sidney, 195
Kira, Alexander, 238, 240
Klute Funeral Home (Richmond, Indiana), 277
Knopf, Alfred, 106
Kramer, Peter, 111–12
Krohn, David, 159
Kunitz, Stanley, 256

The Lady in the Dark (film), 17
Laettner, Christian, 218
Lamb, Charles: *Dissertation on Roast Pig*, 127–28
Langer, Suzanne, 25–26
language: communication and, 27–30, 35; inflated, 164–65. *See also* figures of speech; writing
Latham, Richard, 74, 75, 116
Lauren, Ralph, 85
Lax, Michael, 63
Leavitt, David, 24
Le Corbusier (Charles-Edouard Jean-neret), 264
Lemnitzer, General, 144–45
Lewinsky, Monica, 31
Lewis, Sinclair, 140
licensing, professionalism and, 233
Lilly, John, 241
Lin, Maya, 262, 263, 264–65
Listening to Prozac (Kramer), 111–12
lithium, 112
Little Blue Books, 171
local, 206
Loewy, Raymond, 43, 139, 221
Lois, George, 48
Loman, Willy *(Death of a Salesman)*, 22
Lombard, Carole, 220
Luddites, 59

Macaulay, Thomas, 198–99
McCannel, Malcolm, 14, 15
Mace, Ron, 179, 180
McEwan, Ian, 15n
Macintosh computer, 135–36
Mack, Consuela, 268
McLuhan, Marshall, 217, 274
magic and design, 90–91

New Canaan, Connecticut, 262
Newman, David, 154
New Republic (magazine), 166
New York City, 10, 49, 193–97, 231;
    Central Park zoo, 215; construc-
    tion in, 193–95; School of Visual
    Arts, 255; signage in, 234–35; sub-
    way, 196–97; World's Fairs in, 34,
    220, 221–23
New Yorker (magazine), 152–53, 203
New York Times, 181, 255–56, 268, 270
NGETKBTGTTA. *See* not-good-
    enough-to-keep-but-too-good-to-
    throw-away
niceness training program, 74
Nichols, Mike, 181
Nobody Knows My Name (Baldwin), 11
nondesigners, 13–16, 38–39, 84
nondisclosure agreement, 260
Noonan, Peggy, 20
Norman, Donald, 29
Nostradamus, 279
not-good-enough-to-keep-but-too-
    good-to-throw-away (NGETKBT-
    GTTA), 86–89
nowhereness, 207, 208–9. *See also*
    place, sense of
NPR. *See* National Public Radio
nuclear weapons, 78, 110, 111; Project
    Man and, 144, 145, 147

object lessons, 59
omission, in ads, 184
O'Neill, Tip, 206
On Target Eye Drop Delivery Sys-
    tem, 16
Operation Desert Storm, 42
O'Rourke, P. J., 166

Orwell, George, 49
Osmond, Marie, 180
ownership: of craft process, 67; of
    ideas, 152–55; intellectual property,
    22–26; public domain, 22, 23–24, 153

packing, 82, 87
Page, Satchel, 251
painting, tactility of, 113
Paley, William, 20
Palmer, Cap, 123
Papanek, Victor, 22, 72, 266
paperless revolution, 35
parallel universe, 33–34
Parker, Dorothy, 96
Parsons School of Design, 34
past, the, 255–59; future and, 251
pasta, 81, 189–90
The Pattern of Expectation (Clarke), 279
PBS. *See* Public Broadcasting System
"People think. Machines work.", 120
The People vs. Larry Flynt (film), 274
personal, the, 69. *See also under* private
personal computers, 107, 134–36, 176,
    202. *See also* computers
personal signage, 16, 230–31
Petit St. Vincent Island, 278
Phonemate (answering machine),
    174–75
photography, 262
pictures and words, 47–51, 253–54
Pictures From an Institution (Jarrell), 151
Pininfarina, Sergio, 191
place, sense of, 187; in airports, 207,
    208–9
placebos, 101
plagiarism, 25–26, 154
plastics, 125–26, 191–92; Formica, 107–8

Studebaker (car) designs, 139, 140
Styron, William, 24
subway system, NYC, 196–97
Summer Design Institute, 201–2
Sunday, Billy, 224
Supreme Court, 23
Swift, Jonathan, 160
Swiss Army knife, 78, 111, 243
symbols, respect for, 43–44

Tabibian, Jivan, 161
tableware. *See* flatware design
tactility, 69, 113–17
talking wrong, 27–30
teaching, 176, 199, 200–203. *See also*
    education
Teague, Harry, 43
technology, 234; in education, 202;
    Futurama exhibit, 221–22; hyper-
    bole and, 59; microminiaturiza-
    tion, 72, 116; paperless revolution
    and, 35; special effects, 68; tactili-
    ty and, 113. *See also* computers
"teddy bear" effect, 114–15
telephone answering machine, 174–76
television, 32, 54, 109–10, 266, 272–73;
    commercials on, 180–81; evangel-
    ists on, 224; news trivia, 36–38;
    personal exposure on, 229–30;
    sports announcers on, 217–18
Telnack, Jack, 267
The Tempest (Shakespeare), 275
*Theory and Design in the First Machine
    Age* (Banham), 79
Theory of Games and Economic Behavior
    (Von Neumann & Morgenstern),
    172
Thomas, Dylan, 13

Thompson, Jane, 126
Thurber, James, 25, 71
Time magazine, 138
Toffler, Alvin, 279
toggle-switches, 115
toilet design, 239–40. *See also* bath-
    room design
Toronto, Canada, 237
touch, sense of, 69, 113–16
tourism and travel, 207, 210–14;
    redesign for, 210–11; signage and,
    211, 218–19. *See also* airlines; airports
transformational products, 109–12
trickery in design, 90
Trudeau, Arthur G., 144, 145
TruValue hardware store, 61
Turing, Alan, 121
Turner, Nat, 24
Turner, Ted, 22
Twain, Mark, 105, 189, 205
Tyler, Anne, 207, 213
typewriter, 115

unclear communication, 27–30
United Airlines, 35–36
U.S. Information Agency, 47
universal design, 95–98, 179–80,
    245–46
University of California, 172
University of Michigan, 83
urban construction, 193–95

Vancouver, Canada, 207–8
Van Gogh, Theo, 269
Van Gogh, Vincent, 113, 269, 270–71
Vassos, John, 221
Velcro closures, 97
vending machines, 174, 176–78

The Ventrilo (device), 170
Venturi, Robert, 263
versatility, in objects, 111
Vertigo (Sebald), 251
Vietnam War memorials, 262–63, 264–65
violence, television and, 109
virtual reality, 68, 214, 272–77; Hanson sculpture and, 274–76, 277
visual design, 218; attention and, 247; pictures and words, 253–54. *See also* signage
Visual Thinking (Wolf), 205
Vogel, Susan, 257, 258
Von Neumann, John, 172

Wall Street Journal, 153
The Wall Street Journal Report (TV program), 268
watch design, 121–22
weirdness, 198–99
Weismuller, Johnny, 222
Wesleyan University, 25
wheelchair design, 98
White, E. B., 126, 193, 198
Whitman, Walt, 150, 159–60

Whitney Museum of Art, 86, 275–76
Whyte, William H., 187
Williams, Charles, 24
Williams, Mason, 133
Wilson, Mookie, 269
wine, plastic corks for, 125–26. *See also* corkscrew
The Wizard of Oz (Baum), 162, 168
Wolf, Henry, 204–5
word processing, 115
words and pictures, 5, 47–51, 253–54
World Future Society, 278–79
World's Fair (NYC), 34, 220, 221–23
Wright, Russel, 221
writing, 115; books on, 40; ghostwriting, 19–21; handwriting, 106–8; ownership of, 154–55; personal correspondence, 181–82

Yang, C. C., 172

Zale, Tony, 204
Zapf, Herman, 107
Zeitlin, Steve, 23–24
Zoo Story (Albee), 215